Routledge Guides t(

# The Routledge Guidebook to Thoreau's *Civil Disobedience*

Since its publication in 1849, Henry David Thoreau's *Civil Disobedience* has influenced protestors, activists and political thinkers all over the world. Including the full text of Thoreau's essay, *The Routledge Guidebook to Thoreau's Civil Disobedience* explores the context of his writing, analyzes different interpretations of the text and considers how posthumous edits to *Civil Disobedience* have altered its intended meaning. It introduces the reader to:

- The context of Thoreau's work and the background to his writing
- The significance of the references and allusions
- The contemporary reception of Thoreau's essay
- The ongoing relevance of the work and a discussion of different perspectives on the work.

Providing a detailed analysis which closely examines Thoreau's original work, this is an essential introduction for students of politics, philosophy and history, and all those seeking a full appreciation of this classic work.

**Bob Pepperman Taylor** is based in the Department of Political Science at the University of Vermont.

# ROUTLEDGE GUIDES TO THE GREAT BOOKS

## Series Editor: Anthony Gottlieb

*The Routledge Guides to the Great Books* provide ideal introductions to the work of the most brilliant thinkers of all time, from Aristotle to Marx and Newton to Wollstonecraft. At the core of each Guidebook is a detailed examination of the central ideas and arguments expounded in the great book. This is bookended by an opening discussion of the context within which the work was written and a closing look at the lasting significance of the text. *The Routledge Guides to the Great Books* therefore provide students everywhere with complete introductions to the most important, influential and innovative books of all time.

Available:

Forthcoming:

Routledge Guides to the Great Books

# The Routledge Guidebook to Thoreau's *Civil Disobedience*

Bob Pepperman Taylor

Routledge
Taylor & Francis Group

LONDON AND NEW YORK

First published in The Routledge Guides to the Great Books series in 2015
by Routledge
2 Park Square, Milton Park, Abingdon, Oxon OX14 4RN

and by Routledge
711 Third Avenue, New York, NY 10017

*Routledge is an imprint of the Taylor & Francis Group, an informa business*

© 2015 Bob Pepperman Taylor

The right of Bob Pepperman Taylor to be identified as author of this work has been
asserted by him in accordance with sections 77 and 78 of the Copyright, Designs
and Patents Act 1988.

*British Library Cataloguing in Publication Data*
A catalogue record for this book is available from the British Library

*Library of Congress Cataloging in Publication Data*
Taylor, Bob Pepperman.
The Routledge Guidebook to Thoreau's Civil Disobedience / Bob Pepperman Taylor.
(Routledge Guides to the Great Books)
Includes bibliographical references and index.
1. Thoreau, Henry David, 1817-1862. Civil disobedience. 2. Thoreau,
Henry David, 1817-1862--Political and social views. 3. Politics and literature--United
States--History--19th century. 4. Civil disobedience. I. Title.
PS3051.C5T39 2014
818'.309--dc23
2014023181

ISBN: 978-0-415-81860-5 (hbk)
ISBN: 978-0-415-81859-9 (pbk)
ISBN: 978-1-315-73935-9 (ebk)

Typeset in Garamond
by Taylor & Francis Books

# CONTENTS

# Series Editor's Preface

"The past is a foreign country," wrote a British novelist, L. P. Hartley: "they do things differently there." The greatest books in the canon of the humanities and sciences can be foreign territory, too. This series is a set of excursions written by expert guides who know how to make such places become more familiar.

All the books covered in this series, however long ago they were written, have much to say to us now or help to explain the ways in which we have come to think about the world. Each volume is designed not only to describe a set of ideas, and how they developed, but also to evaluate them. This requires what one might call a bifocal approach. To engage fully with an author, one has to pretend that he or she is speaking to us; but to understand a text's meaning, it is often necessary to remember its original audience, too. It is all too easy to mistake the intentions of an old argument by treating it as a contemporary one.

The *Routledge Guides to the Great Books* are aimed at students in the broadest sense, not only those engaged in formal study. The intended audience of the series is all those who want to understand the books that have had the largest effects.

Anthony Gottlieb

Series editor **Anthony Gottlieb** is the author of *The Dream of Reason: A History of Philosophy from the Greeks to the Renaissance*.

# ACKNOWLEDGEMENTS

It has been a pleasure to work with Andy Humphries, Iram Satti, Siobhan Poole, and everyone at Routledge involved with the development and completion of this book. Patricia Mardeusz of the University of Vermont Bailey/Howe library deserves many thanks for her boundless enthusiasm and helpfulness. Once again, I am indebted to Patrick Neal and Fran Pepperman Taylor for their thoughtful and generous readings of the manuscript.

# 1

## INTRODUCTION

In the summer of 1846, Henry David Thoreau was arrested in Concord, Massachusetts, for not paying his poll tax, a tax levied on each eligible voter in the state. He spent one night sharing a cell with one other inmate, an arson suspect, in the local jail. During the evening of his arrest, some unnamed individual paid Thoreau's tax. In the morning he was released and resumed his normal affairs.

By any measure, this was not at the time a significant political event. Indeed, it looked more than anything else like an eccentric interaction between Thoreau and the constable, Sam Staples. Thoreau had come to Concord village from his cabin on the shore of Walden Pond. He was on an errand to pick up a repaired shoe from the cobbler when Staples confronted him about the unpaid tax. It is likely that Staples, who was responsible for collecting the local taxes, was personally liable for the $1.50 (and perhaps three or four years' worth of unpaid tax as well) regardless of whether or not he collected what Thoreau owed. It appears, nonetheless, that Staples offered, as an act of friendship and neighborliness, either to loan Thoreau the money or just pay the tax himself in the event that Thoreau was short on funds. Thoreau rejected the offer (none too gently, we may infer) and suggested that he was ignoring the tax on principle, not because he was unable to pay. The exchange escalated, Staples threatened jail, Thoreau challenged him to make good on the threat, and Thoreau was taken into custody. The two men were clearly annoyed with one another. When Staples returned home that evening and removed his boots, he was told that someone (probably one of Thoreau's many aunts) had paid the tax for Thoreau. Staples refused to put his boots back on and go out again that evening; Thoreau would have to wait until morning to be released. Thoreau, for his part, refused to leave when Staples arrived the next day, but Staples turned him out before Thoreau could make a bigger deal out of the event than he already had. Thoreau stomped off angrily, and there is every reason to think that Staples was none too happy either. But aside from this relatively small, almost comic confrontation between these two neighbors, and the inevitable village gossip growing from it, this was not the kind of incident one would have recognized at the time as being of great historical importance. In this spirit, one commentator has referred to Thoreau's arrest as "this absurd event."[1]

In time, however, the story of Thoreau's arrest has indeed taken on great historical significance. This significance would grow slowly, however, and as a result of Thoreau's own crafting of our understanding of the event. Over the years, his account has come to speak powerfully to men and women struggling against what they believe to be unjust laws or tyrannical political orders. Such men and women have lived in very different times and places from Thoreau's mid-century Concord, Massachusetts, but the historical and geographical distance between Thoreau and his audience has only served to increase the resonance of his ideas and values for these readers.

In early 1848, a year and a half after his arrest, Thoreau gave two lectures at the Concord Lyceum in which he discussed the details of his arrest and explained what he took to be the moral context in which it occurred. On January 26 he titled his lecture *The Relation of the Individual to the State*, and on February 16 his working title was *The Rights and Duties of the Individual in Relation to the State*.[2] One year after this, in January 1849, he published a version of these lectures in a literary journal under the title

*Resistance to Civil Government.* Very few people appear to have paid much attention to Thoreau's contribution in *Aesthetic Papers*; a single notice came from a reviewer in *The People's Review* in London.[3] The essay had no appreciable impact on the reading public or political thinkers during the remainder of Thoreau's lifetime.

Thoreau died of tuberculosis in 1862 at age 44. Four years later a friend, Ellery Channing, and Thoreau's sister, Sophia, published a volume of Thoreau's essays, including a slightly revised version of *Resistance*, now appearing under the title *Civil Disobedience*. The essay continued to attract very little attention.

Early in the twentieth century, however, *Civil Disobedience* began to gain traction among radicals and political activists in the United States and abroad. American socialists Upton Sinclair and Norman Thomas and anarchist Emma Goldman were all arrested at different times for reading *Civil Disobedience* during public protests.[4] Russian authors Leo Tolstoy and Anton Chekhov read the essay and recommended it to their friends.[5] Mohandas Gandhi first read *Civil Disobedience* when he was a young lawyer in South Africa, and he claimed to have taken a copy of it with him to jail every time he was arrested over the course of his lifetime.[6] "There is no doubt," he wrote, "that Thoreau's ideas greatly influence my movement in India."[7] During World War II, members of the Danish resistance movement struggling against Nazism claimed to have been influenced by Thoreau. British reformers and members of the Labour Party read and promoted Thoreau's writings, and he reportedly influenced French authors Marcel Proust and André Gide.[8] At least one anti-apartheid activist in South Africa suggested that Thoreau's influence was "extremely important" for that movement.[9] Even allowing for exaggeration, it is clear that over the course of the twentieth century Thoreau's ideas, and his arguments in *Civil Disobedience* in particular, have been noted and exploited by political reformers and activists in many nations around the world. Two scholars who have studied the reach of Thoreau's ideas suggest, "It is not unlikely that Thoreau is more widely known, particularly abroad, as the author of *Civil Disobedience* than of *Walden*."[10]

Thoreau's political influence would not fully blossom in his own country until the second half of the twentieth century. American

radicals in the first half of the century occasionally referred to
Thoreau and *Civil Disobedience* (as we have seen with the examples
of Sinclair, Thomas, and Goldman), but the text did not become
central to U.S. protest politics until the civil rights, anti-war, and
student movements of the 1950s, 60s and 70s. Martin Luther
King Jr. reported that *Civil Disobedience* had been central to his
own development as a leader in the civil rights struggle against
American segregation and racial injustice:

> During my early college days I read Thoreau's essay on civil disobedience
> for the first time. Fascinated by the idea of refusing to cooperate with
> an evil system, I was so deeply moved that I re-read it several times.
> I became convinced then that non-cooperation with evil is as much a
> moral obligation as is cooperation with good. No other person has
> been more eloquent and passionate in getting this idea across than
> Henry David Thoreau.[11]

Historian Staughton Lynd, in a 1963 essay, presented Thoreau as
an "admirable radical" to be emulated, suggesting "Henry Thoreau
has become the patron saint of new radicals and of all unadjusted
Americans."[12] Playwrights Jerome Lawrence and Robert Lee, in
their popular 1970 "The Night Thoreau Spent in Jail," unapolo-
getically present Thoreau as a 1960s-style counterculture hero:
"The man imprisoned in our play belongs more to the 1970s than
to the age in which he lived."[13] Like many others, Lawrence and
Lee portray Thoreau as a pacifist hero who "sang out in nonviolent
defiance" as an inspiration to the likes of Gandhi, Tolstoy, and
King.[14] Michael Meyer, who has studied Thoreau's influence in the
United States, notes not only that Thoreau's reputation skyrocketed
during the 1960s,[15] but that "Thoreau has something of a pro-
miscuous reputation; like ladies of easy virtue, his politics have
comforted whomever has bothered to pick them up."[16] In the
words of Walter Harding, perhaps the dean of Thoreau studies
until his death in 1996, "There is hardly an ism in our times that
has not attempted to adopt Thoreau."[17] The impulse to turn to
Thoreau to legitimate acts of political rebelliousness continues in
the twenty-first century. American Congressman John Lewis has
recently praised Edward Snowden, the National Security Agency

whistleblower who exposed the massive NSA collection of personal
data of individuals in the U.S. and abroad (including foreign leaders),
as a practitioner of Thoreauvian civil disobedience.[18]

A significant piece of evidence for Thoreau's influence in
American protest politics is the fact that representatives of the government have from time to time felt the need to attack Thoreau's
influence and ideas. The notorious Senator Joseph McCarthy successfully insisted, in the 1950s, that the U.S. government remove
a particular anthology of American literature from all U.S. Informa-
tion Service libraries around the world because it contained *Civil
Disobedience*.[19] Thoreau's influence was becoming so great among
the government's critics in the 1960s that a high-level official felt
the need to address him directly: Eugene Rostow, the Under-
secretary for Political Affairs in the United States Department of
State felt compelled to use a July 4th speech in the late 1960s to
criticize Thoreau's political ideas.[20] Some political authorities
continue to think of Thoreau's essay as a threat to political order,
patriotism, and stability. A school district in Tucson, Arizona, for
example, has recently banned *Civil Disobedience* (along with many
other texts) from the curriculum of a Mexican American Studies
program. The fear is that Thoreau's essay could encourage unpatriotic
views and attitudes among these high school students.[21]

As trivial as it appeared in 1846, Thoreau's arrest is the incident
around which Thoreau constructed a political essay that has grown
to become one of the most significant and influential political
documents in the American political tradition.

If we were unaware of Thoreau's importance as a political icon
for later generations, there would be little in his biography to alert
us to the likelihood of this development. He never held political
office or joined political organizations. He was little known as a
writer or a political figure outside his local community during his
lifetime. He lived most of his days quietly in his hometown,
rarely traveling beyond his familiar New England. For one who
would become a political hero to many in later generations, the facts
of his life appear at first glance decidedly provincial and unheroic.

To his contemporaries, in fact, Thoreau was not a figure of
great moment or note. Indeed, for many, Thoreau was little more
than a local eccentric. In 1844, just two years before his famous

arrest, Thoreau and a friend were responsible for starting a forest fire that burned approximately 300 acres of woodlot and caused over $2,000 in damages. Thoreau and Edward Hoar had made a fire in an old stump to cook some freshly caught fish. The fire quickly spread out of their control. Hoar was a member of a prominent local family, and this is probably why Thoreau was never charged with a crime in the case.[22] However, he was known by many in his own generation, and by later generations of Concord residents as well, as "the man who burned the woods."[23]

There was more to Thoreau, of course, than this one unfortunate episode. He was born to a middle-class family, although his father had significant financial setbacks during his childhood so the family was not without economic stress and strain. An uncle had a pencil-making business and eventually, in part because of technological innovations introduced by Henry, the whole family became more prosperous as Thoreau's father was taken into the business. Despite economic improvements over time, his mother frequently took boarders into the household, and the family was only affluent enough to send one of the two sons – Henry, since he was more gifted academically – to college at Harvard.

Two other facts about the Thoreau family are worth noting, especially given the emphasis on "manhood" and the critical attitude toward abolitionists we find in *Civil Disobedience*. The first concerns the overwhelmingly feminine nature of the household. Thoreau had an older brother, John, who died in early adulthood when Henry was only 25. He had two sisters (one of whom also died prematurely, of tuberculosis), numerous aunts attached to the household, and female boarders as well. One biographer notes that the Thoreau home was a "predominantly woman's world."[24] Another commentator sourly claims that Thoreau lived "under oppressive female domination."[25] A second fact concerns the strong abolitionist commitments of the women of the household. His mother's table was a regular stop for nearly every abolitionist speaker and reformer who visited Concord; so over the course of his life, Thoreau was intimately exposed to many of the major reform figures in New England and the northern United States more generally.[26] William Lloyd Garrison's newspaper, *The Liberator*, was routinely found along with other liberal and reform publications in the Thoreau home. Concord was a hotbed of abolition, and the women in Thoreau's family were central figures in this movement.

When Thoreau returned to Concord after graduation, he tried his hand at schoolteaching (both, very briefly, as a public school teacher and then as the master of a private school he opened and operated with his brother), looked for but failed to find work as a teacher in other parts of the country, spent less than a year as tutor to a family (Ralph Waldo Emerson's brother's family) in Staten Island, New York, and returned to Concord to find work as a handyman (he was very talented with his hands). Eventually he taught himself surveying, and this became his primary occupation in mature adulthood. Surveying supplied Thoreau with sufficient (even if modest) means by working limited hours and allowed him the freedom to spend a great deal of time wandering the countryside and cultivating his interest as a naturalist and a writer. From the time he returned to Concord after college until his premature death in 1862, his overwhelming focus was as a poet, writer, and observer of nature. He attached himself to Emerson, who became a teacher and friend, although the relationship was not always an easy one. Despite tensions and difficulties in this friendship that developed over the years, however, Thoreau was deeply indebted to his older friend as an intellectual mentor and patron. Emerson's library, encouragement, and friendship were essential for helping Thoreau develop his talents and career as an author.

Edward Emerson (Ralph Waldo's son) tells us that children loved Thoreau, and that he loved them in return;[27] one contemporary reports that 300 of the 400 children in town followed Thoreau's casket to the cemetery for burial.[28] Among adults, however, he was often "a regular hairshirt of a man," in E. B. White's memorable phrase.[29] Two biographers have suggested that "For the most part," his neighbors "looked upon him as a crank and did not hesitate to tell him so to his face."[30] Nathaniel Hawthorne's son Julian, looking back more than 35 years after Thoreau's death, claimed rather dyspeptically that Thoreau's "nature was bitter, selfish, jealous and morbid."[31] While this judgment seems particularly severe (and contrary to some fond memories by others, such as Louise May Alcott and her father, Bronson), it suggests at the very least that White may have been on to something by suggesting that Thoreau was prickly with others. Even as a child, his serious and moralistic personality led to his being given the nickname "the judge."[32]

Two events have defined Thoreau's life for posterity: his arrest and the period of just over two years that he spent living in a simple cabin he built by Walden Pond. To his neighbors, however, he was also known as the man who could be seen walking the local countryside at least half of every day when his health allowed, and this was enough to prove his eccentricity to many contemporary observers. His Aunt Jane probably captured a widespread village opinion when she commented, "I wish he could find something better to do than walking off every now and then."[33] Even Emerson wrote in his *Journal* in 1851, "I fancy it an inexcusable fault in him that he is insignificant here in the town."[34] The most charitable interpretation of his reputation among his contemporaries is probably that he was viewed as a minor local figure with a mixed contribution to the community. Harding and Meyer conclude that "In his own lifetime Thoreau was almost invariably dismissed as an eccentric and unimportant imitator of Emerson."[35] For many who knew him, there was clearly little in Thoreau's behavior or achievements to suggest his future reputation. Even his literary career seemed to many to be a minor footnote to the Concord transcendentalists and to Emerson's towering reputation. Although Thoreau gained a handful of loyal admirers during his lifetime, the gap between his contemporary reputation and his reputation among later generations is striking.

This is not the place to provide a detailed discussion of Thoreau's biography. The observations provided so far, however, suggest that there are a number of paradoxes and surprises to be found. The first of these, as we have seen, could be thought of as the distance between the modest course of Thoreau's life and the worldly, heroic character of the life known to posterity. Thoreau was in many ways a most provincial and unworldly figure. He was a village man who rarely ventured beyond his local community. His travels were confined, until the very end of his life, to New England (including multiple trips to both Cape Cod and Maine), Quebec, and the northeastern United States. His college education was taken a few miles from Concord in Cambridge, and his professional career would be confined almost entirely to his hometown. Thoreau's eyes are said to have swelled with tears after being told by a sister and his mother, soon after graduating from college, that he would have to go out into the world, away from Concord, to seek his fortune.[36] He never married, and appears to have courted only one woman in his early adulthood. His extensive walks, combined with his surveying work and careful observations of nature, gave him intimate knowledge of the local landscape and ecology. From 1845–1847 he lived just outside the village of Concord at Walden Pond. He never traveled to Europe (he once refused an offer of a trip to Rome), and only toward the end of his life, in the hope of improving his health, did he travel as far west as Minnesota. He dryly commented in *Walden* that he had "travelled a good deal in Concord."[37] He lived, in short, a bachelor's life, never far from his family or his native village. While he took brief excursions from time to time to gather material and ideas for his writing, these were always relatively brief regional trips. By the standards of other college educated cultural figures in nineteenth-century America, Thoreau was decidedly uninterested in the conventions of travel to the European continent or even of developing a wider experience outside the northeastern United States (he never traveled further south than Philadelphia, Pennsylvania). It would be hard to imagine a more locally embedded literary and intellectual figure than Thoreau. One of his biographers notes that "No American author – unless it was Whitman – turned so heartily from Europe as Thoreau; for him it was a matter of principle, a proud determination to claim his own place."[38] The novelist Henry James was less charitable, claiming that "he was worse than provincial – he was parochial."[39]

Despite his attachment to his native village, however, Thoreau was in some ways actually the least provincial of thinkers and writers. He had good language skills, reading Latin and Greek and French, as well as some German, Italian, and Spanish.[40] He had a deep interest in the classical literature of Europe, but his interests extended to classical works from India and China as well. He gathered a great deal of archeological and historical material about American Indians, and he hoped to write a book about them one day (he did not live long enough to fully develop this project). Thoreau actually thought of himself as a traveler, even though he rarely left Concord and its surrounding countryside. What he meant by this had more to do with training himself to closely observe and learn from the world around him than it did with ranging far and wide around the globe. Indeed, he thought traveling to distant lands often obscured the kind of attentiveness his traveling was focused on. He was committed to the idea that knowledge was universal and ahistorical, which meant that wisdom could be found both close to home and in the works of the greatest figures in any of the great cultural traditions. No American writer of his generation was less interested in contemporary American literature than Thoreau, but none was more interested in the great literature of the entire world. While in some ways he was a provincial figure, he was clearly a most cosmopolitan thinker as well.

A second paradox concerns our understanding of Thoreau's unique contributions and individuality. Thoreau famously comments toward the end of *Walden*, "If a man does not keep pace with his companions, perhaps it is because he hears a different drummer."[41] He has come to be thought of as almost the archetypal independent man, an eccentric and entirely self-invented individual who refuses to conform to the customs and habits and opinions of his society. Thoreau's reputation serves as a model of independence and individuality, an inspiration for all who feel the need to march, in Thoreau's image, to a different drummer. We often think of him as a person who shows the strength of character to have determined the shape of his own life without regard for reputation or public opinion or social convention. He may have lived his life close to home, but he lived it with a heroic individuality.

In light of this reputation, it is surprising to discover that so much in Thoreau's life was, at least on the surface, unoriginal. As we will see in the chapters that follow, Thoreau's most famous acts were in truth quite derivative. He was clearly following others in Concord by not paying his poll tax and by withdrawing from church membership. A classmate from Harvard had built a simple cabin and lived next to a local pond prior to Thoreau's experiment at Walden. Much of his writing shares a great deal with Emerson's work, and even his speech patterns were said to have mimicked Emerson's.[42] It would be easy to see Thoreau, as many of his contemporaries did, not only as a crank, but as an almost entirely unoriginal crank. This would be a mistake. Thoreau certainly borrowed freely from others, but it has also become clear over time that although he looked like a minor and unoriginal member of Emerson's circle to many in his own lifetime, he was brilliant at taking others' examples and ideas and making use of them in his own way. It is only with the passage of many years, however, that Thoreau's distinctive contributions have come to be widely appreciated.

These paradoxes in Thoreau's biography – the contrast between his provincial and cosmopolitan character, his generally quiet and uneventful life in contrast with his heroic reputation and sense of self, and the tension between his original and unoriginal qualities – are illustrative of the complexity of the man. There is perhaps one paradox, however, that outshines all others for our purposes, and that is the contrast between Thoreau's refusal to become involved in political affairs and his reputation as a political reformer and activist. *Civil Disobedience*, of course, has become a classic of American political thought; two of his other essays, *Slavery in Massachusetts* and *A Plea for Captain John Brown*, also contributed significantly to the abolitionist literature of Thoreau's lifetime. Through these essays, and also through *Walden* and other writings focused on nature and economic life, Thoreau has claimed a significant position in American social and political thought. Yet Thoreau himself could rightly be portrayed as a deeply apolitical or even anti-political individual. He never participated in mainstream politics, even by voting in elections. He loathed political parties and the newspapers that, in his view, were merely extensions of these corrupt institutions. Even political reformers received his uncompromising criticism. Although he shared a hatred of slavery with the abolition movement, he refused to join abolitionist organizations. He did help move individuals along the Underground Railroad, and he gave a few public addresses at abolition events, but he remained jealous of his independence from public life. It would be hard to find any other figure both so personally disengaged from politics yet occupying such a prominent place in American political culture. Even Thoreau's most famous political statement, *Civil Disobedience*, is in large part a challenge to his contemporaries to withdraw entirely from political affairs. Thoreau is, paradoxically, a remarkably apolitical political reformer. He never wished to belong to the kind of organizations that are fundamental to both institutional and protest politics. His contributions to political life are offered from the perspective of a political outsider.

So how did this nineteenth-century character, who little influenced his contemporaries and cultivated very little political experience, come to be such an important and influential figure in the American political tradition? The disjunction between Thoreau's biography and his historical reputation can only be explained in terms of Thoreau's true vocation as a writer. The Henry David Thoreau known to posterity is not so much the Concord resident who died in 1862 as he is a figure introduced in Thoreau's own writings. Thoreau did not write what we think of as conventional fiction, in the manner of his contemporaries Hawthorne and Melville. His essays and books, however, were much more personal than many of the essays crafted by Emerson. Almost everything Thoreau wrote was autobiographical, self-consciously presented from the perspective of the carefully crafted character, Henry Thoreau. The working title of the early drafts of *Walden* was, tellingly, *The History of Myself.*[43]

The brilliance with which Thoreau presents himself is reflected in the attraction of later audiences to the experiences, sensibilities, character, and moral commitments of the Henry Thoreau found in his texts. One biographer has called *Civil Disobedience* Thoreau's "most often read – and taught – essay and one of the great Western statements on the importance of conscience."[44] The reason for this popularity is in large part the result of the way Thoreau weaves his own story into more formal arguments about the "relation of the individual to the state." One of Thoreau's most sensitive commentators has noted his unique approach to moral and political reform: "persuasion and example were his only weapons."[45] Many of the arguments Thoreau presents are similar to those found in Emerson's essay, *Politics*. Thoreau's character, however, embodies these ideas in *Civil Disobedience*. It is his skill in animating his essay with the personality, sensibilities, and experiences of the figure

Henry Thoreau that has allowed Thoreau the author to captivate later audiences and speak more directly and clearly to them than Emerson ever would in *Politics*. As an exemplary figure in his own writings, it is understandable that some readers have been annoyed, even repelled, by what they take to be the arrogance or conceit of the Thoreau they find in texts like *Walden* and *Civil Disobedience*. But many others are inspired by the example they find here. It is the morally principled character of Thoreau himself, as we find him living in Thoreau's writings, that has inspired so many readers in the twentieth – and now the twenty-first – century.

What follows in the remainder of this book is designed to introduce readers to *Civil Disobedience*, Thoreau's most influential and widely read essay. The essay itself is reproduced in the Appendix at the end of the book. Readers will find each paragraph numbered for easy reference; light annotation is also provided. Before moving to Chapter 2, it is probably best to carefully read *Civil Disobedience* in its entirety. Returning then to Chapter 2, readers will find a close reading and explication of the text. In Chapter 3, some of the essay's most important historical and intellectual contexts are discussed. The following chapter (4) exposes readers to the main currents of interpretation found in the scholarly secondary literature. The final substantive chapter (5) provides some suggestions for how we might think about the relationship between Thoreau's essay and some of the great themes of Western political theory. In the Postscript (Chapter 6), we will again briefly explore the relevance of Thoreau's essay for political engagement and protest.

## NOTES

1  Stanley Edgar Hyman, "Henry Thoreau in Our Time," in Sherman Paul, ed., *Thoreau: A Collection of Critical Essays* (Englewood Cliffs, NJ: Prentice-Hall, 1962), p. 24.
2  Henry D. Thoreau, *Essays*, Jeffrey S. Cramer, ed. (New Haven, CT and London: Yale University Press, 2013), p. xxvii.
3  Walter Harding, *The Days of Henry Thoreau* (NY: Alfred A. Knopf, 1966), p. 207.
4  Henry David Thoreau, *The Variorum "Walden" and the Variorum "Civil Disobedience,"* Walter Harding, ed. (NY: Washington Square Press, 1968), p. 335.
5  Walter Harding and Michael Meyer, *The New Thoreau Handbook* (NY: New York University Press, 1980), p. 221.

6 Sujit Mukherjee, "Thoreau in India," in Eugene F. Timpe, ed., *Thoreau Abroad* (Hamden, CT: Archon Books, 1971), p. 162.

7 William Stuart Nelson, "Thoreau and American Non-Violent Resistance," in John Hicks, ed., *Thoreau in Our Season* (Amherst, MA: University of Massachusetts Press, 1967), p. 14.

8 Maurice Gonnaud and Micheline Flak, "Thoreau in France," in Timpe, ed., *Thoreau Abroad*, p. 38.

9 Rev. Trevor N. W. Bush, "Thoreau in South Africa," in Hicks, ed., *Thoreau in Our Season*, p. 27.

10 Harding and Meyer, *New Thoreau Handbook*, p. 42.

11 Rev. Martin Luther King Jr. "A Legacy of Creative Protest," in Hicks, ed., *Thoreau in Our Season*, p. 13.

12 Staughton Lynd, *From Here to There* (Oakland, CA: PM Press, 2010), p. 32.

13 Jerome Lawrence and Robert E. Lee, *The Night Thoreau Spent in Jail* (NY: Hill and Wang, 1970), p. vii.

14 Ibid.

15 Michael Meyer, *Several More Lives to Live* (Westport, CT: Greenwood Press, 1977), p. 152.

16 Ibid., pp. 83–84.

17 Quoted in ibid., p. 9.

18 John Lewis, "Veteran Civil Rights Leader: Snowden Acted in Traditon of Civil Disobedience," *The Guardian*, 7 August 2013. Available at: www.theguardian. com/world/2013/aug/07/john-lewis-civil-rights-edward-snowden. (accessed June 2014).

19 Harding and Meyer, *New Thoreau Handbook*, p. 210.

20 Meyer, *Several More Lives to Live*, p. 181.

21 *Daily Kos*, "The Banning of Mexican American Authors in Tucson," 16 January 2012. Available at: www.dailykos.com/story/2012/01/16/1055318/-The-Banning-of-Mexican-American-authors-in-Tucson# (accessed June 2014).

22 Henry Seidel Canby, *Thoreau* (Boston, MA: Houghton Mifflin, 1939), p. 211.

23 Harding and Meyer, *New Thoreau Handbook*, p. 7.

24 Canby, *Thoreau*, p. 24.

25 Henry David Thoreau, *Consciousness in Concord*, Perry Miller, ed. (Boston, MA: Houghton Mifflin, 1958), p. 8.

26 Harding, *Days of Henry Thoreau*, p. 201.

27 Harold Bloom, ed., *Henry David Thoreau* (NY: Bloom's Literary Criticism, 2008), p. 70.

28 Walter Harding, "The Last Days of Henry Thoreau," in Walter Harding, ed., *The Thoreau Centennial* (Albany, NY: The State University of New York Press, 1962), p. 45.

29 E. B. White, "Walden – 1954," *Yale Review* 44, 1954, p. 22.

30 Harding and Meyer, *New Thoreau Handbook*, p. 204.

31 Harding, *Days of Henry Thoreau*, p. 309.

32 Canby, *Thoreau*, p. 33.

33 Ibid., p. 22.

34  Robert D. Richardson, *Henry Thoreau* (Berkeley, CA: University of California Press, 1986), p. 299.

35  Harding and Meyer, *New Thoreau Handbook*, p. 221.

36  Michael Sims, *The Adventures of Henry Thoreau* (NY, London, New Delhi, Sydney: Bloomsbury, 2014), p. 32.

37  Henry David Thoreau, *A Week on the Concord and Merrimack Rivers; Walden, or, Life in the Woods; The Maine Woods; Cape Cod* (NY: Library of America, 1985), p. 326.

38  Sherman, Paul, *The Shores of America* (Urbana, IL: University of Illinois Press, 1958), p. 39.

39  Bloom, ed., *Henry David Thoreau*, pp. 136–137.

40  Harding and Meyer, *New Thoreau Handbook*, p. 97.

41  Thoreau, *A Week, etc.*, p. 581.

42  Sims, *The Adventures of Henry Thoreau*, p. 97.

43  Richardson, *Henry Thoreau*, p. 183.

44  Ibid., p. 175.

45  Paul, *The Shores of America*, p. 246.

# 2

# READING *CIVIL DISOBEDIENCE*

Reading Thoreau's *Civil Disobedience* is more challenging than is often appreciated. Even the title we recognize, "Civil Disobedience," may mislead us; it is not the title under which the essay was originally published, nor do we even have any evidence that Thoreau ever spoke or wrote the phrase "civil disobedience" himself. The current title was given to the document when it was posthumously published in a collection of his work in 1866, four years after his death. When Thoreau first presented the lecture that would become the essay, in January and then again in February 1848, he suggested that it was an investigation of "the relation of the individual to the state." When he published the lecture as an essay the following January (1849), he gave it the title *Resistance to Civil Government*. Although it is possible that Thoreau approved the title *Civil Disobedience* – he edited many of his papers for publication or re-publication during his final illness – we have no evidence about this one way or the other. *Resistance to Civil Government* is the only title we can be sure that Thoreau approved for this essay.

So even before we get to the body of the document, we are confronted with a dilemma. In the twentieth century, "civil disobedience" has come to mean something very specific: the breaking of a law claimed or assumed to be unjust, while respecting the more general legal and constitutional structure by engaging in this targeted law-breaking in an open, well-publicized manner and willingly accepting the legal consequences for this behavior. In the nineteenth century, civil disobedience was not yet so clearly identified with this particular form of political protest. But at the very least, the phrase seems to commit the disobedient person to a kind of civility, a general respect for the broad constitutional and legal order. If we read the essay with the title *Resistance to Civil Government*, we expect to confront a more radical document, one less respectful of government in general, less "civil," more belligerent toward political authority. Indeed, if we hear that someone wants to speak to us about "resisting civil government," we may expect that person to speak about revolution rather than reform, and we may not be surprised if that individual defends not only illegal resistance, but possibly violent, secretive, and subversive resistance. Thus, the title most commonly identifying Thoreau's famous essay leads us to expect the kind of patriotic, nonviolent, and civil acts of disobedience many of us identify with the examples of Mohandas Gandhi and Martin Luther King Jr. The only title we can be certain that Thoreau approved, however, leads us to think in very different terms. While *Civil Disobedience* has become the most widely recognized title for the essay, we need to be very careful not to allow this title to inappropriately shape or predispose our reading of the text. Even if Thoreau did approve the posthumous title of *Civil Disobedience*, and there is no reason for us to be confident that he did, we need to remember the radical and pugnacious title Thoreau first selected for the essay.

There are a number of other differences between the 1849 and 1866 editions of *Civil Disobedience*. Most of these are minor editorial matters such as changes in punctuation and corrections of mistranscriptions and misspellings, and they have no significant impact on the text's meaning. There are three substantive changes in addition to the difference in title, however. In the second paragraph, the third sentence of the 1849 edition describes the American government as follows: "It is a sort of wooden gun to the people themselves; and, if ever they should use it in earnest as a real one against each other, it will surely split." This sentence, published just a little over a decade before the American Civil War, seems to recognize that there are real possibilities for Americans using the military power of government against one another. When the essay was edited for publication by Thoreau's sister, Sophia, and his friend, Ellery Channing, the second half of the sentence was removed to now read: "It is a sort of wooden gun to the people themselves." The meaning of the first part of the sentence is thereby retained – that is, the government is a violent tool of the people, but an inept and highly imperfect tool (like a practice rifle rather than a real one;[1] wood, after all, is not the proper material to contain the explosive power of a firearm). The foreboding prediction of civil war is removed, presumably out of respect for the recent trauma experienced by the nation in the "War Between the States."

In addition to the change of this sentence, a passage from George Peele's *The Battle of Alcazer* (1594) was added to paragraph 40, and a reference to Confucius ("the Chinese philosopher") was added to the final paragraph (45). Of these four substantive differences between the 1849 and 1866 editions, the first two (the title and the alteration of the sentence in paragraph 2) are of the greatest significance.

The posthumous edition of the essay, bearing the title *Civil Disobedience* and other substantive changes and editorial corrections, has become the most widely used edition of the text. Although there are reasons to prefer the 1849 edition since it was the only edition definitively approved by Thoreau (some editors hold the 1849 text to be authoritative, and my personal sympathies are with them), convention dictates that we think of the 1866 edition as the standard text. It is this later edition that has been reproduced in the Appendix. For ease of reference as you read through this chapter and those that follow, paragraphs have been separated and numbered. Notes have been supplied in the Appendix to identify the substantive differences between the 1849 and 1866 editions, as well as to explain unfamiliar terms, references, and allusions.

There are two other general sources of confusion for readers of *Civil Disobedience*, especially those encountering it for the first time. The first of these is the rhetorical style Thoreau employs throughout the essay. This style is often sharp and sometimes exaggerated.

Thoreau once wrote in his *Journal* that "We live by exaggeration," and in a letter to a friend he admitted that he is personally a great exaggerator.[2] He is sometimes sarcastic, sometimes punning and joking, and often extremely critical and judgmental. In *Walden*, for example, Thoreau claims, "I have lived some thirty years on this planet, and I have yet to hear the first syllable of valuable or even earnest advice from my seniors."[3] We have seen that Thoreau's childhood nickname was "The Judge," and a college classmate reported that as a student at Harvard he was "cold and unimpressionable."[4] Some readers view these attributes as evidence of courage and strength of character and applaud them with pleasure and approval. Others view them as evidence of egotism and a deep lack of sympathy with others and cringe in disgust. Regardless of how they strike any individual reader's sensibility, however, it is important not to allow our emotional connection to the text to mislead us or blind us to its meaning. Likewise, we need to be very aware of Thoreau's sarcastic edge, so as not to be misled by certain passages. For example, when Thoreau says of the United States government, in paragraph 2, that "It is excellent, we must all allow," it is important to recognize the deep sarcasm that can be inferred from the context of the rest of the paragraph. Taken out of context, and read without this sarcastic edge, the comment could be significantly misleading to our overall reading of Thoreau's message.

The third element to keep in mind when reading *Civil Disobedience* is Thoreau's intended audience. We have seen that people all over the world, in different times and places, have found this essay to speak to them in meaningful ways. Thoreau himself, however, is clearly addressing a very limited and particular audience: his fellow citizens of Concord and of Massachusetts more generally. This means, first, that he only feels the need to frame his argument within this limited moral and political context. It means, in addition, that there is much that Thoreau feels he does not need to explore or defend, since he can assume he shares a similar view with his audience (on the immoral nature of slavery and concerning the war with Mexico, for example). In the United States in 1849, there were certainly significant numbers of American citizens who suffered no moral pain over slavery or the war with Mexico. But this broader citizenry is not being addressed in Thoreau's essay.

Thoreau feels no need to explain in detail the moral horror of either of these realities. On the contrary, he assumes he shares this sense of horror with his audience. In *Civil Disobedience* his focus is limited, so he does not provide a more general defense of anti-war abolitionism. Instead, his project is to explain how best to channel and act upon these shared moral sensibilities and commitments.

When reading *Civil Disobedience*, then, always remember to be sensitive to the problems posed by the competing versions of the text, Thoreau's style and rhetorical habits, and his self-consciously chosen audience.

Once we get past the title and turn to the body of the essay, we find there are at least two obviously distinct but related projects in the text. One is to reflect philosophically on the obligations that do or do not bind individuals to the law, the political community, and political authorities; remember that the theme of the original lecture upon which the published essay is based was "on the relation of the individual to the state." Another task is to tell the story of his arrest, on either July 23rd or 24th, 1846 (we are uncertain which day it was), for failure to pay his poll tax. The entire essay consists of 45 paragraphs. Paragraphs 28–35 tell the story of Thoreau's night in jail, with the remaining paragraphs consisting of more abstract and less biographical reflections and arguments. The philosophical reflections are intended to illuminate and explain the biographical events. Thoreau's lecture, out of which the essay grew, was conceived as a kind of explanation to his neighbors for the behavior that led to his arrest.

The distinction between these two broad projects in *Civil Disobedience* is a helpful starting point, but it is also possible to recognize a more fine-grained division of the text. Paragraphs 28–35 are obviously of central importance for providing the biographical context and excuse for the abstract reflections in the rest of the essay. But the 37 "philosophical" paragraphs are themselves noticeably divided in important ways. We might usefully think of *Civil Disobedience* as being made up of the following eight sections:

1. Broad introductory comments and reflections (paragraphs 1–2).
2. The philosophical heart of the essay, what I will refer to as a "treatise on expediency," which constitutes the longest and

philosophically most complex elements of the essay (paragraphs 3–24).
3. A three-paragraph transition connecting the treatise on expediency to Thoreau's personal story (paragraphs 25–27).
4. Telling the story of his arrest, night in jail, and release (paragraphs 28–35).
5. A two-paragraph transition away from his autobiography, restating his philosophical position in light of this personal story (paragraphs 36–37).
6. Imagining a moral position different from the one he has defended thus far (paragraphs 38–40).
7. The reaffirmation of his position (paragraphs 41–43).
8. Placing these reflections back into the broad context initially sketched in the opening two paragraphs (paragraphs 44–45).

Sections 1 and 8 (the beginning and end) are important mirrors of one another, as are Sections 3 and 5 (the "bookends" around the biographical sketch). The central moral content of the essay is explored, explained, and defended primarily in Section 2.

## SECTION 1

In the opening sentences of *Civil Disobedience*, Thoreau famously declares that he accepts the motto that "That government is best which governs least." This slogan, taken from the masthead of a widely read political newspaper, the *Democratic Review* (a newspaper, it should be noted, in which he had published an essay in 1843), is pushed to an even more radical conclusion; namely, that "That government is best which governs not at all." We are presented in these very first sentences with a distinction that will be dropped in paragraph 3, but that we will return to in the final passages of the essay in Section 8. This is the distinction between the best practical ideal and the ideal itself. As will become clear in Section 2, Thoreau wants to focus in *Civil Disobedience* on what he takes to be the best practical goal – that government which governs least. But he raises an even higher ideal – that government which governs not at all – even though he recognizes that men are not yet "prepared" for it. That anarchist goal may not yet be practicable, but it is an animating goal nonetheless. It is only mentioned here (and at the end) to situate the body of the essay within a broader moral and political context and to remind the reader that even though he tells us in the first sentence of paragraph 3 that he will attempt to "speak practically and as a citizen," there is a deeper vision of human well-being than the world he addresses in the body of the essay.

Having framed his discussion within this ideal set of moral commitments and ideas, Thoreau declares that government is "at best but an expedient." That is, at its best, government is a practical device, in the service to some broader goals or goods of a community. It is frustrating that Thoreau does not develop this idea here. Just what *are* the functions and tasks appropriate to "expedient" government? We are left quite unsure about this, but Thoreau does immediately develop the negative to the point: governments are most commonly inexpedient, and the American government is no exception to this pattern. Americans who flatter themselves that their government is in some way an exception to this pattern ignore the reality. Thoreau correctly points out that the current war with Mexico has been engineered and pursued by a small minority who has taken to using the government "as their tool," that is, the tool to promote the interests of that minority. Americans have always been sensitive to the problems associated with standing armies – permanent professional armies, as opposed to citizen militias. In the Declaration of Independence, standing armies are declared to be an instrument through which the King of Great Britain came to tyrannize the colonies. Thoreau uses this widely shared fear as leverage for explaining his point. Standing armies are easily manipulated by factions (most commonly an overbearing executive) against the interests or intensions of the broader political community. In a like manner, the entire mechanism of government can be captured and exploited for narrow and inappropriate ends. When governments become "inexpedient," they are dangerous and violate the rights, the consent, of the people at large. They abandon their purpose and thereby lose their legitimacy.

Thoreau develops this point in paragraph 2 by reminding the reader that the government is "but a tradition." It has not been given to Americans by "nature," it has no standing in the moral universe beyond the fact that it is a young set of institutions developed by a particular group of individuals in the recent past. As good as it may have originally been, it has already become inexpedient and is thus "each instant losing some of its integrity." Most of the remainder of paragraph 2 is a rhetorical flourish, a reminder that government is supposed to serve, rather than be served, but that the contemporary American government (like virtually all others) attempts to reverse this appropriate ordering of things. To make this point, Thoreau denies the good that government has done to promote education, settle the West, and so on. This is an especially flamboyant claim to make in the late 1840s, as the country was vigorously debating the role of the federal government in promoting "internal improvements," that is, infrastructure investment in roads and canals and other public works to stimulate economic development (Whigs strongly promoted such investments, while Democrats opposed such extensive government spending and the growth of the federal government's importance in regulating and shaping the economy). Thoreau's point is that regardless of the degree to which we find government involved in the development of American social life, the vital energy and action required for achieving social goods comes not from government but from the people themselves. While not denying that there are proper roles for government to play as an "expedient" to democratic society, Thoreau loudly proclaims that what good we find in America has been produced despite the government, rather than because of it.

Recall the important sentence from paragraph 2 describing the American government as a "sort of wooden gun to the people themselves." We have seen that the sentence originally appeared in 1849 with an additional clause ("and, if ever they should use it in earnest as a real one against each other, it will surely split") that seemed to foresee the grave danger of sectional conflict that was to erupt into the American Civil War a little more than a decade later. Even with the second half of the sentence removed, however, we see Thoreau's view that the American government is at best an imperfect tool; its aim is limited to maintaining order through violence, or the threat of violence, and it is poorly constructed even for this limited purpose (without the steel required for a true weapon). Even though Thoreau believes the government has grown increasingly "inexpedient" over the 60 years since the creation and adoption of the Constitution, he also appears to believe it was a significantly imperfect political order to begin with.

What we have in these first two paragraphs, Section 1, are a number of important preliminaries. First, there is the initial contrast between the best government and a world without the need for any government at all. Second, we find the idea that the best government is at best a practical expedient. Third, we have the view that Thoreau's own government has succumbed to the disease so common to political authority; it has become inexpedient, an increasingly unjust and imperial force, instead of playing its proper role as society's servant. Americans commonly think of the Founders in heroic, even reverential, terms. Thoreau's image of the "wooden gun" suggests that even these revolutionary beginnings were significantly imperfect.

## SECTION 2

What we are thinking of here as Section 2 is by far the most extensive and complex set of passages in *Civil Disobedience*. In these 21 paragraphs (paragraphs 3–24), nearly half of the paragraphs in the essay, Thoreau develops all his essential themes and arguments. We referred above to this section as a "treatise on expediency" since Thoreau's understanding of the uses (and abuses) of government and politics is cast in terms of expediency and inexpediency. This is the conceptual key to unlocking his argument.

Thoreau begins this section by making a claim he repeats a number of times thereafter: that he intends to speak practically. Although in the opening paragraph he imagines a world developed well beyond current practical possibilities (and he will return to that theme in the concluding paragraph), for the sake of his argument in this essay he will try to address the world as he currently finds it. He distinguishes himself, in this important sense, from "no-government men," and claims that he will take the perspective in this essay not as one of these, but as a citizen, as one who accepts his status as a member of a political community. So, what is a "no-government man"? In general we might think it is a person who objects to the idea of government altogether, an anarchist. There were such individuals in Concord, friends of Thoreau's in fact, who held views quite like this. Many radical abolitionists, including Thoreau's friend Bronson Alcott, were pacifists who objected to all political power on the ground that it was ultimately based upon force. These idealists held that only moral suasion and the appeal to what they took to be Christian ethics were acceptable when confronting threats either from institutions, such as slavery, or individuals, such as criminals. This position was commonly called "non-resistance," and Alcott had actually twice debated Thoreau and Thoreau's brother, John, in the Concord Lyceumon on this matter of non-resistance; both times Alcott defended non-resistance and Thoreau criticized it.[5] This helps frame the importance of Thoreau's original title to this essay, *Resistance to Civil Government*. That title alone suggests that Thoreau wished to distance himself from no-government men, just as he clearly explains in this paragraph.

Although the distancing from Alcott's position is clear, this should not be taken to mean that Thoreau unambiguously opposes no-government men like Alcott and other utopian abolitionists and "non-resistants." In *Walden*, Thoreau refers to Alcott admiringly as "One of the last of the philosophers,"[6] and the opening and closing paragraphs of *Civil Disobedience* suggest Thoreau's sympathy with Alcott's views, at least in some future time "when men are prepared for it." Alcott had himself refused to pay his poll tax and had been arrested for it in 1843, three years before Thoreau, and it is likely that Thoreau was motivated to refuse to pay his tax by Alcott's example. In addition, the non-cooperation with government that we find Thoreau defending in this essay is not as different from "non-resistance" as we might expect. For now, however, Thoreau will explain his refusal to pay his poll tax not as an act of non-resistance, but rather as the opposite, as a kind of active resistance. He is taking what he claims to be a practical stance, one that assumes, at least for the time being, a world where expedient government may be imaginable and perhaps necessary. Instead of insisting on the abolition of government, he will explain the kind of government that would "command his respect."

The distinctions Thoreau presents in paragraph 4 allow us to see the rough shape of the argument to come. If we are going to speak practically about government, as he has chosen to do, we have to admit that the relationships our current government generates are based upon force rather than consent or agreement. We obey the majority not because of some abstract or presumed commitment identified by political philosophers, but rather because the majority is simply stronger than the minority. Once this becomes the case, government has become the mechanism by which one group imposes its will upon another. In this way, government compromises its moral position. From this time forward in the essay, Thoreau will refer to his standing in relation to the government not as a citizen, but as a subject, and his implication is that this is the *practical* reality for all of us. This is the reality of practical political life, that the government is a power claiming the right to treat us as objects to be commanded and manipulated at will. To the degree that we accept this relationship, we jettison what Thoreau calls our manhood, by which he means our capacity to be morally responsible and self-governing. When government becomes thus inexpedient, the appropriate relationship between citizens and government is perverted and reversed. Citizens are treated as subjects, and governments take into their own hands the sovereignty that rightly belongs in the hands of the people alone.

Here and in what follows, then, Thoreau makes clear that when we allow ourselves to accept our status as subjects and submit to the superior force of the government, we compromise our natures and become less than fully human – as he says, we are reduced to the likeness of "horses and dogs," if not "wood and earth and stones" (paragraph 5). To lose our conscience is to lose our manhood, and to lose our manhood is to lose our human dignity. For all of the terrible things said about soldiers in this passage, it is interesting to note that Thoreau apparently never objected to his obligation to muster with the local militia – an obligation assumed of every able-bodied man of military age, and which he seems to have performed annually.[7] His insults are directed not at soldiers in general, but at those soldiers who allow themselves to be manipulated to unjust ends. Inexpedient government turns the moral universe upside down. The government, which should be the tool or the machine wielded by another, becomes itself the sovereign force. As citizens become subjects, in practical terms they themselves become machines at the service of the government. So perverse does this moral universe become that the true man, the individual taking full responsibility for his own decisions by consulting his own moral considerations – his conscience – will be thought a selfish enemy of the government rather than its greatest friend. Thoreau ironically refers to Hamlet's egalitarian observation that Alexander the Great died and turned to dust just as any man does to suggest that we can wait to be mere objects until we die ("A wise man will only be useful as a man, and will not submit to be 'clay,' and 'stop a hole to keep the wind away,' but leave that office to his dust at least") (paragraph 5). He refers to comments of Louis, heir to the throne of France in Shakespeare's *King John*, to inspire all subjects – not just aristocrats like Louis – to become citizens, to insist upon their moral independence ("I am too high-born to be propertied,/To be a secondary at control,/Or useful serving-man and instrument/To any sovereign state throughout the world") (paragraph 5).

Given the perversion of the political world, a true citizen necessarily finds himself in an antagonistic relationship with the actual government. Only a subject, one who has abdicated his moral responsibilities, can view "that political organization as *my* government which is the *slave's* government also" (paragraph 7). A citizen, in contrast, will be disgraced by this relationship and will be required to disassociate from the political organization in order to maintain his moral integrity. Thoreau concludes this first set of considerations, in paragraph 8, by focusing his attention on a conventional set of political beliefs. "All men," he says, "recognize the right of revolution." This may not be true in all times and places, but it certainly was true for Thoreau's audience in Massachusetts, who traced with pride their revolutionary heritage back beyond the Declaration of Independence of 1776 to the battle of Lexington and Concord in 1775. The conventional wisdom in mid-nineteenth-century Concord was that the Founders were justified in resisting the British government. It was much less widely believed by Thoreau's contemporaries, however, that they, like their forebears, might also justly engage in "resistance to civil government." Thoreau nonetheless insists that the political situation in his own lifetime is dramatically more "inexpedient" than was the situation during the Revolutionary period. The main complaint of the colonists against the government of Great Britain concerned an increase in taxes on certain commodities. But this is a trivial consideration in comparison with the political conditions found in nineteenth-century American public life. A sixth of the American population was currently held in servitude, and the government was currently pursuing an imperial war against its neighbors in Mexico – a war largely framed by and pursued in the interests of the slaveholding states. For Thoreau, these evils dwarf the wrongs committed by the British government against the colonies. All Americans who believe the colonists were right to rebel must admit, if any moral consistency is to be maintained, that the case for rebellion in 1848 is dramatically stronger and of much greater urgency.

In bringing his audience back to their own admitted political principles, and insisting that these principles lead them in directions they have been reluctant to go, Thoreau continues to develop the metaphor of machinery. The "friction" and the "machine" metaphors refer back to paragraph 2, where he suggests that government is a machine the people create for their own purposes. He wants to emphasize in paragraph 8 that his orneriness is not a matter of resisting every little friction caused by such a machine. He implies that it would be morally irresponsible to object to every minor inconvenience and unfairness produced by the daily function of government. When he says that now the "friction" has come to have its own "machine," he is suggesting again that things have been turned upside down, that the friction, the injustice, has come to define and direct the government itself. The injustices the machine of government now serve, such as slavery and imperial war, are so morally grotesque that we must admit that we are not facing mundane political trivialities (such as, perhaps, a modest growth in taxes); we are facing dire injustices that must drive "honest men," those who would be true citizens in a just political order, to consider rebellion and revolution.

Although Thoreau suggests that the widely held popular belief in the right to revolution should lead us to a much more radical posture toward the current government than is generally admitted, he understands there is a conventional moral wisdom leading in the opposite direction. This common perspective is consequentialist, or broadly utilitarian, and assumes that an ethical approach to politics is fundamentally a balancing of expected political outcomes, a weighing of the expected benefits of a particular political act against the likely negative consequences. The art of politics thus becomes the art of utilitarian calculation. William Paley was an eighteenth-century moral philosopher Thoreau had read as a student at Harvard. Paley's greatest work of political philosophy, *The Principles of Moral and Political Philosophy*, included a chapter entitled "The Duty of Submission to Civil Government Explained." Thoreau almost certainly had this chapter in mind when originally entitling his essay *Resistance to Civil Government*. In his chapter, Paley introduces the idea of expediency and thus frames and provides the terms of Thoreau's arguments in this central section of *Civil Disobedience*. "The lawfulness of resistance, or the lawfulness of a revolt," Paley argues, "does not depend alone upon the grievance which is sustained or feared, but also upon the probable expense and event of the contest."[8] Paley's view is that justified rebellion is always dependent upon a kind of calculation, an evaluation of expected costs and benefits. Indeed, he holds that "all civil obligation is resolved into expedience."[9] Put another way, political morality for Paley is always a form of political calculation and prediction, a process of imagining if expected outcomes are better or worse than the current situation.

This view is ubiquitous in political life; Thoreau points out that "in their practice, nations agree with Paley" (paragraph 10). In truth, it is not only "nations" that agree. Many citizens think of political obligations in just such consequentialist terms. This is precisely the point at which Thoreau can make clear his own position and contrast it with this conventional wisdom. Expediency is not a moral category for Thoreau. It is, rather, a non-moral calculation, rather like efficiency. It is a matter of expediency, for example, to decide which side of the road cars should drive on; no great moral question is at stake in choosing the left or the right. There needs to be an agreement on one side or another for the sake of safety and efficiency, but there is no reason to believe that any principles beyond basic efficiency are at stake in coming to a decision. In contrast, Thoreau holds that moral issues are of a qualitatively different nature from such matters of utility and efficiency. As he sarcastically suggests, Paley might find it "inexpedient" to refrain from wresting a plank from a drowning man in order to save his own life. But moral life requires just such a commitment to principles beyond utility or expediency. There are times when we are required by moral principle, for example, to perish rather than harm another person. Thoreau makes clear that he believes this is not only true for individuals; he believes the same principles apply to political communities.

The important distinction between Thoreau's position and Paley's is not that Thoreau dismisses expediency. Rather, he holds that it is a perfectly normal part of the administration of daily life. However, he denies that expediency is itself a guide for moral evaluation and decision-making. It is a non-moral form of calculation that is incapable in itself of providing significant moral guidance. In fact, thinking of expediency as a moral principle creates a kind of blindness, an inability to think beyond the logic of a particular situation and view it from a broader moral perspective. In his first book, *A Week on the Concord and Merrimack Rivers* (written while Thoreau was living at Walden Pond, the same period during which he also worked on the lecture that would become *Civil Disobedience*), Thoreau writes: "However flattering order and expediency may look, it is but the repose of a lethargy, and we will choose rather to be awake, though it be stormy, and maintain ourselves on this earth and in this life, as we may, without signing our death-warrant."[10] When we consider "order and expediency" to be our guiding moral principles, he believes we are not being sufficiently alert to moral considerations. Thoreau recognizes that when we act from principle, "stormy" relations and events my result. He even uses the principled rebellion of Antigone against her uncle Creon, in contrast to her sister Ismene's initial moral uncertainty, as an illustration of his point.

*Antigone* takes place in the aftermath of a civil war. Antigone's two brothers have been slain while fighting on opposite sides in the war. Eteocles fought for the victorious Creon and was awarded full funeral honors. Creon declares Polynices a traitor, however, and decrees that his body must be left unburied. Antigone and Ismene both believe this order violates their familial obligations to bury family members. Antigone rebels immediately, but Ismene dithers and declares that she is too weak and uncertain to rebel. Even though Antigone's challenge to Creon produced significant "storminess" (the stage is littered with corpses at the end of the play), there is no doubt in Thoreau's mind that Antigone is a moral hero for being unwilling to evaluate her moral obligations to her brother in consequentialist terms.[11]

To confuse expediency with morality as Paley does, then, threatens to turn us into individuals like the drowning man referred to above, who forgets that there are some things we simply should not do regardless of the consequences. Moral principles, in other words, grow from values greater than utility or even survival. For Thoreau, moral principle is what is needed to inform expediency; for Paley, expediency is moral principle itself. Of all the confusions caused by "inexpedient" government, this is perhaps the most fundamental: the moral universe is inverted, and principle becomes sacrificed to utilitarian calculation.

We can see that for Thoreau this leaves the individual confused, impotent, and cut off from his moral obligations. While there are thousands who understand that slavery and imperial war are wrong, they "sit down with their hands in their pockets, and say that they know not what to do, and do nothing" (paragraph 10). But the story is even worse than this. It is not only that we are confused by consequentialist calculation (it is hard, after all, to fully imagine all the potential outcomes of various political options; it is harder yet, if not impossible, to consistently predict which of these outcomes will occur). In addition, utilitarianism reduces all values to a common calculus. In this way, economic calculation comes to hold an equal consideration to calculations concerning, say, individual liberty. Once this happens, the moral game is up: we find ourselves corrupted by our economic interests ("What is the price-current of an honest man and patriot to-day?") (paragraph 10). After all, utilitarianism gives us permission, when evaluating what to do about slavery, to give significant moral weight to our material interests, even if the enslavement of human beings is a wrong so great that calculations of profit and loss should be irrelevant. Instead of considering the justice of the situation, we ask about its costs. The "question of freedom" thus becomes reduced to the question of free trade, and we find ourselves privileging our economic interests in our moral calculations. Thoreau assumes his

Concord and New England audience agrees in general with the anti-war abolitionism he defends. However, the utilitarianism of conventional political wisdom has deeply corrupted both their moral understanding and their moral integrity. This is what he means when he charges, at the end of paragraph 10, that there are "nine hundred and ninety-nine patrons of virtue to one virtuous man." How can we act responsibly when our own material interests corrupt us? If we are to cease being mere "patrons of virtue," and actually become virtuous individuals, we will have to separate our moral evaluations from economic considerations. Only then will appropriate moral action become clear.

The remaining paragraphs (11–24), in what we are calling Section 2, focus on the contrast between participation in conventional forms of democratic political life, on the one hand, and what Thoreau takes to be moral or just behavior, on the other. He begins with one of his most provocative claims, in paragraph 11, that voting, far from being a virtuous civic duty, is a "sort of gaming." When we engage in the practical act of voting, he claims we are doing nothing other than "feebly" expressing our preference to others. This expression is feeble since it holds no stake in the outcome of the election; if my view prevails, good, but if it doesn't, I accept the outcome as a matter of course. This is the sense in which Thoreau equates voting with gambling. We prefer to win, but we understand that our preferences are subject to a process that we can control no more than the cards we are dealt or the numbers that appear when we roll the dice. Morality (his reference in this paragraph is to a "wise man") requires that we be more invested in the promotion of right than we are by merely voting and following majority rule. If Thoreau is right that there is "but little virtue in the action of masses of men," majority rule will often produce decisions of little virtue. In fact, he suggests that the majority will only vote for the right, that is, the abolition of slavery, if they either become indifferent toward it or if there remains very little slavery left to abolish – a damning observation that turned out to be all too true as American history unfolded. We let ourselves off the moral hook, Thoreau, suggests, by thinking our duty toward justice is merely to register our vote.

The system of party politics that developed in the United States to organize elections reflected the same lack of moral integrity found in the practical experience of voting. When Thoreau refers to the Democratic Party presidential nominating convention, he feels nothing but contempt for the candidates (whom he calls demagogues) and the professional politicians and newspaper editors comprising the bulk of party activists. Rather than appealing to our consciences, the goal of the party is to nominate a candidate who appeals to our interests, and politics is thus reduced to the same kind of mutual aid society Thoreau illustrates by reference to the Odd Fellows. Instead of promoting our independence (most importantly, our moral independence), such politics flatter our interests and make us dependent on the system itself. In contrast, Thoreau makes his famous plea for a "man who is a *man*," and "has a bone in his back which you cannot pass your hand through!" (paragraph 12). This image of a man with a strong backbone, which is one Thoreau used in a number of his writings,[12] contrasts with the morally weak and dependent – if gregarious – subjects Americans have become. In *Walden*, similar points are also made in very strong language: "But, wherever a man goes, men will pursue and paw him with their dirty institutions, and, if they can, constrain him to belong to their desperate odd-fellow society."[13] While political institutions are thought to ensure our independence, the reality for Thoreau is that they come to function in such a way as to rob us of the very good they are supposed to protect.

Everything Thoreau wants to suggest about our political obligations rests on this contrast between political participants and those who resist political power, between political expediency and moral action, between Odd Fellows and true citizens, between those who are governed by their interests (and, thus, by demagogues) and *men*. Moral life, and the practical citizenship informed by it, is for Thoreau manhood itself. Conventional political participants may object to the "character and measures of a government," yet nonetheless "yield to it their allegiance and support" (paragraph 14). These individuals, like the voters he has criticized, actually prevent meaningful reform by giving their support to the unjust political order. They believe they must obey unjust laws until they are able to provide political remedies for them and thus, again, find themselves granting legitimacy to the injustices themselves (paragraph 16). Thoreau criticizes even those who have petitioned to dissolve the United States (paragraph 14). In 1842, John Quincy Adams presented a petition from residents of Haverhill, Massachusetts to the United States House of Representatives requesting "peacefully to dissolve the union of these States."[14] Motivated by a hatred of slavery and distressed about the degree to which they believed the slave interests were dominating federal policy, these citizens (represented by a former president of the United States, who was himself the son of the nation's second president) believed dissolution preferable to associating with slave states. Thoreau suggests, however, that even a radical petition such as this is inadequate, since it recognizes the authority of the government to accept or reject the petition. Best to deny this authority altogether, and simply refuse recognition of all inexpedient political authority.

Most damning of all, these conscientious subjects, even those who say they hate slavery and its consequences, benefit from the injustices they claim to deplore. Thoreau alludes to an event involving his "esteemed neighbor," former Congressman Samuel Hoar (paragraph 21). South Carolina had passed a law requiring that "any free negro, or person of color" coming to South Carolina on a merchant ship had to be jailed while that vessel anchored in port. The captain of the ship, when he wished to leave, was required to pay the cost of that individual's jailing before he would be released back to the ship. Hoar was sent by the Governor of Massachusetts to bring suit against this law. When he landed in South Carolina, that state's legislature censured Hoar and ordered him expelled. This proved unnecessary, as he was driven from the town by threats of violence before the legislature's order could be enforced. For Thoreau, this incident illustrates exactly the problem represented by "conscientious" political subjects. Massachusetts found itself suffering the humiliation, first, of the arrest of its free black citizens, and second, of the expulsion of its representative sent to protest and remedy this injustice. All this happened because Massachusetts desired to profit from trade with South Carolina. Because of this desire, citizens of Massachusetts, even abolitionist citizens, find themselves both supporting and profiting from the slave system in the South. The point, Thoreau believes, is not to protest to South Carolina in the hope of maintaining our mutually lucrative trading relationship without submitting to the humiliating treatment of Massachusetts' citizens. The point is to refuse to enter into such a relationship in the first place, to refuse to benefit from the slave system in any way.

Reform, Thoreau observes with contempt, "keeps many scores of newspapers in its service, but not one man" (paragraph 21). So, how does "a man" act? It is important to note that Thoreau's "wise" or independent and moral man is not, in the first place, a political creature at all. Rightly understood, politics derives its legitimacy not from its own logic, but instead from the degree to which it conforms to principles and purposes derived beyond itself. So, too, the man "with a bone in his back which you cannot pass your hand through." Such a man may very well be devoted to "other pursuits and contemplations," just as Thoreau is (paragraph 13). Thoreau makes clear that he "came into this world, not chiefly to make this a good place to live in, but to live in it, be it good or bad" (paragraph 19). Even so, he needs to take care that his ability to enjoy these other pursuits does not come at the expense of other individuals. This, indeed, is his first obligation: to see that he does not enjoy his own independence by "sitting upon another man's shoulders" (paragraph 13). Thoreau imagines that there may be some injustices that simply grow from the necessary "friction of the machine of government" (paragraph 18). It is hard to understand exactly what Thoreau might mean by this. Perhaps it is that political institutions and the laws that define them are blunt instruments; even when applied equitably, they may fail to recognize the full array of differences in the circumstances of citizens. Or perhaps Thoreau simply means that even with the best intentions, political actors will make mistakes, make decisions that we dislike, or "drop the ball" from time to time – simply by virtue of being human. As he has said before, there are many such issues that will either remedy themselves over time or may not be worth the effort to protest and correct. There are also, however, injustices that are so profound that when we obey the law conscientiously, and participate actively in political affairs, we are thrust into the position of reinforcing and perpetuating these injustices.

Disengagement from political life thus becomes Thoreau's model for moral behavior. He will not adopt "the ways which the State has provided for remedying the evil," since they "take too much time, and a man's life will be gone" (paragraph 19). He refuses to grant the state the right to determine the appropriate methods for pursuing his responsibility to do no harm to others. To make this point, Thoreau employs some of the most radical language in the essay. To confine oneself to conventional methods of political reform is to cede moral authority to political institutions built upon a Constitution that is itself evil (paragraph 19). Refusing to recognize the Constitution's authority is the truly radical path; Thoreau compares such a refusal to events that convulse the body, like birth and death. He had spoken earlier about the need for men to rebel and revolutionize (paragraph 8); here, he seems to understand very well the radical implication of language like this. He even imagines that his rebellious men may provoke bloodshed. He answers this concern, however, by pointing to the violence already inflicted on our humanity (our consciences) by the slave order; his view is that we are currently bleeding to "an everlasting death." Remedying this evil may require literal acts of bloodshed (paragraph 22).

Radical as the language is, the political posture of "*one* HONEST man" is less about aggressive confrontation than it is about the withdrawal from political life. The task is to find a way to remove oneself from the social system built upon slavery, and the political system supporting it (paragraph 21). The most immediate way to achieve this is to refuse political allegiance in its most basic form: refuse to pay your taxes. Just as the Protestant revolutionary, John Knox, had argued that "a man with God is always in the majority," so Thoreau suggests that if abolitionists "at once effectively withdraw their support, both in person and property, from the government of Massachusetts," they will be in a position of being "more right than" their neighbors and therefore members of the only majority that matters (paragraph 20). This is the way that citizens of Massachusetts can literally separate themselves from slave interests and slave power. This is what Thoreau means by an individual who ceases to hold slaves (paragraph 21). Such is the form of resistance to civil government Thoreau champions. Conventional political reformers give too much legitimacy to the institutions requiring reform. In Thoreau's view, what the state fears most is a loss of its status, the refusal of subjects to recognize its overawing power – he will later suggest that in the face of such refusals the state acts "half-witted," and is as "timid as a lone woman with her silver spoons" (paragraph 26). Withdrawing one's support is more subversive, in Thoreau's view, than any other possible act. This is the only way to maintain moral integrity in the face of the moral obtuseness of the slave state and the slave society from which it grows.

Thoreau was fond of paradox as a rhetorical device, and he frequently invoked it to startle his readers and to drive home his points (this quality actually annoyed Thoreau's friend and mentor, Ralph Waldo Emerson, who found the technique gimmicky). We see a classic Thoreauvian use of paradox in the claim that the freest man in an unfree society is found in jail. Indeed, the only place for a man of integrity in an unjust political order is prison, and it is here that victims of injustice should look for him; Thoreau mentions the fugitive slave, the Mexican prisoner on parole, and the Indian who has come to plead for justice (paragraph 22). Prison, where the state intends to punish and terrify those who resist its power, is actually the space where free individuals can "abide with honor" (paragraph 22). Thoreau's moral idealism suggests that truth is always stronger than falsehood and that the state cannot exist without the moral recognition of its subjects. Rather than silencing rebellious individuals, imprisonment emphasizes the degree to which the imprisoned have refused to grant the state the recognition it craves and requires. Non-cooperation with political power is the greatest threat to that power, and this is the sum of the political strategy recommended in *Civil Disobedience*.

In the years to come, Thoreau's position appears to have changed on this point in two important ways. First, in *Slavery In Massachusetts*, written five years after *Resistance to Civil Government* was published, Thoreau begins to doubt the degree to which it is possible for a practical citizen to effectively withdraw from the slave power. The Fugitive Slave Act of 1850 required northern citizens to actively aid in apprehending escaped slaves for the purpose of returning them to bondage. Citizens of Massachusetts, in this way, were required by law to be active agents of slave power. As Thoreau grew to understand that withdrawing into nature would not release him from these corrupt legal obligations, his thoughts became "murder to the State,"[15] and he was able to imagine a more active form of political engagement and rebellion. Second, and related to his growing pessimism about the ability to attack the slave authority by merely withdrawing from cooperation with it, he strongly and without hesitation supported John Brown's attack on Harper's Ferry in 1859. The movement from *Civil Disobedience* to *Slavery in Massachusetts* and then on to *A Plea For Captain John Brown* represents less a turning away from pacifism and nonviolence (which, as we saw above, it is not at all clear Thoreau supports in *Civil Disobedience*) than it does a growing pessimism about the possibility and effectiveness of withdrawing from interactions with the institutions supporting slavery. In *Civil Disobedience*, however, Thoreau clearly casts his lot with non-cooperation as the most appropriate form of resistance to "inexpedient" political authority.

Such non-cooperation requires the courage to face the prospect of prison when we cast our "whole vote, not a strip of paper [a ballot] merely" (paragraph 22). This is the way, for Thoreau, to assert one's entire influence, to refuse to compromise with unjust institutions, and to maintain one's integrity as a moral individual. But aside from fear of imprisonment, there is an additional impediment to maintaining one's "manhood," in Thoreau's sense, and this is our attachment to material goods and wealth. This leads him, in the final two paragraphs of what we are thinking of as his "treatise on expediency," to reflections that can be thought of as a summary of ideas he discusses in detail in *Walden* and in essays such as *Life Without Principle*. Thoreau suspects that people with the greatest freedom, the greatest moral autonomy, will not be worldly in a conventional economic sense (such individuals "commonly have not spent much time in accumulating property") (paragraph 23). Wealth always threatens our integrity in two important ways. First, it simply comes to preoccupy us and thus distracts us from more important and appropriate concerns. As Thoreau puts it, wealth "puts to rest many questions" the wealthy individual should be concerned with, "while the only new question which it puts is the hard but superfluous one, how to spend it." The greater the wealth, the more we are pulled away from matters and commitments that define a free life of moral integrity; with wealth, a man's "moral ground is taken from under his feet" (paragraph 23). In another nice example of Thoreau's love of paradox, we find the claim that our life opportunities actually decrease with growing wealth – the exact opposite of our conventional wisdom.

Second, the production and maintenance of wealth is fundamentally dependent on the protection and support of governments, even very unjust governments. Thoreau brags that he likes to think that he never relies on the state for protection (paragraph 24). This is mainly because he has no wealth to tempt others to threaten him. "You must live within yourself, and depend upon yourself always tucked up and ready for a start, and not have many affairs" (paragraph 24). If we live simply, and are willing to get along with only life's basic necessities, we will find ourselves liberated from the need for the state. Wealth enmeshes us in a relationship of dependency and thereby compromises our moral integrity. In *Walden*, Thoreau counsels us to "Simplify, simplify, simplify!"[16] The more we own, the more wealth we control, the less we are able to retain our independence. The point is the same in *Civil Disobedience*. The state's authority grows from our dependence upon it, our fear that we will not be safe or secure without it. If, however, we live in voluntary poverty, if we live very simply, the state loses this leverage and we gain our freedom.

This lesson completes the full range of arguments in what we have thought of as Thoreau's "treatise on expediency." The reason we can think of these paragraphs (3–24) in this way is because here we find Thoreau challenging what he takes to be the conventions of social and political thinking and more or less turning them upside down. While attempting to speak "practically and as a citizen," Thoreau suggests that we must never allow the "expedient" (utilitarian, practical, administrative) world of politics to determine our moral perspective. Personal integrity requires looking for moral principles beyond the political world. American slave society had provoked the invasion of Mexico for crude and immoral purposes; to engage in political negotiation with these forces, through conventional political participation, would be to grant a level of legitimacy to interests that simply do not deserve it. To think clearly and ethically about political life, we must look beyond the political world, from the practical and relative to the moral and absolute. Once we make this move, we can see the need to detach ourselves from "inexpedient" political life. We can also see the need for fearlessness about our bodily liberty, just as we need to divest ourselves of superfluous wealth and worldly concerns in order to maintain our moral clarity. The overall lesson of this treatise is the importance of maintaining moral and material independence from the slaveholding elements of American society and politics. In these central passages of *Civil Disobedience*, withdrawal and non-cooperation is the form that "resistance to civil government" takes.

## SECTION 3

The occasion for Thoreau being asked to lecture, in 1848, on the "relation of the individual to the state," was his arrest and one night of imprisonment in late July two years earlier. Paragraphs 25–27 serve as a short transition from the abstract theory of the first half of *Civil Disobedience* to an autobiographical account of the night Thoreau spent in jail.

By way of introduction, he explains that his objection to paying certain taxes pre-dates his conflict over the poll tax. In 1841 he objected to contributing to the public support of the local clergy. Massachusetts had abolished state-mandated support for the clergy eight years earlier, in 1833. Citizens were still considered members of their local church parish, however, and could be assessed for a tax to support the clergy unless they formally revoked their church membership. When Thoreau tells the story in paragraph 25 of revoking his church membership, it appears that he significantly exaggerates the details. It is not clear why he would have been fined for not paying that tax, since he was free to withdraw from church membership if he so desired. Perhaps Concord had insisted that he pay for the previous four years (he returned home from Harvard in 1837), during which time he had not formally revoked his church membership; if so, there is no public record of this. In addition, the town would have been behaving quite unusually in his case, since it was common for people's names simply to be removed, upon request, from the roll of those owing the tax (indeed, more than half the citizens of Concord removed their names from this roll in just a few years after the 1833 law was passed).[17] It is thus quite unlikely that the state would have confronted Thoreau in the manner he suggests, insisting that he must pay or be jailed. Of all the autobiographical material in *Civil Disobedience*, this appears to be the most exaggerated. Regardless of the degree to which he may play fast and loose with the details of this case, Thoreau's important point is that prior to his conflict over the poll tax he had already made claims about the limits of the state's authority to tax him without his consent.

The poll tax was a general tax levied on eligible voters in Massachusetts. As we observed above, Thoreau was not the only citizen in Concord to refuse to pay this tax, and it is possible that he was motivated to take this step (probably in 1842 – six years prior to when he gave the speech, rather than six years prior to the publication date) as a result of Bronson Alcott's example. Thoreau's reflection on his arrest suggests the degree to which he feels deeply alienated from his fellow citizens, and the degree to which he views the state as the representative of the majority of those around him. His earlier claims about the lack of virtuous individuals now become personal; they – his "townsmen" – are unable to understand him, they are "underbred," they "plainly did not know how to treat me" (paragraph 26). He equates these townsmen with the state and makes his famous comment about how half-witted and timid it appears (paragraph 26). Popular opinion, and the state that represents it, is a blunt instrument of force and violence; it is incapable of touching the essential humanity of a free individual. The goal of the many is to "force me to become like themselves." Most people cannot understand a person who prefers the *right* to the *safe*, someone who thinks that the comfort and liberty and even the life of the body are less important than a commitment to what is true and good. Such people appear as a moral rebuke to the many. But *men*, Thoreau claims, can never be forced through physical imprisonment or violence to abandon that which makes their life valuable to them. Thoreau is echoing Socrates' claims in *Crito* here, and he explicitly juxtaposes the opinion of the many with the view of the wise. He goes even further than Socrates in that famous dialogue, however, when he claims that he owes nothing to the "successful machinery of society." He denies that he is the "son of the engineer," that is, those who control the machinery of society (paragraph 27). As he suggested throughout what we have called his "treatise on expediency," Thoreau's moral authority (and the moral authority of expedient government) is located in sources beyond political life.

There is a threatening belligerency in these comments, which should remind us of Thoreau's comments about bloodshed and violence in paragraph 22: he is willing to resist the government and to see who proves the stronger in the long run. Of course the state can imprison him; it may even kill him if it becomes threatened enough. At the end of the day, however, it has only tools for attacking Thoreau's senses, his body. It is blind to the higher purposes and gratifications of life. Thoreau directly challenges the state. Do your worst, he suggests, and we will see who is stronger in the most important ways: "I was not born to be forced. I will breathe after my own fashion. Let us see who is the strongest. ... They can only force me who obey a higher law than I" (paragraph 27). With these words, Thoreau has connected the moral claims of Section 2 to the story of his arrest and imprisonment, which now follows.

## SECTION 4

The centerpiece of *Civil Disobedience* is, of course, the night Thoreau spent in jail. That this story gives life to such an important and influential essay might be thought remarkable both because the act that precipitated Thoreau's arrest was not original and the consequence of his act – a single night in the local jail – is quite trivial in comparison with the suffering of so many other political actors we might think of. What gives power to Thoreau's account of the story, then, is neither the event's heroism nor its originality, but rather the skill with which Thoreau, as a writer and thinker, presents the story to us.

In the original 1849 edition of the essay, paragraphs 28–35 were typeset in smaller print to emphasize that here we find the autobiographical narrative that gives life to the broader discussion in the rest of the essay. It is important to note that Thoreau does nothing to exaggerate the danger and sacrifice of his experience. He begins the story by suggesting that his experience was "novel" and "interesting" (as compared, say, with "horrible" and "terrifying"), and it is clear from his description that the prison was well managed, peaceable, and relatively humane (paragraph 28). He ends the story with the simple sentence that "This is the whole history of 'My Prisons'" (paragraph 35). The reference here is to a book by Silvio Pellico, an Italian writer arrested as a revolutionary in 1820. After a decade in prison, Pellico's account of his sufferings, *Le Mie Prigioni*, was published in 1832 (translated into English as *My Prisons* in 1836) and widely read in Europe and the United States. By humorously comparing his experience of a single night in the Middlesex jail with Pellico's terrible ordeal, Thoreau is gently and ironically reminding us that the importance of his story does not grow (as it had for Pellico) from any significant suffering on his part. The value and power of his experience is found elsewhere. When Thoreau was released from jail after his single night, eyewitness accounts suggest that he was angry and agitated,[18] but this grew from his insistence that he *not* be released, that he be allowed to stay in jail to make his political point, rather than from the trauma of being imprisoned. Sam Staples, the constable and a friend of Thoreau's, would not allow Thoreau to remain in jail any longer, since the fine had been paid the previous evening.

Instead of an account of suffering and barbarism, Thoreau's account of his experience takes the form of a travel narrative: "It was like travelling into a far country, such as I had never expected to behold" (paragraph 31). What he discovers immediately is that the jail represents its own world. It has its own literary history and traditions (that is, gossip, tall tales, and jailhouse poems) that are the legacy of the inmates and of which the outside world of Concord knows nothing. Thoreau is fascinated enough by this new world that his cell mate finally instructs him to go to sleep, even though Thoreau has many more questions to ask (Thoreau's gregariousness provides a marked contrast with his criticism of gregariousness in paragraph 12). He feels as if he is not only far away, but that he is also traveling backward in time to medieval Europe (Concord is a "shire town" – that is, a county seat – which connects the institutions of his own time to more ancient institutions). As the jail was located in the center of Concord, Thoreau feels that he is now seeing his town in a new way; this was "a closer view of my native town" (paragraph 31). He calls the jail "one of our peculiar institutions," tying it to slavery (Southerners such as Senator Calhoun of South Carolina defended slavery as the South's "peculiar institution") (paragraph 31). A clear implication is that for Thoreau the jail calls into question our conviction that we have progressed far beyond earlier and unjust social orders.

By gaining this new view of his village, Thoreau feels all the more alienated from his fellow citizens. The prison walls between him and the village become symbols of the moral distance between himself and his neighbors, who now appear in his eyes as distant to him as "Chinamen and Malays" (paragraph 33). He accuses them of being untrustworthy, of being unwilling to take risks for what is right, of hoping that their conventional behavior will allow them safety and prosperity. There is a kind of willful ignorance about the institutional supports (such as the local jail) that allow them to live their shallow and self-preoccupied lives. Thoreau, an individualist of the first order, accuses his fellows of being bad neighbors and friends. This feeling would linger. In 1852 Thoreau remarked in his *Journal*, "My countrymen are to me foreigners."[19]

We do not know who invites Thoreau to join the huckleberry party when he is released from jail, but we do know that Thoreau loved to take children huckleberrying for both recreation and what we might today call environmental education.[20] Even if we do not know the composition of the group involved in that particular excursion, we do know that they provide a notable contrast to those residents of Concord Thoreau so bitterly criticizes in the previous paragraph. At least some of Thoreau's neighbors – be they adults or children or some combination of both – recognize his leadership qualities, for "they were impatient to put themselves under my conduct" (paragraph 34). When Thoreau died in 1862, Emerson gave the eulogy at his funeral (and later published his remarks as an essay). He was very critical of Thoreau's interest in leading huckleberry parties: "I cannot help counting it a fault in him that he had no ambition. Wanting this, instead of engineering for all America, he was the captain of a huckleberry-party."[21] This criticism seems, in light of Thoreau's comments here in *Civil*

*Disobedience*, to miss Thoreau's point and to miss it quite spectacularly. Thoreau's contrast between the corrupt village of Concord, with the jail located at its very center, and the countryside he retreats to in order to gather berries, is the contrast between a world corrupted by injustice and a world where "the State was nowhere to be seen" (paragraph 34). The entire thesis of what we have called Section 2 had been the need to withdraw one's support from slavery and the political institutions that protect it. Here, at the end of Section 4, in the telling of his release from prison, he suggests there is an alternative to the mainstream of Concord life with its inexpedient politics. There is a landscape beyond the village where Americans can live independently and withdraw from the support of injustice. Thoreau does not retreat to a huckleberry party because, as Emerson implies, he lacks ambition. On the contrary, the huckleberry party symbolizes an alternative America for those who understand the need to "resist civil government." In that alternative America, the relationships (even the leadership and subordination implied in his description of his own role in the group) are based upon a kind of solidarity and neighborliness that threaten no individual's "manhood" or independence. Here is a hint of a social order more free and just than that which enslaves and imprisons and engages in imperial war.

## SECTION 5

The two paragraphs following the "whole history of 'My Prisons'" provide a brief restatement of Thoreau's thesis and the connection of his philosophical commitments to his practical political decisions and opinions. He wishes to "refuse allegiance to the State, to withdraw and stand aloof from it effectually" (paragraph 36). This non-cooperation with the government does not extend to those specific elements that he has explicitly consented to, such as his highway tax. But his reason for paying that tax is to be a good neighbor; it does not reflect a belief in the state's right to demand general obedience and allegiance (Thoreau cannot give that general commitment, for he desires to be a "bad subject"; to give such a general commitment would be for him the height of servility). His resistance to civil government grows from a general distrust of political institutions and an unwillingness to grant them undeserved moral legitimacy. He is aware that the poll tax he refuses to pay does not directly finance the Mexican war he objects to, since it is a state and local tax rather than a federal one. His claim about the moral corruption of all levels of American government is that they share a commitment to "inexpedient" ends and values. He will therefore "quietly declare war" on the state as a whole – "State" being his term for the entirety of governmental institutions in this case – by standing aloof from it.

There is another comment in paragraph 36 that requires notice. Thoreau says he will not pay a school tax, since he is already "doing my part to educate my fellow-countrymen now." Most people think of Thoreau as a writer, naturalist, and, perhaps, a surveyor. As we saw in the previous chapter, however, Thoreau's first career was as a teacher, much as it was for many Harvard graduates like him. Thoreau was not alone in his own family in pursuing a career as an educator; a sister and brother taught school for part or most of their adult life (his brother, John, had founded a school and shared the teaching duties with Henry prior to his premature death). His extended family included more schoolteachers. Thoreau is very much the pedagogue in *Civil Disobedience*, and his own self-image as an educator is clearly indicated by his remark.

Thoreau continues to be very critical of whoever paid his tax (it is reasonable to assume that he knew who this was, and that members of at least his lecture audience may have had a strong sense of who this was as well). His lack of generosity toward (most likely) his aunt makes some readers very impatient with Thoreau, and it does make this pedagogue sound didactic, judgmental, and moralistic to the extreme. Be that as it may, Thoreau is consistent in his contempt of the view that avoiding punishment is more important than the moral obligation to resist unjust political authority.

## SECTION 6

The paragraph that immediately follows (38), however, softens what we might think to be the arrogant self-righteousness of the preceding passage. Here, Thoreau admits that the view he has been defending throughout the essay is merely his view "at present."

He implicitly recognizes that in the future he might come to believe that his current position is wrong, or incomplete, or misleading, and he would be required to adjust his views in light of his evolving thoughts. He explicitly recognizes that moral argument can be "biased by obstinacy," and we certainly get a sense of Thoreau's stubborn nature simply by reading his account of his tangle with Sam Staples and the tax laws of Massachusetts. He also notes that we can become corrupted by a desire for recognition from others. Thoreau has enough self-knowledge to understand that those most concerned with behaving nobly (and who is more concerned with this than Thoreau himself?) are the most susceptible to being corrupted by vainglory. While the overall tone of *Civil Disobedience* is profoundly self-confident (to say the least!), Thoreau acknowledges that despite our good intentions we can easily go astray in our thinking and deceive ourselves about our own motives. This may be a rare moment of humility in *Civil Disobedience*, but it is also refreshing and essential for considering the next brief passage.

In this mood, Thoreau critically evaluates the position he has defended throughout the essay. There are two initial possibilities he considers. The first is to simply condescend to his neighbors and assume they are hopelessly ignorant, and that it is therefore a waste of time and effort to challenge and chastise them. He has to reject this impulse for two reasons. First, he suggests that his sympathy for their ignorance does not excuse the significant pain that they inflict through this ignorance. Second, and implicit in the rest of the paragraph, is his refusal to admit that their ignorance is irredeemable; they are human and, at least potentially, humane and capable of learning to see the world in new and more justifiable ways. Patronizing them would be to express a level of arrogance greater than anything we find Thoreau expressing in *Civil Disobedience*. It would require the arrogance of believing that he, Thoreau, was alone in being capable of understanding moral imperatives. It would require the arrogance of thinking most people are incapable of moral education or moral growth. It would require a conviction that most people are less than fully human. This is a conviction he rejects.

A second temptation is to view the power of the state and the body of citizens as a natural power, like fire and other brute forces.

This would suggest that fatalistic submission, rather than resistance, would be the wisest course; there is no virtue in objecting to the power of, say, gravity. Yet Thoreau understands, again, that resistance signifies a kind of respect. If political power is a natural power like gravity, it would be no more capable of moral reform than are the laws of nature. Thoreau's resistance grows from a belief in the humane potential of those involved in political affairs and the citizenry as a whole. Thoreau believes, and must believe in order to act as he does, that he can resist this government "with some effect" (paragraph 39). There is certainly no assurance that the government, and the slave society upon which it is built and which it defends, will reform and become expedient at last. There is this possibility, however, and therefore a reasonable justification (perhaps even a necessity) for resistance to injustice.

Thoreau suggests that he is, in truth, all too inclined like the rest of us to obey the law without giving it much thought. It takes energy, time, and effort to resist. Resistance also makes us look quarrelsome and self-righteous. There is an alternative view to the position he has defended in the essay, and this is the view he is tempted by when he is off his guard, when he is inclined to simply submit to political authority without making a fuss. This perspective is captured in the verse quoted (not quite accurately) in paragraph 40. The author, George Peele, captures a position we find defended as far back in Western political theory as Plato's *Crito*. Our country is like our parents, it creates the conditions under which we appear in the world, and these are the conditions that allow us to grow into the particular person we become. Although we tell ourselves stories about our independence and self-cultivation – that we are "self-made" men and women – the reality is (from this view) that the political environment from which we spring profoundly shapes us. We therefore owe the political community gratitude comparable to that which we owe our parents or guardians. Thoreau appears to equate this perspective with what he calls the "lower point of view" (paragraph 40). This perspective represents a form of common sense, and Thoreau concedes that despite all its problems and injustices, there is much to recommend the American Constitution and government in comparison with all the other governments that are and have been found in the world.

But is this the correct way to view the situation? Thoreau acknowledges this alternative view, captured in Peele's verse and defended from a "lower" perspective from that which he has assumed throughout the essay. From the view "a little higher" than this comparative view, however, our political institutions are as he has described them throughout, and from the highest view of all they lose their moral importance altogether – in the sense we have discussed earlier, since moral life is to be found outside, rather than inside, the political universe. Some readers are tempted to see paragraph 40 as an illustration of Thoreau's softening or weakening his position toward the end of the essay.[22] They suggest that here he loses his radicalism. But if we are right in our reading, this passage reinforces the exact message he has presented in the earlier "treatise on expediency." The softened, less radical, submissive and accepting view is rejected as altogether unpersuasive. It is a temptation produced by an inadequate understanding of our proper relation to both morality and political authority.

Peele's verse was added to *Civil Disobedience* in 1866. Although we cannot know with certainty that it was Thoreau himself (rather than the editors of the 1866 edition) who made the decision to add the Peele material, we may conclude that regardless of whose decision it was, it was added to clarify the meaning of the paragraph. When we look at the actual content of Peele's play, *The Battle of Alcazar*, from which this verse is drawn, we can see that it is used more to lampoon than to champion the position it represents. Peele was a contemporary of Shakespeare's, and his play was an account of the Battle of Alcacer Quibir in Morocco in 1578. The Portuguese King, Sebastian I, led Portuguese and allied Moorish troops against the Ottoman-Moroccan army led by the Sultan of Morocco. The Portuguese wanted to re-establish control of trade in the Mediterranean and along the European and African coast of the Atlantic Ocean. The battle was, therefore, a commercially driven imperial war, much like the American war on Mexico. Unlike the American war, however, Alcacer Quibir ended disastrously for the imperial forces: the Portuguese were routed and destroyed by the Moroccans. The moral position of obedience defended in the verse, in short, grew from an imperial political context we know Thoreau disapproves of. In addition, it produced disaster for the Portuguese, as if to suggest the danger facing Thoreau's own nation, morally if not materially, by pursuing a comparable path. When we recognize that Peele's moral position was at one with the defense of imperial war, Thoreau (and/or his editors) gives us good reason to read this passage as satirical, as a reason not to trust this alternative position he is considering. Such a reading of the Peele verse adds more ammunition to understanding this paragraph as a rejection of the "lower point of view" (that is, the point of view emphasizing the comparative goodness of the American political order, and a strong obligation to political authority more generally). Instead of sympathizing with this perspective, Thoreau gives us reasons to reject it.

## SECTION 7

Unlike those who revere political institutions and hold political obligations among our highest duties, Thoreau remains persuaded that if we allow political life to generate its own moral principles and purposes we end up with a morally perverse world, one where the greatest evils – such as slavery and imperialism – are viewed as necessary and inevitable instead of as outrageous, evil, and indefensible. He returns to his claim that to live a morally serious life is to live, as much as possible, beyond the world of politics. "If a man is thought-free, fancy-free, imagination-free, that which *is not* never for a long time appearing *to be* to him, unwise rulers or reformers cannot fatally interrupt him" (paragraph 41). There is an unreality to the moral universe of "unwise rulers and reformers"; they fail to see the deeper moral principles and truths. As Thoreau writes in *A Week on the Concord and Merrimack Rivers*,

> To one who habitually endeavors to contemplate the true state of things, the political state can hardly be said to have any existence whatever. It is unreal, incredible, and insignificant to him, and for him to endeavor to extract the truth from such lean material is like making sugar from linen rags, when sugar-cane may be had.[23]

To illustrate this point, Thoreau considers the career of the most illustrious politician in Massachusetts and perhaps the whole of the northern United States, Daniel Webster. Known by many as the "Defender of the Constitution," Webster illustrates perfectly the conflict between expediency and principle introduced in Section 2. Thoreau allows that there is a role for expediency in politics and that we need to accept this within its proper limits. Among professional politicians, Webster is the best. Even so, "his quality is not wisdom, but prudence" (paragraph 42). Because he is tied to defending the Constitution, he is blind, perhaps willfully blind, to its moral flaws. Instead of being a leader, Webster is therefore merely a follower, and his own words convict him of wearing moral blinders. A true genius for legislation would bridge the gap between the moral and political worlds. Thoreau suggests, however, that — Webster and perhaps even the Founders notwithstanding — "No man with a genius for legislation has appeared in America" (paragraph 44). While these words are likely to offend some patriotic Americans, what follows is an even more audacious challenge to popular conviction: Thoreau suggests that both the Bible and the Constitution are satisfactory sources of moral guidance only for those unwilling to think seriously for themselves. Both of these esteemed texts provide a partial representation of truth, as opposed to truth itself. Whatever truths they capture are imperfect expressions of deeper moral realities. Thoreau casts his lot with "they who behold where" truth "comes trickling into this lake or that pool" (that is, into traditional sources such as the Bible or the Constitution) and "gird up their loins once more, and continue their pilgrimage toward its fountainhead" (paragraph 43). Contrary to the common view, Thoreau believes we must look behind our political and religious texts to seek the deeper truths they draw on.

It is hard to imagine a stronger claim about the limited meaning of political life and conventional political and moral (religious) opinion than this. We might think of the single sentence constituting paragraph 43 as the climactic restatement of the thesis defended in Section 2. Political life, that is, must always be informed by nonpolitical moral principles if its "expediency" or prudential logic is to avoid being corrupted by injustice and moral shortsightedness. Thoreau brings us back to the logic of non-cooperation with the current "inexpedient" political order. Justice requires political disengagement and moral commitment to the "fountain-head" of higher principle.

## SECTION 8

As suggested at the outset, the final two paragraphs of *Civil Disobedience* provide a kind of mirror image of the first two paragraphs. The penultimate paragraph, like paragraph 2, suggests that to the degree moral progress is to be found in our society, it has come from the people rather than from legislators and politicians. The main difference in paragraph 44 is that Thoreau extends the critique from American history to the whole of Western history since the writing of the New Testament. In the final paragraph, as in the first, Thoreau offers a glimpse of two ideals. The first is of a state that respects the independent judgment of every individual as superior to its own – a state that, in the most radical sense imaginable, derives all its authority from the active consent of every citizen. This state "can afford to be just to all men" and will view the civic relationship as essentially the same as neighborliness (paragraph 45). This is the perspective that Thoreau defends early on as a "practical" perspective, one in which he accepts his status as a citizen and thus separates himself from "no-government men" (paragraph 3).

Being "just to all men," this state would likely produce individuals who live apart from it, as Thoreau has made clear he wishes to do. These individuals would satisfy the duties of "neighbors and fellow-men," but would not necessarily identify as citizens (paragraph 45). Their moral values and duties to themselves and others would be, as we have seen throughout *Civil Disobedience*, derived from non-political sources of inspiration. Such philosophers, Thoreau implies, could "prepare the way" for an even "more perfect and glorious State, which also I have imagined, but not yet anywhere seen" (paragraph 45). Just as in the opening paragraph Thoreau imagines a government that governs not at all, so here in the final sentence Thoreau imagines a state that ceases to be a state altogether. He shares with no-government men a vision of a world without the need for politics, even if such a world is not yet "practical." In *Civil Disobedience*, he does not speak as a no-government man, but he shares a vision with his anarchistic neighbors of the best future world.

## NOTES

1 Henry David Thoreau, *Essays*, Jeffrey S. Cramer, ed. (New Haven, CT and London: Yale University Press, 2013), p. 145.

2 Henry David Thoreau, *Journal of Henry D. Thoreau*, vol. 1, Bradford Torrey and Francis H. Allen, eds. (Boston, MA: Houghton Mifflin, 1949), p. 412; Henry David Thorau, *Familiar Letters of Henry David Thoreau*, F. B. Sanborn, ed., (Boston, MA and NY: Houghton Mifflin, 1894), p. 220.

3 Henry David Thoreau, *A Week on the Concord and Merrimack Rivers; Walden, or, Life in the Woods; The Maine Woods; Cape Cod* (NY: Library of America, 1985), p. 330.

4 Henry David Thoreau, *Collected Essays and Poems* (NY: Library of America, 2001), p. 646.

5 Robert D. Richardson Jr., *Henry Thoreau: A Life of the Mind* (Berkeley, CA: University of California Press, 1986), p. 177.

6 Thoreau, *A Week, etc.*, p. 535.

7 Walter Harding, *The Days of Henry Thoreau* (NY: Alfred A. Knopf, 1966), p. 168.

8 William Paley, *The Principles of Moral and Political Philosophy* (London: printed for F.C. and J. Rivington, 1822), p. 288.

9 Ibid., p. 289.

10 Thoreau, *A Week, etc.*, p. 108.

11 Ibid., pp. 108–109.

12 See Thoreau, *Collected Essays and Poems*, pp. 85, 180.

13 Thoreau, *A Week, etc.*, p. 459.

14 Thoreau, *Essays*, Cramer, ed., p. 153.

15 Thoreau, *Collected Essays and Poems*, p. 346.

16 Thoreau, *A Week, etc.*, p. 395.

17 John Wood Sweet, "The Liberal Dilemma and the Demise of the Town Church: Ezra Ripley's Pastorate in Concord, 1778–1841," *Proceedings of the Massachusetts Historical Society* 104, 1992, p. 102.

18 Henry Seidel Canby, *Thoreau* (Boston, MA: Houghton Mifflin, 1939), p. 233.

19 Thoreau, *Journal*, vol. 3, p. 194.

20 See Thoreau, *Collected Essays and Poems*, p. 500.

21 Ralph Waldo Emerson, "Thoreau," in Harold Bloom, ed., *Henry David Thoreau* (NY: Bloom's Literary Criticism, 2008), p. 25.

22 See Barry Kritzberg, "Thoreau, Slavery, and Resistance to Civil Government," *Massachusetts Review* 30, no. 4, 1989, p. 540.

23 Thoreau, *A Week, etc.*, p. 104.

# 3

## CONTEXTS

There are many ways to think about Thoreau's relationship to the world he lived in and the way in which this relationship is reflected in *Civil Disobedience*. In this chapter, we will focus on four different contexts in which, and through which, Thoreau's essay may be understood: the philosophical milieu of his hometown of Concord; the abolition movement; the anti-war movement; and the more general body of Thoreau's own writings. Each of these contexts gives us insights into *Civil Disobedience*. Together they allow us a more nuanced and expansive understanding of the essay than we can gain by focusing on any one of them alone.

### EMERSON AND TRANSCENDENTALISM

We noted in Chapter 1 that much in Thoreau's biography – from his refusal to pay his poll tax, to his experiment at Walden Pond, to even the speech patterns he cultivated upon returning home from college – appears unoriginal and derivative. One biographer writes, "His ideas are all borrowed."[1] More than one contemporary critic thought of him as an insignificant disciple of

Emerson, with little or no originality and no unique contribution beyond Emerson's ideas.

Looking at Emerson's *Politics*, an essay published in 1844, four years before Thoreau delivered the lecture that would become *Civil Disobedience*, could certainly reinforce this point. While Emerson did not have a personal story to tell about "resistance to civil government," his opinions about politics will look familiar to anyone who has studied Thoreau's essay. Like Thoreau, Emerson reminds his readers that our political institutions are of recent origin, that they were designed by imperfect individuals, and that they should aim to serve (rather than dominate) individual citizens:

> In dealing with the State, we ought to remember that its institutions are not aboriginal, though they existed before we were born; that they are not superior to the citizen: that every one of them was once the act of a single man.[2]

Like Thoreau, Emerson emphasizes that even the best political institutions are significantly flawed and that we need to maintain a skeptical attitude toward laws and political authority: "Every actual State is corrupt. Good men must not obey the laws too well."[3] Emerson is therefore skeptical, like Thoreau, about the use of political force and authority, and he suggests that our goal should be for less government: "Hence, the less government we have, the better, – the fewer laws, and the less confided power."[4] Like Thoreau, he imagines a good state producing individuals for whom the state no longer remains necessary: "To educate the wise man, the State exists; and with the appearance of the wise man, the State expires. The appearance of character makes the State unnecessary."[5] Like Thoreau, Emerson suggests that we are not yet at the end of human progress and that there is much more we need to do to produce the kind of "wise men" Emerson has in mind: "We think our civilization near its meridian, but we are yet only at the cock-crowing and the morning star. In our barbarous society the influence of character is in its infancy."[6] (We can also note the images of the cock-crowing and the morning star, both of which Thoreau will borrow freely in his masterwork, *Walden*.) Finally, although Emerson uses the language of friendship where Thoreau speaks of neighborliness, the end point of a new form of civil association is similar to what Thoreau means by "expedient" politics. Emerson writes that we must not "doubt that roads can be built, letters carried, and the fruit of labor secured, when the government of force is at an end. ... Could not a nation of friends even devise better ways?"[7] It is clear that Thoreau's own ideas are intimately related to those of his friend and mentor.

It is, therefore, hard to argue with the claim that many of Thoreau's key ideas in *Civil Disobedience* "are all borrowed." The biographer who made this observation adds another point, however, that is also essential for thinking about Thoreau's essay: "the originality is in the blending."[8] Yes, Thoreau's gesture of refusing to pay his poll tax was derivative. And yes, many of his political ideas and opinions are found in others' earlier works. But *Civil Disobedience* combines these ideas with a discussion of Thoreau's arrest in a unique and compelling way, so that Emerson's *Politics* is mainly read and studied by scholars today while Thoreau's essay continues to resonate with a much wider audience. All thinkers and writers grow within an intellectual and artistic milieu, and all borrow ideas that can be traced to others. The contribution is not always made from a pure originality, but from "the blending," the use to which these ideas are put, and the form in which the ideas are expressed.

The literary and philosophical movement associated with mid-nineteenth-century Concord, Massachusetts, within which Emerson is usually thought of as the central intellectual force, is American transcendentalism. Exactly what we mean by transcendentalism is not entirely clear, as the label was given by a critical outsider, rather than generated by those associated with the movement.[9] Those we today call transcendentalists embraced the label ironically, as if to say, "so you want to call me that, fine, I'll accept this label even though it was not given to me as a compliment." A group of Concord intellectuals met and discussed philosophical topics regularly, and they also briefly published a journal, *The Dial*, first edited by Margaret Fuller and then by Emerson. (Most of Thoreau's early published works were placed in *The Dial*.) If you were to read the standard intellectual histories of transcendentalism, you would find discussions of the influence of both German idealism and romanticism. The influential authors included Madame de Stael, a French woman of letters, and Thomas Carlyle, a Scottish critic and thinker, as well as poets like William Wordsworth. The term "transcendentalism" is taken from Kantian philosophy, and suggests a process through which the human mind processes and creates meaningful experience (it does not refer to "transcendent" things, or things beyond humans, as many people expect it to). While this is not the place to give a lesson in either German idealism or romanticism, there are two critical points to mention. First, from German idealism the view was adopted (sometimes in more sophisticated and sometimes in quite informal forms) that the human mind is constructed so as to understand and interpret human experience in a manner that is both real and true. That is, our minds function in such a way that our own intellectual perceptions are to be trusted as constructive of a true, even an "objective" world. This side of transcendentalism encourages a trust in, indeed a commitment to, individual character and conscience – character is essential so that conscience is not corrupted by selfish or partial considerations. Assuming good character, conscience or personal vision and perception is a trustworthy construction of what is true and right. Second, from romanticism the transcendentalists gained a strong respect and appreciation for nature. From a combination of these two intellectual roots, we find transcendentalists interested in thoughtful individuals who immerse themselves in the natural world.

We can see these elements in Emerson's own description of transcendentalism. In "The Transcendentalist" he writes, "What is popularly called Transcendentalism among us, is Idealism; Idealism as it appears in 1842."[10] The idealist "takes his departure from his consciousness, and reckons the world an appearance."[11] It is our consciousness that takes and gives form to the world of appearance, and thereby creates reality. "His thought, – that is the Universe."[12] "I – this thought which is called I, – is the mould into which the world is poured like melted wax."[13] Note the individualism of these ideas. For Emerson, this construction of reality is a very personal, even a private, affair:

> From this transfer of the world into his consciousness, this beholding of all things in the mind, follow easily his whole ethics. It is simpler to

> be self-dependent. The height, the deity of man is, to be self-sustained,
> to need no gift, no foreign force.[14]

When Thoreau writes in *Civil Disobedience* of his longing for a
"man who is a *man*, and has a bone in his back which you cannot put
your hand through," he is referring to just such an independent,
self-assured individual. Emerson understands we might fear that
this doctrine will generate a chaos of divergent realities for different
individuals; might not there be as many different realities as there
are individuals, after all? How are we to make peace within a
society of individuals who all reach different conclusions about
important moral matters? Emerson's answer is captured in this
comment: "What is the privilege and nobility of our nature,
but its persistency, through its power to attach itself to what is
permanent?"[15] The process of thinking honestly about important
matters, he is suggesting, ties all individuals into something
"permanent," a reality and a truth that is not capricious or subjective, but is objective and shared by all. Yet, each individual
must approach it independently.

If we think of Emerson as representative of transcendentalism,
understanding full well that this group of thinkers was only
loosely united around some general ideas and commitments, we will
not be surprised by the priority of education over political life in this
intellectual movement. In an essay entitled *Culture*, Emerson writes:

> Let us make our education be brave and preventive. Politics is an
> after-work, a poor patching. We are always a little late. ... What we
> call root-and-branch reforms of slavery, war, gambling, intemperance,
> is only medicating the symptoms. We must begin higher up, namely,
> in Education.[16]

Political life is symptomatic rather than formative; it expresses the
kind of people we are, rather than shaping us in the first place. If
political life is perverse or unjust, these problems can only be
addressed by looking at ways to educate, to reform, individuals prior
to their participation in political affairs. Just as the corrupt character
of individuals corrupts political affairs, so the reform of politics
lies with the reform of individuals in their pre-political incarnations.

The mid-nineteenth century was a time of great educational reform and experimentation, not only by individuals associated with transcendentalism. Bronson Alcott, for example, was identified as a part of the transcendentalist circle, and his experimental school in Boston, in which the formidably talented Elizabeth Peabody aided him, looked to develop humane and child-centered methods of teaching children. Horace Mann, the great educational leader and first Secretary of the Massachusetts Board of Education, was not intimately involved with the intellectual life of the Concord transcendentalists (although he was on the periphery of this world), and his orientation was much more as a Whig politician than a philosopher and intellectual. His work in constructing the Massachusetts common school system, which became one of the prominent models for the public schools in the rest of the country in the second half of the nineteenth century, was, however, very much of a piece with the transcendentalist emphasis on the (moral) education of individuals as the first step in any meaningful political reform. In this sense, the transcendentalists were clearly in step with much New England reform sentiment.

The transcendentalists were thus driven by a reform temperament, but the reform they had in mind was aimed at private life more than at political institutions and civic participation. An illustration of this impulse is found in the utopian agricultural community at Brook Farm, in the mid 1840s, and then Brook Farm's very short-lived successor, Fruitlands, at the end of the decade. These cooperative communities grew out of the idealistic impulses of transcendentalism; the farms were to be jointly owned by the community of farmers, with shared labor, significant gender equality, and an attempt to wed manual labor and intellectual life. The first these, located in West Roxbury, Massachusetts (just outside Boston), attracted Nathaniel Hawthorne, who later satirized the experiment in his novel *The Blithedale Romance*. While there were dozens of utopian cooperative communities in mid-nineteenth-century America, Brooke Farm and Fruitlands were the only explicitly secular cooperatives of this sort. Neither experiment proved economically viable, and there was conflict and disagreement among the members as well. Thoreau rejected the invitation to join Brook Farm, writing in his *Journal*, "As for these communities, I think I had rather keep a bachelor's hall in hell than go to board in heaven."[17] He was clearly much too private and individualistic in his lifestyle to wish to live in a cooperative community. However, there is much to be said for the parallel between these utopian communities and Thoreau's own experiment at Walden Pond as a one-man attempt to develop a simple, virtuous, and satisfying way of life.

The United States was a bustling (some would say chaotic) commercial society in Thoreau's lifetime, and the transcendentalist inclination was to be wary of the degree to which commercial markets and economic materialism were defining and channeling the greater part of American energy and effort. One of the great historians of the early American republic, Gordon Wood, reports that by 1815, the United States was the most "thoroughly commercialized society in the world."[18] Another, Joyce Appleby, has suggested that in the early nineteenth century, "Materialism and morality fused" together; that is, morality became infused with a concern for economic prosperity and success.[19] Although there was no single response to the growth of capitalism in transcendentalist circles, there was a general distrust among these intellectuals of moral ideals that celebrated economic life as an end in itself.

One deep American tradition that informed much of the transcendentalist sensibility as a whole, and helped shape its response to emerging capitalism, is what we might think of as Jeffersonian agrarianism. This can be seen in the utopian cooperative agricultural experiments as well as in Thoreau's experiment at Walden, and even in classic transcendentalist texts such as Emerson's first book, *Nature*. In his *Notes on Virginia*, Jefferson had argued that independent farmers made the best citizens:

> Those who labour in the earth are the chosen people of God, if ever he had a chosen people, whose breasts he has made his peculiar deposit for substantial and genuine virtue. It is the focus in which he keeps alive that sacred fire, which otherwise might escape from the face of the earth.[20]

Jefferson's idea was that being a farmer developed both intellectual and moral qualities of the highest order. Intellectually, independent farmers needed to solve for themselves the problems of agricultural production, itself a "science of the very first order."[21] Yet, if farming requires the continued use and development of our intellectual powers of systematic observation, experiment, planning, and so forth, Jefferson was even more enthusiastic about the moral virtues he believed farming encouraged. Most importantly, farmers who owned and controlled their own land, even if poor, were independent, self-reliant, and committed to the community within which they farmed (after all, land is not transferrable the way that many other forms of wealth are). Because they produce for themselves, under conditions they control, they are less apt to need to subordinate themselves to others in the course of their work and by caring for their basic needs. This suggests that on ethical and civic matters, farmers are likely to come to their own views without great concern for the opinion of others.

Wage workers, Jefferson feared, would lose the independence of livelihood that encourages the independence of character required by democratic citizens. For this reason he hoped we would "let our workshops remain in Europe."[22] While small family farms produce prudent and independent citizens, jealous of their liberty and loyal to their localities, Jefferson feared that commerce produces dependence, a loss of independent judgment, rootlessness, and a preoccupation with material goods and wealth above all else. In a letter to Madison from 1787, he wrote, "I think our governments will remain virtuous for many centuries; as long as they are chiefly agricultural."[23] If our family farms are replaced by cities and commerce and wage workers, however, Jefferson feared a degeneration of citizens' characters. Such a development would threaten the health of free government from within.

Although the transcendentalists differed from Jefferson in many ways, they shared a belief that a life "close to nature" was in many ways a more virtuous life than what could be found in commercial and urban environments. In *Nature*, a very influential work among transcendentalists, Emerson paid his respects to the role that nature plays in allowing for "commodity" – that is, production of economic goods – in human well-being. But this is only the first level of benefit we get from nature, in his view, and must not be confused with the higher moral lessons and experiences we gain by interacting with the nonhuman world. While we cannot ignore the problem of getting our living, we must solve that problem in a way that frees us to pursue human goods beyond material pleasures and comforts. Emerson and many of his colleagues shared a vision of a pastoral environment in which individuals would be able to develop their moral characters in a way that allows for the greatest independence and personal integrity. Markets and commerce may be necessary, but they must be disciplined and subordinated to higher goods if we are to maintain our deepest freedoms and develop our greatest potential. In the later passages of *Nature*, Emerson encourages his readers to "Build, therefore, your own world."[24] A life lived in close contact with nature, he believed, would produce individuals capable of building free and independent lives.

In his eulogy for Thoreau, Emerson commented that Thoreau was "a born protestant."[25] His meaning is purposely ambiguous; Thoreau was a protestor, as we know from *Civil Disobedience*, but he also had a moral disposition that tied him, even if not literally or doctrinally, to the Protestant religious traditions of New England. As mentioned in Chapter 2, Thoreau withdrew from participation in organized religion when he returned home to Concord after college. In many ways he differed dramatically from his Puritan forebears – think of the comments he made in *Civil Disobedience* about the imperfection of the Bible; think, as well, of his skeptical approach to (some would say contempt for) social and political authority. But there are two elements of Thoreau's disposition and attitude that tie him to his New England religious tradition: his moral intensity and his moral individualism. Thoreau was not even remotely a conventional Christian, if he was any kind of Christian at all, yet his attitudes and inclinations were significantly shaped by the moral style and traditions of Protestant Christianity.

In this way, Thoreau was representative of the more general transcendentalist community. Emerson began as a Unitarian minister but resigned his pulpit when it was clear he could no longer conform to the traditions and customs and dogmas of organized religion; he was much more optimistic about human potential than the conventional Puritan emphasis on original sin would allow, and he found the traditions of institutionalized Christianity inhibiting for original and meaningful individual religious experience. In a speech to graduates of the Divinity School at Harvard in 1838, Emerson told his audience of new ministers, "Yourself a newborn bard of the Holy Ghost, – cast behind you all conformity, and acquaint men at first hand with Deity."[26] In contrast to a more orthodox Protestant view of human depravity that separates us from God, and that requires God's grace to reconcile us with God, Emerson speaks of the sublime within each individual. "That is always best which gives me to myself. The sublime is excited in me by the great stoical doctrine, Obey thyself. That which shows God in me, fortifies me."[27] In what would become one of the famous passages in American literature, Emerson had written in *Nature*,

> Standing on the bare ground, – my head bathed by the blithe air, and uplifted into infinite space, – all mean egotism vanishes. I become a transparent eye-ball; I am nothing; I see all; the currents of the Universal Being circulate through me; I am part or particle of God.[28]

This idea that we are able, through the mediation of nature, to achieve such unity with God, is heretical to a more orthodox Puritan Protestantism. Yet, even though Emerson and many transcendentalists left the Congregationalist and Unitarian churches of New England, they retained the fundamental Protestant perspective that the individual is both responsible for, and to a significant degree capable of, seeking his or her own relationship with the divine (or, in more secular versions, with the right and the true). Calvinist theology may have dropped away in transcendentalism, but moral individualism and moral intensity remained aplenty. An unfriendly commentator has called Thoreau a "Puritan in decadent form."[29] A more friendly interpretation would be to suggest that he retained elements of his Puritan inheritance despite turning away from Christianity per se.

One scholar of the Concord transcendentalists has drawn a parallel between the "new consciousness" of the 1840s with the "alternative lifestyles" in American society in the 1960s and 70s.[30] We should be careful about this parallel (the transcendentalists by no means sought sexual liberation or a more general liberation of the senses, such as that promoted by youth culture in the 1960s and 70s), but it is true that there was resistance to conventional manners and customs among the transcendentalists, just as there was to religious conventions. This same scholar suggests that the transcendentalists were the first American generation to confront a world of "too much."[31] In this sense, we might think of them as our first middle-class rebels, preaching a kind of "revolutionary abstinence."[32] Thoreau certainly embodied both an asceticism in regard to wealth, and an individual eccentricity regarding conventional mores of polite society – he was known for wearing corduroy pants, the blue jeans of his day, which were the garb of Irish laborers. To this degree, he was participating in what might be thought of as America's first middle-class counterculture.

One of Thoreau's most pointed critics was a contemporary author and editor, James Russell Lowell. Lowell had tangled with Thoreau when he was the editor at the *Atlantic Monthly* and had removed what he took to be an offensive comment from *Chesuncook*, an essay Thoreau had submitted for publication about his travels in Maine. In a review of a posthumous collection of Thoreau's writings, Lowell refers to Thoreau as one among the "pistillate plants kindled to fruitage by the Emersonian pollen."[33] Thoreau was dismissed as a misanthropic egotist (Lowell calls him "cold and wintery" in his "purity"),[34] but most importantly, as an insignificant disciple of Emerson. While Thoreau has come to be recognized in the twentieth century as a great writer in his own right, there is disagreement among interpreters concerning his relationship to Emerson and transcendentalism: some view him as a central figure in the transcendentalist movement, while others see him as breaking away from transcendentalism and branching out into new directions. The important element to stress here, however, is that regardless of the degree to which Thoreau may eventually grow away from the world revolving around his mentor, it is obvious that when we read *Civil Disobedience* we can see a close relationship to central ideas identified with transcendentalism and the broader intellectual life in Concord.

## ABOLITIONISM

Interpreters disagree about whether or not it is appropriate to consider Thoreau an abolitionist. The reason for the debate has nothing, really, to do with Thoreau's personal opposition to slavery; there is no doubt about this, as Thoreau was consistent in this opposition throughout his life. The debate, instead, focuses on Thoreau's relationship to organized abolitionist groups. If we only think of abolitionists as members of the recognizable abolition organizations, it is clear that Thoreau never personally joined any of these. As we have seen in *Civil Disobedience* (see paragraphs 21, 41), Thoreau was actively antagonistic toward "reformers" of all types, and tended to lump them with professional politicians more generally. Despite this hostility, however, Thoreau expressed abolitionist sentiments publicly in *Civil Disobedience*, and increasingly made his views public in the years that followed. Later in life he personally addressed abolitionist gatherings (filling in for Frederick Douglass at one of these), and less publically but perhaps more importantly, he was active in helping move a number of escaped slaves along the Underground Railroad. He was among the most forceful white defenders – perhaps *the* most forceful – of John Brown after the raid at Harper's Ferry. If being an active member of an abolitionist organization is required to make one an abolitionist, Thoreau clearly and willfully fails to reach this threshold. If, however, an abolitionist was anyone who publicly criticized slavery, supported abolitionist speakers (such as Wendell Phillips) when they visited Concord's lyceum, and performed deeds aimed at weakening and defying the institution of slavery, Thoreau was clearly in the abolitionist camp. Sandra Harbert Petrulionis captures the reality of these two perspectives on Thoreau's abolitionism by suggesting that "He was and was not a radical abolitionist."[35]

For our purposes, these debates are somewhat beside the point. Understanding the abolitionist politics that quite literally surrounded him in his family and village life significantly illuminates Thoreau's language and arguments in *Civil Disobedience*. William Lloyd Garrison was the most influential radical abolitionist in Boston, and the female members of Thoreau's household – which included his mother, two sisters, and numerous aunts, to say nothing of frequent women boarders – were either active members of the Garrisonian cause or sympathetic to it. We mentioned earlier that we can be certain that every major figure in New England abolition passed through Concord at some time or another during Thoreau's lifetime, and they frequently dined at the Thoreau home.[36] Petrulionis notes that Frederick Douglass became friends with Thoreau's sister, Helen.[37] When we venture beyond the walls of Thoreau's household and look at the village life of Concord, we find a remarkably active abolitionist community – a community, it should be noted, which included a large number of remarkably capable and fearless women, but also male participants such as Bronson Alcott. Thoreau and Emerson were both reluctant to join abolitionist organizations, but they had active abolitionists all around them and could not but help to be familiar with their views, methods, and debates.

There are a number of elements in New England abolitionism, most particularly within the strain growing out of Garrison's organization and journalism, that were moral commonplaces in Thoreau's social environment. The first and most obvious of these is simply the appeal to moral laws that are believed to be greater than political laws or even the Constitution itself. In his *Declaration of Sentiments of the American Anti-Slavery Convention* in Philadelphia in 1833, Garrison wrote:

> That all those laws which are now in force, admitting the right of slavery, are therefore, before God, utterly null and void; being an audacious usurpation of the Divine prerogative, a daring infringement on the law of nature, a base over-throw of the very foundations of the social compact, a complete extinction of all the relations, endearments and obligations of mankind, and a presumptuous transgression of all the holy commandments; and that therefore they ought instantly to be abrogated.[38]

The language Garrison uses is clearly religious, and in this he was not exceptional; one historian of abolition has commented, simply, "No religion, no abolitionism."[39] Early nineteenth-century America was a hotbed of religious enthusiasm, and abolitionism grew out of these religious impulses. How could human laws be respected or obeyed if they violated what was clearly God's (or "nature's") law? While Thoreau does not use language as explicitly theological as Garrison's, it is clear that he shares with Garrison a faith in the existence of a "higher law" than those proclaimed by political institutions or elites and a corresponding belief that lower laws are legitimate only to the degree that they conform to the higher.

The degree to which this claim was fundamental to abolition is illustrated by the need for abolition's opponents to challenge it. A classic example of this comes from Daniel Webster, whom Thoreau uses to illustrate the moral blinders of political elites in the final paragraphs of *Civil Disobedience*. In 1851, just two years after the publication of the first edition of *Civil Disobedience*, Webster gave a speech in Virginia in defense of the Fugitive Slave Act of 1850 (which he helped broker). He lampoons the idea of a higher law as mystical and incoherent.

> Gentlemen, this North Mountain is high, the Blue Ridge higher still, the Alleghenies higher than either, and yet this "higher law" ranges further than an eagle's flight above the highest peaks of the Alleghenies! No common wisdom can discern it; no common and unsophisticated conscience can feel it; the hearing of common men never hears its high behests; and, therefore, one would think it is not a safe law to be acted upon in matters of the highest practical moment.[40]

Webster believes that when people like Thoreau and Garrison appeal to higher laws to demonstrate the immorality of slavery, they are appealing to principles no person can see and no two individuals can agree upon. How am I to know what the higher law is when it is impossible for me to come to agreement with others about exactly what it teaches? Better to depend upon the Constitution and the compromises of statesmen found in our nation's laws than to look to the heavens for a form of guidance that can only, in the end, lead to disagreement and conflict. Our concern here is not with whether or not Webster's claim is persuasive, but rather with the fact that he felt the need to make it. Appeal to higher laws than the Constitution and laws of the United States was fundamental to the abolitionist position. The commitment to the Constitution as constituting our highest obligations required the denial of just such a higher law. While it would be possible to argue for Webster's policy position of compromise with the South on grounds other than those he chose (one could say, for example, that although the Compromise of 1850 was significantly imperfect in comparison to the higher law, it was the least imperfect option available in the real world of politics), it is telling that a politician of Webster's stature found the appeal to higher law a dangerous option. The reason he felt this way was clearly because of the use that had been made by higher law reasoning in the abolitionist community.

As the original title to *Civil Disobedience* suggests, Thoreau defends a position he calls *resistance* to civil government. The choice of language was significant since in the Garrisonian abolitionist community a position called *non-resistance* was widely held and practiced; in fact, seven female members of Thoreau's family identified with this position.[41] Non-resisters refused to cooperate with any force outside the teachings of evangelical Christianity; any use of force or coercion was viewed as a usurpation of God's rightful authority. Since the institutions of government rely on physical force – both to defend the nation from external foes and to maintain civil order by enforcement of criminal law – they are corrupted by wielding (or threatening) illegitimate violence. Non-resistance, therefore, was a form of Christian and pacifist anarchism in which the individual refused to cooperate with political institutions. This could include the refusal to pay taxes, or vote, or, among the most extreme non-resisters, even rely upon the police for protection from criminal behavior. Non-resistance was committed to reforming the world by persuading those violating Christian teachings to change their ways. The practitioners of non-resistance were convinced that the power of truth was greater than any physical force. Their approach to abolition, therefore, was built entirely on a commitment to moral suasion. Rather than using law, let alone violence in extra-legal forms, non-resisters wished to appeal directly to the Christian consciences of slaveholders to recognize the violence slavery commits against the Christian values of peace and equality. As Garrison said, "We have no force but the force of truth."[42]

This position, emerging and flourishing in Concord abolitionist circles in the 1830s and 40s, was both deeply optimistic and deeply anti-political – optimistic about the "force of truth," and anti-political in its view of the profound moral corruption of all organized political life. While this kind of millennial evangelical Protestantism was not unique to abolitionists, it did significantly shape the early years of the abolitionist movement. It also created one of the early sources of tension and disagreement within the radical abolitionist community fairly soon after the movement became organized and recognizable. In November 1837, Elijah Parish Lovejoy, a minister and abolitionist journalist in Alton, Illinois, was murdered by a mob attacking his printing press and abolitionist publications. This was just the most famous incident in the growing mob violence abolitionists faced in the 1830s. This violence produced significant disagreement among abolitionists about their commitment to pacifism and to working outside political institutions. The following fall, in 1838, Garrison sponsored a convention of peace activists and abolitionists in Boston. Members of the American Anti-Slavery Society and the American Peace Society objected both to Garrison's philosophy of non-resistance, as well as his insistence that women be able to participate as full voting members at the convention. When the members of these two groups realized that Garrison's maneuver to allow female participation would put him in a position to dominate the proceedings, a schism occurred and they walked out of the convention. Thus was formed the New England Non-Resistance Society. Forty-four individuals, 20 of whom were women, signed the *Declaration of Sentiments* from the convention.

The creation of the New England Non-Resistance Society, ten years prior to Thoreau's lecture that would become *Civil Disobedience*, marked the degree to which the abolitionist movement would struggle with the issue of violence. The Garrisonians in the Non-Resistance Society attracted a more radically pacifist and anti-political constituency than other abolitionist groups such as the American Anti-Slavery Society. According to historian John Demos, the non-resisters tended to have a deep distrust, even hostility, toward human institutions. Many were "come-outers," that is, individuals who had left their churches because of what they took to be the desire of ministers and congregations to coerce dissenting individuals into doctrinal conformity. Conservative abolitionists increasingly rejected the radical pacifism of non-resisters, especially as violence against abolitionists grew. They also distrusted the Garrisonian reluctance to participate in conventional political processes and activities. Much of the debate in the 1830s was over the "no-government" question, with the radical position looking increasingly less practical and defensible to large sectors of the population. In Demos' words, "the popular image of non-resistance was scarcely flattering."[43] Over time, the pacifist and anti-political position would lose support: "The decline of non-violent abolition in the 1850s was nothing short of total collapse."[44] The abolition movement would eventually be taken over by the Republican Party (growing out of the 1840 Liberty Party, and then the Free Soil Party of 1848 and 1852), working with more conventional political tools and strategies. The election of Lincoln as the first Republican president in 1860 made it clear to the Southern slave states that their "peculiar institution" was doomed if they remained in the United States under Republican leadership, and thus the American Civil War was sparked.[45]

While non-resistance and the appeal to higher law were central components of what we might think of as the radical strain of New England abolitionism, what some have referred to as the "perfectionist" elements in the abolition movement, there were two other elements we can recognize as significant for understanding *Civil Disobedience*. The first of these is sometimes called "immediatist."[46] The meaning is simply that abolitionists demanded that slavery be abolished immediately. The alternative view to immediatism would be to think of slavery much the way the Founders did, as an unfortunate reality that will eventually fade away if we design laws and institutions appropriately. It may have been impossible to abolish slavery at the time of the Founding; the compromises needed to hold the new union together were simply too extensive to allow for immediate abolition. In this view of the American Founders, they assumed the Constitution had instituted a political community in which slavery would become increasingly less viable over time. And, indeed, slavery was abolished in the Northern states in due course. The invention of the cotton gin at the end of the eighteenth century, however, made slave production of cotton highly profitable in the Southern states, so free labor was unable to replace slave production in the normal course of economic development in that region. The Republican Party and its predecessors, however, pursued public policies to isolate slavery as a local anomaly within an overall free nation, making it impossible for it to prosper and thrive in the long run. For the immediatist, this gradualist and Constitutional approach to abolition was too slow and too compromising with the evils endured by the slave. Even if it required the dissolution of the Union, immediatist abolitionists insisted on the present rather than future or gradual elimination of slavery.

A second element of radical abolition is closely related to immediatism: the view that political disunion is better than cooperation with slavery. In 1844, Thoreau's sisters supported a resolution at the New England Anti-Slavery Convention in Boston supporting "disunion" with the slave states.[47] In a public meeting a few years after Thoreau published *Civil Disobedience* Garrison referred to the U.S. Constitution as "a covenant with death and an agreement with hell."[48] From his perspective, and unlike the view of the Republicans outlined above, the Constitution was implicated in the protection and promotion of slavery. If disunion and dissolution of the nation were necessary to prevent New England from being implicated in the institution of slavery, so be it. Immediatism and disunion naturally reinforced each other in the perfectionist abolitionism of Garrison and his allies.

When we compare Thoreau's position in *Civil Disobedience* with the perspective of much of the abolitionism shared by his family, friends, and neighbors, it is difficult to sort out the degree to which he is distancing himself from these views, on the one hand, and sharing these views, on the other. Three elements of Garrisonian abolition discussed here – appeal to higher law, immediatism, and disunion – are present in Thoreau's essay. We have seen that he clearly insists on the existence and moral priority of higher law. He insists as well on immediately canceling all association with the slave powers. On these matters, he expresses views very close to if not the same as those of the Garrisonians. The one obvious difference concerns the issues of non-resistance; after all, he purposefully titled the essay *Resistance to Civil Government* in 1849. Just as Thoreau had desired to carve out a position distinct from non-resistance when he debated Alcott on this issue years earlier (in 1841), so he wanted to distinguish himself from the "no-government" (non-resistance) position in his public lecture of 1848 and his published essay the following year. Despite the many views that Thoreau clearly shares with abolitionist members of his community, he is also clearly adamant in his claim that he has a unique or differing position in some important sense. In part, as we saw in Chapter 2, his differences with "no-government men" are more about current strategy than long-term goals. He, like they, can imagine a day when political associations more or less dissolve into neighborly ones. But what is the meaningful distinction between his view of resistance and what we see to be the widely held abolitionism in his own social environment?

Perhaps the answer is found in an essay Thoreau published in 1844 about an abolitionist newspaper editor in New Hampshire, Nathaniel P. Rogers. The essay, *Herald of Freedom*, took its name from the New Hampshire Anti-Slavery Society's newspaper, which Rogers edited. Thoreau's essay is an admiring portrait of Rogers as a writer and abolitionist. He approves of the answer Rogers once gave to the charge that "Jesus Christ never preached abolitionism."[49] Rogers answered, first, "I deny your proposition. ... That single precept of his – 'Whatsoever ye would that men should do to you, do ye even so to them' – reduced to *practice*, would abolish slavery over the whole earth in twenty-four hours."[50] The second answer Rogers gives, however, draws Thoreau's approval as well. "Secondly, granting your proposition to be true – and admitting what I deny – that Jesus Christ did not preach the abolition of slavery, then I say, *he did'nt* [sic] *do his duty*."[51] Rogers' view here is very much like the position Thoreau would later defend in *Civil Disobedience*, that the moral power of the Bible comes from principles beyond the Bible itself. Even Jesus Christ could have been criticized if he had not supported abolition. Thoreau, that is, has found a kindred spirit in Rogers, who appeals to moral principles beyond our conventional religious (and political) common sense. Thoreau explains, in addition, that Rogers is exemplary in discovering these principles more through his conscience than impartial reason. "His was not the wisdom of the head, but of the heart."[52] This is as if to say, in language Thoreau would use four years later in his great essay, that Rogers is an admirable man because he has a backbone you cannot put your hand through.

What Thoreau does not talk about in *Herald of Freedom*, or in his minor revision of the essay two years later after Rogers' death, are many of the specific views that Rogers defended, including a firm belief in gender as well as racial equality (views many Garrisonians fully support). Most important for Thoreau, Rogers advocated the dissolution of abolitionist societies on the grounds that all human organizations threatened the moral autonomy of their membership. Just as the "come-outers" left their churches in order to avoid the coercive attempts of congregations and clergy to control the beliefs of the members, so Rogers believed anti-slavery and abolition societies represented comparable threats to their members' moral independence. Rogers split with the Garrisonians over this issue in 1844, the year Thoreau wrote admiringly of him. Thoreau scholar Wendell Glick argues that "Rogers broke with Garrison in 1844 on the very issue which prevented Thoreau from making common cause with Garrison, even though his less critical sisters and aunts were rabid Garrisonians."[53]

If Glick is right that Thoreau was an admirer not only of Rogers' literary abilities, but of his moral and political views as well, then we start to get a sense of how Thoreau viewed his own abolitionism as differing from that of many of his friends and relatives in Concord. Over the course of the 1840s, many abolitionists would drift away from the non-resistance of the Garrisonians by becoming more willing to consider the use of force to confront and end slavery, as well as the conventional political tools such as political parties and voting. As we have seen, Demos writes of the almost complete collapse of the nonviolent abolition movement by the 1850s. Certainly, the majority of criticisms of the Garrisonian position within the abolitionist movement would come from the political and non-pacifist position, beginning in the 1830s and growing progressively over the next decade or so. Thoreau was clearly not committed to the pacifism of many Garrisonians (like his own relatives). The position he carves out in *Civil Disobedience*, however, follows Rogers by moving in the opposite direction from the drift of abolitionist politics as a whole. Rather than criticizing the Garrisonians for not being political enough, Thoreau agrees with Rogers in distrusting even the organization of political pressure groups – groups not competing for political power, but agitating for general moral and political reform. That is, Thoreau's complaint was not that the Garrisonians were too anarchic and apolitical; it was that they were too organized and did not stress individual integrity enough. Glick writes that "Rogers was Thoreau's early 'man of principle.'"[54] It is precisely such a man with the most pure and honorable personal integrity that Thoreau is defending in *Civil Disobedience*. Only this heroic individual could embody the independence of mind and body to allow for a complete "disunion" with the slave society. Thoreau, like Rogers, held that the citizens of New England were called to live such independent lives. This independence would produce the moral integrity that would put an end to slavery. Organizing into reform groups is not what is called for. Purification of one's own interests and motives, and taking care to make certain that one is not "sitting upon another man's shoulders," (paragraph 13) constitutes "resistance to civil government" for Thoreau.

## THE MEXICAN AMERICAN WAR

The American war with Mexico, although playing a central rhetorical role in *Civil Disobedience*, was not truly integral to either the instigation of events leading to the writing of the essay or to the essay's legacy. In 1845, the United States annexed Texas, which had declared itself to be an independent republic but which Mexico considered a rebellious province of its own national union. Annexation provoked war between the United States and Mexico, which commenced in 1846 and ended two years later in 1848. Thoreau's decision to withhold his poll tax was probably made in 1842, and so was clearly made well before the war and therefore for reasons quite independent of it. When Thoreau delivered the lectures that would become the essay in early 1848, the war was already coming to a close; when the essay appeared in 1849, the war was over. Although the injustice of the war, and its connection to the protection and proliferation of slavery, are central to Thoreau's charges against "civil government," the essay was neither influenced deeply by other anti-war activists nor did it play any important role in the anti-war movement that did develop. Most readers of *Civil Disobedience* today have only the slightest sense of the historical reality of the war itself, and the legacy of Thoreau's influence is generally independent of readers' appreciation for the historical reality of the war.

Nonetheless the war provides a crucial context for understanding Thoreau's claims because it provides such a powerful illustration of what he calls the "inexpedience" of our political institutions. Thoreau insists that inexpedient political institutions violate moral principle in two ways. First, they act independently of the wills and interests of the individuals they purportedly serve, and thus reverse the appropriate relationship between government and citizen. Second, their acts are apt to be unjust on their own merits, regardless of the ways in which policy is shaped and pursued. Put simply, inexpedient government is both undemocratic and tends to be unjust. The war with Mexico provides as dramatic an example of both of these pathologies as one could imagine. Ulysses S. Grant, who would become a crucial force leading the Union Army in the Civil War, which in turn would propel him into the American presidency, is not usually thought of as unpatriotic or prone to radical political critique. He was a young officer in the Mexican war, however, and when reflecting back on it 30 years later, he commented: "I do not think there was ever a more wicked war than that waged by the United States on Mexico. I thought so at the time, and when I was a youngster, only I had not the moral courage to resign [his military commission]." Later, at the end of his life, he said that the war was "one of the most unjust waged by a stronger against a weaker nation," and that the American Civil War was "our punishment" for that "transgression."[55] Grant was by no means eccentric in his evaluation. We might very well agree with him that this was truly a wicked war on three counts: the conditions under which it was instigated; the manner in which it was pursued; and the intention of the war policy (and the outcome that in turn reflected this intention).

The war was instigated by the Polk administration in a manner that can be frankly described as fraudulent. James Polk emerged as the surprise nominee for president for the Democratic Party in 1844. A deeply divided party was unable to nominate the favored candidate, Martin Van Buren (Van Buren received a simple majority of delegates on the first ballot of voting, but was unable to muster the super-majority required for nomination). Polk emerged as the nominee only after the eighth ballot. He was a Southerner from Tennessee and a slaveholder who, unlike Van Buren, supported the extension of slavery into the Western territories. Polk won a second surprising victory by defeating the very popular Whig, Henry Clay, in the general election. Polk ran on a platform that included the annexation of Texas, which had declared its independence from Mexico in 1836. Both Van Buren and Clay opposed annexation, as did other powerful politicians such as John Calhoun. Even pro-slavery Southerners like Calhoun feared that annexation would be destabilizing to the delicate balance between South and North and that it would inevitably draw the nation into war with Mexico, which had never recognized Texas' independence. Historian Amy Greenberg comments that Polk's upset defeat of Clay was very much a result of his promotion of U.S. expansionism. As she puts it, Polk understood better than Clay the power of "Manifest Destiny" in the voting population at large, that "Manifest Destiny was every-thing in 1844."[56] (It is interesting to note that the term "Manifest Destiny" was coined by the Democratic journalist John O'Sullivan in the *Democratic Review* in 1845 – the same newspaper whose slogan – "That Government is Best Which Governs Least" – Thoreau uses to open *Civil Disobedience*.)

Polk had a broad and ambitious vision of a continental United States, and this vision included not only the annexation of Texas, but the acquisition of the Mexican holdings in California and the British holdings in Oregon as well. Leading a Democratic Party that was itself deeply divided on this issue, and facing a Whig opposition altogether opposed to annexation and war, Polk and elements of the Democratic Party promoted an aggressive posture toward Mexico. For example, Walt Whitman, the editor of a Democratic newspaper in Brooklyn, New York, wrote that "Mexico must be thoroughly chastised. ... Let our arms now be carried with a spirit which shall teach the world that, while we are not forward for a quarrel, America knows how to crush, as well as to expand!"[57] After annexation in 1845, Polk engaged in negotiations that were transparently cynical and designed to insult and provoke Mexico.[58] He then aggressively sent General Zachary Taylor with an army into disputed territory beyond the Nueces River, which was recognized by Mexico (and many Americans) as the border between Texas and Mexico. An incident was provoked between a group of Taylor's forces and a larger Mexican force, and Polk was able to use this incident as justification for declaring war. In a message to Congress, Polk portrayed the skirmish as an entirely unprovoked and vicious act of aggression by the Mexicans and demanded that Congress vigorously support what was now, in fact, a condition of war between the two nations. Given the popularity of this aggression in the population at large, Polk was able to successfully provoke and pursue a war that a significant number of America's political elites believed was imprudent at best and entirely unjustified at worst. John Quincy Adams, a former president and then a Congressman from Massachusetts, referred to "this most outrageous war." To a colleague, he hoped out loud that military officers would refuse to fight and soldiers would desert.[59] The majority of representatives, Whigs as well as Democrats, felt cornered into supporting the war, however, and Polk had won his support in Congress with the passage of a War Bill. Senator Charles Sumner of Massachusetts would call this bill "the wickedest act in our history."[60]

In many ways, Polk's scheming was exactly the kind of elite manipulation of political institutions and popular opinion that Thoreau fears is endemic to "inexpedient" government. Polk was a slaveholder, with a slaveholder's perspective on national politics (even while serving as president, he purchased 19 slaves).[61] While he may have genuinely believed he was representing the national interest, the critical point was that he defined the national interest as a slaveholder would. It certainly seemed clear to many in the North that Polk's concern with Texas and expansion generally was intimately tied to his support for slavery and the racialist politics that viewed "white" civilization as thoroughly justified in dominating and displacing nonwhite peoples in Mexico, the far West, or anywhere else. Polk's maneuvers both reflected and manipulated widespread racist and expansionist sentiment. Abraham Lincoln, a then one-term representative from Illinois, called the war a "war of conquest fought to catch votes."[62] It was certainly defensible to view the war as provoked by undemocratic and demagogic policies in support of the interests of an elite minority of slaveholders.

War broke out in 1846 and concluded in 1848. It was brutal, with a casualty rate of about 17 percent among American forces (only the Civil War recording a higher casualty rate in the history of American warfare).[63] Over 8 percent of American forces deserted.[64] Many soldiers in the regular army were recent immigrants and Catholics and were thus unenthusiastic about fighting against Catholic Mexicans. Perhaps the most terrible elements of the war, however, concerned atrocities committed by American volunteers. These volunteer units, sent by the states, were organized in response to the call from the president. American popular mythology often romanticizes volunteer regiments in respectful terms (think of the symbol of the revolutionary minutemen), while distrusting regular army units. Historian Jill Lepore has commented that the United States is "a nation founded on opposition to a standing Army."[65] In the war with Mexico, however, the volunteer regiments, fueled by racist hatred of Mexicans, raped, murdered, and pillaged to such a degree that Army officers were unable to control them. A private under Taylor's command wrote to his family,

> The majority of the Volunteers sent here are a disgrace to the nation; think of one of them shooting a woman while washing on the bank of the river – merely to *test* his rifle; another tore forcibly from a Mexican woman the rings from her ears. Their officers take no notice of these outrages.[66]

General Winfield Scott, writing to the Secretary of War, declared that

> Our militia & volunteers, if a tenth of what is said to be true, have committed atrocities – horrors – in Mexico, sufficient to make Heaven weep, & every American, of Christian morals, blush for his country. Murder, robbery & rape of mothers & daughters, in the presence of the tied up males of the families, have been common all along the Rio Grande.[67]

Embedded journalists with the American armies initially fueled the pro-war sentiment throughout the country, but as the war progressed, the press corps began to report on the atrocities committed by American soldiers. These reports fueled the development of a significant anti-war movement in which elites (like Henry Clay and Abraham Lincoln) as well as common citizens at large began to recognize the viciousness of the war and the terrible behavior of many of the Americans fighting the war. There was significant opposition to American imperialism by the time Thoreau gave his lecture in spring 1848. *Civil Disobedience* was just one expression of an anti-war sentiment that had become quite widespread and vocal by then. It was a sentiment stimulated by press reportage of significant American atrocities.

The anti-war movement also reflected a broad recognition that this was a war of conquest fought to some significant degree for the purpose of protecting and extending American slavery. The outcomes of the war included the expansion of the American empire from the Atlantic to the Pacific, and this expansion made the question of the extension of slavery an increasingly impossible one for the nation to resolve. We saw above that Ulysses Grant believed the Civil War was the price we paid for this act of imperial aggression. In historian Daniel Walker Howe's words, "Above all, westward expansion [of which the war with Mexico was a central component] rendered inescapable the issue that would tear the country asunder a dozen years later; whether to expand slavery."[68] As we know in retrospect, this question would be settled only by a devastating civil war, which claimed the lives of three quarters of a million Americans between 1861 and 1865.[69]

In *Civil Disobedience*, Thoreau argues that unjust ("inexpedient") government behaves undemocratically, allows the apparatus of the government to be captured by the interests of a few, and loses its moral bearings through this behavior, and that the outcomes of such injustices are bloody and immoral. The American War with Mexico is a textbook illustration of the points he wants to make. While his attitude toward government developed prior to the war, and his refusal to pay his poll tax also pre-dated it, the war provided a perfect example of the problems he hoped to explain in *Civil Disobedience*. Thoreau was neither initially motivated by the war nor unique in his criticism of it, but he was particularly forceful in using the war as a case study of what we can expect from unjust political institutions.

## THOREAU'S OWN WORK

For readers of Thoreau's work as a whole, there is much in *Civil Disobedience* that is expected and familiar. Stylistically, for example, Thoreau's moral extravagance and exaggeration (noted in Chapter 2) is found in many of his writings, as is his tendency to pun and make dry jokes. One of the narrative techniques in *Civil Disobedience* is to cast his experience as a journey; being arrested and put in jail takes the form of a voyage through both time and space. Thoreau's first book, *A Week on the Concord and Merrimack Rivers*, was cast explicitly as a river journey. One of his most widely read essays is *Walking*, which ties his practice of walking to the medieval wanderers, "Saunterers," for whom walking was a religious pilgrimage. "If you are ready to leave father and mother," he writes, "and brother and sister, and wife and child and friends, and never see them again, – if you have paid your debts, and made your will, and settled all your affairs, and are a free man, then you are ready for a walk."[70] This passage serves both to illustrate Thoreau's wonderfully effective rhetorical extravagance (he certainly gets our attention by stressing our need to "settle our affairs" just to take a walk!), as well as his insistence that free individuals are "homeless" or, perhaps, best understood as on a journey of great importance even when we are close to home.

It is noteworthy that one of the books in Thoreau's library was John Bunyan's *Pilgrim's Progress*, the Puritan masterwork describing the pilgrimage of a character named Christian. Thoreau never traveled much beyond his native village and the surrounding countryside; he traveled to Quebec and Maine to the north, Cape Cod to the east, the Berkshires and Vermont to the west, New York City, Staten Island and Philadelphia to the south, and once further west to Minnesota toward the end of his life when he ventured that far in the hope of calming his tuberculosis. He did, however, famously say he traveled extensively in Concord, and this is actually not only funny but quite true – he walked at least four hours among the woods and fields of his local landscape during most days when he was healthy. His walking was never merely for exercise (although health was a welcome consequence of this activity) but was a spiritual and artistic activity, even a meditative one, in which Thoreau studied his natural surroundings and turned his observations into the raw material for his writing (in his *Journal* he comments that it "takes a man of genius to travel in his own country, in his native village").[71] While not a conventional or practicing Christian, Thoreau certainly inherited the Puritan sense of pilgrimage. He lived his life as a wanderer, even if within the confines of a fairly restricted locale, and he models much of his writing on the template of the pilgrimage or voyage of discovery. He comments in *Walden* that "I have learned that the swiftest traveller is he that goes afoot."[72] We noted earlier that he rejected the opportunity for European travel. He focused instead on the local spiritual and philosophical pilgrimage. As he says in *Walden*, "Every man is the lord of a realm beside which the earthly empire of the Czar is but a petty state, a hummock left by the ice."[73] We do not need to leave home to live a satisfying and admirable life. We simply need to develop the eyes for seeing the world around us. Wherever we are, we need to "voyage" in our daily life. Distant travel may actually distract us from the difficult and serious moral traveling that can give meaning to our lives.

Most of Thoreau's traveling took place in the pastoral countryside, away from villages and cities (an exception is his description of his trip to Montreal in *A Yankee in Canada*; likewise, much of his traveling in Maine, described in *The Maine Woods*, was in less populated wilderness than is found in many of his other rambles). For a reader of Thoreau's works it is no surprise to learn in *Civil Disobedience* that after being released from jail he retreats from the village to the huckleberry field. In *Walden*, Thoreau constructs a cabin on the shores of a local pond (on property owned by Emerson), and lives there for two years, two months, and two days. Living in an area just outside the village allows him a perspective on his world that is just slightly removed from the conventions of society. While he is not in an unpeopled wilderness (such wilderness rarely appears in his writings), he is in nature, and he finds that here he is able to cultivate his independence and freedom. In *Walking*, one of the most famous of Thoreau's comments is found: "in Wildness is the preservation of the world."[74] He claims that "From the forest and wilderness come the tonics and barks which brace mankind."[75] Nature, for Thoreau, is not only an endlessly interesting and appropriate object of study (he was, indeed, a naturalist, and he became increasingly skilled and obsessed with his careful observations of nature as he grew older). More importantly, nature is a moral teacher. The experience of nature, he suggests, can direct us away from the trivial and superficial, toward the real and meaningful. He comments in *A Week* that "All our lives want a suitable background."[76] Nature provides us with just such a background.

The premise of Thoreau's investigations in *Walden* is that the "mass of men lead lives of quiet desperation."[77] That is, even though we are a relatively free country, we are also surrounded by people searching for happiness in all the wrong places; for example, through wealth and social status. "Most men, even in this comparatively free country, through mere ignorance and mistake, are so occupied with the factitious cares and superfluously coarse labors of life that its finer fruits cannot be plucked by them."[78] Thoreau's experiment in simple living at Walden Pond allowed him to become "convinced, both by faith and experience, that to maintain one's self on this earth is not a hardship but a pastime, if we will live simply and wisely."[79] He offers two resources for escaping our desperation and learning to make life playful, a pastime, a pleasure. The first of these is great books. Thoreau was convinced that the greatest works of world literature held real insight into the demands of moral life (he was captivated by Eastern as well as European classics). The reader of *Civil Disobedience* might be surprised by the degree to which he promoted public support for the fine arts, at least at the local level: "In this country, the village should in some respects take the place of the nobleman of Europe. It should be the patron of the fine arts. It is rich enough."[80] He suggests, in appropriately extravagant Thoreauvian form, that

> New England can hire all the wise men in the world to come and teach her, and board them round the while, and not be provincial at all. That is the *uncommon* school we want [a joking reference to the public *common* schools for children in Massachusetts]. Instead of noblemen, let us have noble villages of men. If it is necessary, omit one bridge over the river, go round a little there, and throw one arch at least over the darker gulf of ignorance which surrounds us.[81]

If we saw hints of Thoreau's lineage as an educator in *Civil Disobedience*, in *Walden* we see an explicit support for the public promotion of literacy and high culture. He argues here that "By such a pile [of the great books] we may hope to scale heaven at last."[82] A reflective and meaningful life can be learned from the greatest cultural artifacts left to us through the ages.

Despite this trust in great literature, the overall solution offered in *Walden* to the problem of unhappiness and confusion lies in a different resource from books and high culture; nature has the great advantage that it is available to the literate and illiterate alike. One of the most optimistic messages of the book is that "The setting sun is reflected from the windows of the alms-house as brightly as from the rich man's abode; the snow melts before its door as early in the spring."[83] The overriding metaphor of the book is melting, thawing, awakening, overcoming sleep, and learning to be fully awake to life and its possibilities. "The commonest sense is the sense of men asleep, which they express by snoring."[84] Our conventional views and thoughts and lifestyles grow from a kind of sleepwalking, an unthinking common sense that does not address our deepest needs and possibilities. Instead of living wide awake, we become burdened with "factitious cares and superfluously coarse labors." The climax of the book takes place in the spring, when Walden Pond, a symbol for Thoreau's own education, thaws and comes to life again. Awake like the pond and its surrounding landscape, Thoreau prepares to leave Walden and embark on his next adventure in life. This idea of awakening was a particularly powerful and literal one for Thoreau, who suffered, along with an uncle, from narcolepsy.[85] Even with his physiological struggle with wakefulness, Thoreau understood that such a physical challenge was trivial when compared with our need to be morally awake, to live life meaningfully and with pleasure.

Nature "awakens" us by teaching us beauty and novelty and challenging our imaginations. One of the greatest services of nature, however, is that it literally brings us to our own senses. It teaches us to experience and appreciate the moment:

> We should be blessed if we lived in the present always, and took advantage of every accident that befell us, like the grass which confesses the

> influence of the slightest dew that falls on it; and did not spend our
> time in atoning for the neglect of past opportunities, which we call
> doing our duty.[86]

We commonly become so preoccupied with the past and the
future in our conventional lives that we are unable to focus on
and enjoy – to fully experience – the present. Wild nature is thus
a "tonic."[87] It awakens us to a world beyond ourselves and our
small concerns. It not only brings us to the moment, it also teaches
us humility. As Thoreau puts it, we learn to "witness our own
limits transgressed, and some life pasturing freely where we never
wander."[88] The appeal of this humility, this recognition of a
natural world of great beauty and complexity and importance
beyond our own personal lives, must seem like a paradox to most
of us: the more we are able to enjoy and lose ourselves in the
experience of nature, the more our life becomes a pleasure and a
satisfaction to us. "It is life near the bone where it is sweetest."[89]
In *Walking*, Thoreau puts it this way: "I believe that there is a
subtle magnetism in Nature, which, if we unconsciously yield to it,
will direct us aright."[90] A life lived in nature makes us physically
healthy by exercising our bodies. Much more importantly, such a
life provides the experiences we need to become morally awake, to
help us develop an independent and humane sensibility. These
themes are consistent throughout Thoreau's body of writings and
make it clear that the retreat to a huckleberry party at the end of
*Civil Disobedience* was not an accident or a symbol without meaning
to Thoreau's larger philosophical project.

Another consistent element in Thoreau's ideas, and one related
to the project of learning to live in and learn from nature, is his
distrust of wealth and commerce. He is not opposed to all trade
and commercial life – after all, he traded some of the beans he
grew at Walden for rice, which he much preferred and could not
grow in the Massachusetts climate. He did consistently object,
however, to the production of wealth for wealth's sake, and to the
promotion of forms of individual and social life defined almost
entirely by economic activity. Such, he held, are distracting from
humane concerns, and corrupting as well. In *Walden* he argues
that "The luxury of one class is counterbalanced by the indigence

of another."[91] When we produce great wealth, we inevitably produce poverty and inequality that infects our common life. As individuals, the economic process that should serve us governs us instead: "But lo! Men have become the tools of their tools."[92] His own experience suggests that "trade curses everything it handles,"[93] and his best solution has been to learn "to want but little."[94] In *Life Without Principle*, one of his last and most powerful essays, Thoreau explodes: "I think that there is nothing, not even crime, more opposed to poetry, to philosophy, ay, to life itself, than this incessant business."[95] American society was becoming so corrupted by its commercial spirit that it was losing the opportunity to cultivate the freedom it professed to serve.

> America is said to be the arena on which the battle of freedom is to be fought; but surely it cannot be freedom in a merely political sense that is meant. Even if we grant that the American has freed himself from a political tyrant, he is still the slave of an economical and moral tyrant. Now that the republic – the *res-publica* – has been settled, it is time to look after the *res-privata*, – the private state.[96]

In 1861, when he wrote these words, Thoreau was as distrustful of the corruption of capitalist economics as he was in 1848. The fear of economic injustice and servility is found throughout his writings, and is in no way unique to *Civil Disobedience*. His greatest book, *Walden*, as well as his essays and lectures, comes back to this concern again and again.

Thoreau's loving portraits of nature are thus deeply connected to his critique of contemporary economic life. Learning to observe, appreciate, and experience nature can help us slow down, turn our ambitions away from "this incessant business" and toward a more spiritually satisfying and morally edifying life. Nature teaches us to turn away from material wealth for the sake of artistic, philosophical, and moral wealth. It teaches us the deepest forms of independence and to spurn the artificial independence built upon the accumulation of goods and social status; these prove, in the end, to be among the most insidious forms of dependency. Thoreau's retreat to the huckleberry field at the end of *Civil Disobedience* connects his observations about "resistance to civil government" with his broader, lifelong concern to teach an alternative to America's developing commercial culture and his use of nature as the moral educator in this project. In this sense, *Civil Disobedience* is just one element of a broader political project. Thoreau's ambition may have been unconventional, but he was remarkably ambitious nonetheless. He hoped to shape, and even redirect, America's public life through his writings. This comment from *Walden* suggests the degree to which such redirection was central to his work:

> the only true America is that country where you are at liberty to pursue such a mode of life as may enable you to do without these [luxuries], and where the state does not compel you to sustain the slavery and war and other superfluous expenses which directly or indirectly result from the use of such things.[97]

Despite this broad social ambition, most of Thoreau's writings do not deal directly with political affairs, or they comment about political life only in passing. Such comments tend to be deeply disparaging about politics generally. For example, in an early essay, *Natural History of Massachusetts*, he comments that "The merely political aspect of the land is never very cheering; men are degraded when considered as the members of a political organization."[98] The most positive reflections on American politics are probably found in *A Yankee in Canada*, written a few years after *Civil Disobedience*, where comparison with his neighbors to the north provoked Thoreau's most obviously patriotic and optimistic claims about the American political order. Even though American politics looked good to him in comparison with Canadian politics, however, the structure of the arguments he develops in his discussion do not change dramatically between 1848 and 1853, when the first parts of *A Yankee* were published.

In his trip to Montreal in 1850, Thoreau observed soldiers being drilled. His fear that military service under autocratic and unjust regimes violates soldiers' moral integrity is as clear here as it is in *Civil Disobedience*. It would be impossible to give any of these soldiers a good education, he reflects, without making them deserters; the soldier's "natural foe is the government that drills him."[99] It is remarkable, however, to see the degree to which

Thoreau's contempt for this military display provokes him to imagine a just and inspiring human community.

> If men could combine thus earnestly, and patiently, and harmoniously to some really worthy end, what might they not accomplish? They now put their hands, and partially perchance their heads, together, and the result is that they are the imperfect tools of an imperfect and tyrannical government. But if they could put their hands and heads and hearts and all together, such a co-operation and harmony would be the very end and success for which government now exists in vain, – a government, as it were, not only with tools, but stock to trade with.[100]

Nonetheless, when he compares the United States with Canada, it is not the positive potential of collective action he is drawn to, but the degree to which the government is simply less involved in the lives of citizens that makes his own country more attractive to him:

> Give me a country where it is the most natural thing in the world for a government that does not understand you to let you alone. ... What makes the United States government, on the whole, more tolerable, – I mean for us lucky white men, – is the fact that there is so much less of government with us.[101]

While he may prefer his own nation to Canada, it is for reasons that will not surprise the reader of *Civil Disobedience*. Despite hints here and elsewhere about positive political functions (as we saw, for example, concerning the local promotion of literary culture), his casual reflections on politics generally reflect the kind of distrust of political institutions, and desire for less rather than more political power, readers of *Civil Disobedience* expect. A cranky comment from a late (1858) *Journal* captures a view of political institutions similar to that found in *Civil Disobedience* and throughout his writings: "I think the law is really a 'humbug,' and a benefit principally to the lawyers."[102]

There are two important essays written in the years following *Civil Disobedience* in which readers have sensed a shift in Thoreau's political views, at least as they relate to the specific matters raised in the earlier essay, resistance or rebellion to unjust government. The first of these, *Slavery in Massachusetts*, was written and delivered at an anti-slavery rally in Framingham, Massachusetts, organized by William Lloyd Garrison on the 4th of July, 1854. The occasion for writing the essay was the arrest in Boston of a fugitive slave, Anthony Burns. The Fugitive Slave Act of 1850 required all law enforcement officials – that is, state as well as federal officials – to apprehend and return any individual suspected of being a fugitive slave to his or her claimed owner (the slaveholder's word was sufficient evidence to require law officials' cooperation). In addition, any citizen could be prosecuted for aiding a suspected fugitive slave and punished with up to six months' imprisonment and a $1,000 fine. This law, growing from the Compromise of 1850, significantly strengthened the earlier Fugitive Slave Act of 1795, which was a law binding only on federal law enforcement and widely ignored or even actively subverted in practice in Northern states. Anthony Burns had escaped from bondage in Virginia in 1853 and come to Boston. The following year he was arrested and tried under the law of 1850. Two days after his arrest, on May 26, abolitionists stormed the courthouse where he was to be tried in an attempt to free him. Violence ensued and a federal marshal was fatally stabbed. President Franklin Pierce sent federal troops to help enforce the law. The police maintained control of Burns, his trial was held, and he was returned to Virginia. The entire affair had the effect of radicalizing many New Englanders and illustrating the degree to which the North had become increasingly complicit in the protection of Southern slavery. (Burns was later ransomed; he returned to Boston, was then educated at Oberlin College in Ohio, and moved to Canada where he lived until his premature death from tuberculosis in 1862.)

*Slavery in Massachusetts* shares themes and arguments with *Civil Disobedience*. As he had in the earlier essay, Thoreau suggests that those captured by the logic of politics are unable to make the kind of moral distinctions guided by principles greater than those generated by the political world. For that reason, he charges those "who have been bred in the school of politics" with precisely the failing that politically involved people tend to accuse apolitical individuals of embodying: a failure "now and always to face the facts."[103]

Those who view the Fugitive Slave Act as a necessary compromise assume that finding an agreement with the slave powers is the highest moral objective. As such, they prove themselves to actually be the party least able to understand the full moral stakes involved. "The fact which the politician faces is merely, that there is less honor among thieves than was supposed, and not the fact that they are thieves."[104] The Fugitive Slave Act, in other words, is simply an immoral compromise. Professional politicians have become so invested in the contemporary political order that they are unable to recognize the most significant moral categories and obligations. When a Massachusetts judge was presented with the demand to hear the charges against Anthony Burns, he used political authority not for "expedient" purposes, but for the sake of enforcing injustice. Just as Thoreau says in *Civil Disobedience* that the "law never made a man a whit more just," he claims here that "The law will never make men free; it is men who have got to make the law free."[105] He concludes this thought by appeal to higher laws than those embodied in our Constitution or legal codes, just as he does in *Civil Disobedience*: "They are the lovers of law and order, who observe the law when the government breaks it."[106] What this requires is that we behave like men, in the sense Thoreau uses the term in both essays; that is, like independent, free, moral individuals. "I would remind my countrymen, that they are to be men first, and Americans only at a late and convenient hour."[107]

Thoreau is, in short, working from the same general moral theory in *Slavery in Massachusetts* as he does in *Civil Disobedience*. While he uses the language of "good government" rather than "expedient" government in 1854, he still recognizes a potentially legitimate role for political institutions: "The effect of good government is to make life more valuable, – of a bad one, to make it less valuable."[108] As in *Civil Disobedience*, however, he believes our government has become deeply involved in injustice. In truth, he is even more disgusted than he was six years earlier. His anger has reached a boiling point. "If there is any hell more unprincipled than our rulers, and we, the ruled, I feel curious to see it."[109] In *Civil Disobedience*, the state is unjust, but also bumbling and morally pathetic – he equates it with a scared old woman protecting her silver spoons. In *Slavery*, the state (and the supporters of the state) more devilish yet, more actively insidious, and not merely cowardly and defensive.

In one of the most famous comments in the essay Thoreau says, "The remembrance of my country spoils my walk. My thoughts are murder to the State, and involuntarily go plotting against her."[110] Although the thesis of *Civil Disobedience* is about resisting unjust government, the language of *Slavery in Massachusetts* has become more active and violent, not merely about withdrawal. "It is not an era of repose. We have used up all our inherited freedom. If we would save our lives, we must fight for them."[111] This alone does not necessarily suggest anything significantly different from what was said in *Civil Disobedience*, but the point is stated more aggressively than it had been earlier. The emphasis in *Civil Disobedience* is on independence from the political world, and this perspective is present in *Slavery in Massachusetts* as well: "Let each inhabitant of the State [of Massachusetts] dissolve his union with her, as long as she delays to do her duty [of resisting the Fugitive Slave Act]."[112] But the language in *Slavery in Massachusetts* includes a higher pitch of moral rage as well as an implication of greater active assault upon political institutions. It is clear that Thoreau is in sympathy with those who attempted to rescue Anthony Burns and that such direct assaults upon injustice are justified in his mind. This does not contradict the claims of *Civil Disobedience*, but it does extend them in the direction of thinking of "resistance" as a kind of rebellious engagement – a direction not pursued in the earlier essay.

If we reflect on the comment quoted above that thinking about political life spoils his walk, we get a sense of a noticeable shift that has occurred for Thoreau between 1848 and 1854. The general moral theory remains, but the understanding of the appropriate response to inexpedient political power has enlarged somewhat. The reason for this clearly appears to be the Compromise of 1850. The government of Massachusetts, and not only the federal government, was now even more directly implicated in slavery than it was in 1848. The power of the state, in short, was becoming increasingly intrusive in Thoreau's life. The strategy presented in 1848 of withdrawing to a huckleberry party no longer seems as viable. As long as the government of Massachusetts abides by the Compromise,

Thoreau is more directly implicated in and personally threatened by political injustice. Simple withdrawal no longer appears to capture the full range of reasonable resistance. Withdrawing support from the state may require more active forms of engagement than Thoreau had imagined prior to 1850.

In this extended passage from *Slavery in Massachusetts*, we see Thoreau struggling with these new developments:

> I have lived for the last month, – and I think that every man in Massachusetts capable of the sentiment of patriotism must have had a similar experience, – with the sense of having suffered a vast and indefinite loss. I did not know at first what ailed me. At last it occurred to me that what I had lost was a country. I had never respected the Government near to which I had lived, but I had foolishly thought that I might manage to live here, minding my private affairs, and forget it. For my part, my old and worthiest pursuits have lost I cannot say how much of their attraction, and I feel that my investment in life here is worth many per cent less since Massachusetts last deliberately sent back an innocent man, Anthony Burns, to slavery.[113]

A sense of loss, rage, and the impossibility of avoiding the political world has been amplified as a result of the Burns affair. Developments in American national and local politics have made themselves more present and unavoidable in Thoreau's life than he found them to be just a few years earlier.

Nonetheless, the ending of the essay follows a similar form as *Civil Disobedience*. Thoreau remembers a water lily he smelled the other day, and he refers to it as an "emblem of purity" that grows from the "slime and the muck" of the earth.[114] He uses this flower as a symbol of the potential virtue of even these unprincipled men he has severely criticized in the essay. "If Nature can compound this fragrance still annually, I shall believe her still young and full of vigor, her integrity and genius unimpaired, and that there is virtue even in man, too, who is fitted to perceive and love it."[115] Once again, nature is capable of helping direct us toward the higher moral principles, if only we can get beyond the conventions of our political life.

> So behave that the odor of your actions may enhance the general sweetness of the atmosphere, that when we behold or scent a flower,

we may not be reminded how inconsistent your deeds are with it; for all odor is but one form of advertisement of a moral quality, and if fair actions had not been performed, the lily would not smell sweet. The foul slime stands for the sloth and vice of man, the decay of humanity; the fragrant flower that springs from it, for the purity and courage which are immortal.[116]

Just as the huckleberry party shows us a new moral life in *Civil Disobedience*, so the water lily stands as the symbol of such a life in this essay.

There is one other comment in *Slavery in Massachusetts* worth noting. *Civil Disobedience* provides us with a very damning criticism of Thoreau's hometown of Concord, which was very much a country village. In *Slavery in Massachusetts*, however, he is led by events in Boston to consider the contrast between cities and country, and how they each stand in relation to the kind of morality that can be found beyond the narrow logic of politics. "On any moral question," he writes,

I would rather have the opinion of Boxboro than of Boston and New York put together. ... When, in some obscure country town, the farmers come together to a special town meeting, to express their opinion on some subject which is vexing the land, that, I think, is the true Congress, and the most respectable one that is ever assembled in the United States.[117]

Thoreau is not consistent in this sentiment. He would write in his *Journal* in 1859 that there is "nothing but confusion in our New England life. The hogs are in the parlor."[118] In *Slavery in Massachusetts*, nonetheless, he suggests that direct democratic debate in country villages is significantly more to be trusted than the sophistication of professional state and national level politicians. The reason for this is clear, given Thoreau's overall moral perspective: the farmers he is referring to are much more apt to be independent and well tutored by nature rather than by politics. Their moral principles will be less constrained or misshapen by the conventions and demands of political power. This friendly comment may surprise us, in light of how critical Thoreau often is of his rural neighbors. But his overall moral theory has not changed here: those closer to nature and less removed from the commerce and national perspective of the cities are more likely to be open to the higher law of morality.

The second important political essay to appear after *Civil Disobedience* was *A Plea for Captain John Brown*, delivered as a lecture in 1859 in Concord, Boston, and Worcester, Massachusetts after news reached the North about John Brown's raid on Harper's Ferry. Brown had been in Concord twice, in 1857 and earlier in 1859, and Thoreau had made a modest contribution to Brown during the first visit. When he heard of Brown's failed attack on Harper's Ferry, Thoreau became one of Brown's strongest supporters among white anti-slavery figures (African Americans tended to be much less critical of Brown than white abolitionists; indeed, the former often portrayed Brown as the one virtuous white man).[119]

When we recall the recommendation in *Civil Disobedience* to retreat from political life, Thoreau's defense of John Brown's insurrectionary methods may seem contrary if not contradictory to his earlier views. It is certainly true that Thoreau's praise of Brown is not the praise of one who withdraws to a huckleberry party. Thoreau had written in *Civil Disobedience* that he was not responsible for correcting all the wrongs of the world, although he *was* responsible for not contributing to them. He also seemed to believe that "disunion" with slaveholders was possible, if we could just learn to live simple, independent lives. In *Slavery in Massachusetts*, the final passage about the water lily reminds us of the huckleberry party in *Civil Disobedience* and the common message from both 1848 and 1854. Even after the outbreak of the Civil War, Thoreau appeared to continue to think of disunion with the South as the preferred strategy, rather than defending the union and purging it of slavery altogether as President Lincoln and the Republican Party aimed to do. In a letter from 1861, he wrote:

> If the people of the north thus come to see clearly that there can be no *Union* between freemen & slaveholders, & vote & act accordingly, I shall think that we have purchased that progress cheaply by this revolution. A nation of 20 millions of freemen will be far more respectable & powerful, than if 10 millions of slaves & slave holders were added to them.[120]

Disunion, rather than saving the union through active universal abolition, appears to have tempted Thoreau through the end of his life (he died the spring following these comments).

Nonetheless, we have seen in *Slavery in Massachusetts* that Thoreau had begun to sense, after the Compromise of 1850, the impossibility of simply removing himself from being implicated in the institution of slavery. Thoreau's defense of Brown continues to move in this new direction. He writes, "If private men are obliged to perform the offices of government [i.e., protecting fugitive slaves], to protect the weak and dispense justice, then the government becomes only a hired man, or clerk, to perform menial or indifferent services."[121] And our current government, we know, has become just such a "hired man" for slave interests (in Thoreau's view). "When a government puts forth its strength on the side of injustice, as ours to maintain Slavery and kill the liberators of the slave, it reveals itself a merely brute force, or worse, a demoniacal force. It is the head of the Plug Uglies [a notorious street gang in Baltimore]. It is more manifest than ever that tyranny rules."[122] As in *Civil Disobedience*, Thoreau suggests that a person in the right is not required to appeal to majority sentiment when faced with injustice of this magnitude: "When were the good and the brave ever in a majority?"[123] Here he takes the argument one step further and suggests that such an individual – in this case Brown – comes to represent legitimate government itself. "The only government that I recognize, – and it matters not how few are at the head of it, or how small its army, – is that power that establishes justice in the land, never that which establishes injustice."[124] Brown, he claims, was perhaps the most significant force in preventing Kansas from becoming a slave territory.[125] And at Harper's Ferry, despite his small army, Brown worked to perform the appropriate task of government by attempting to establish justice.

More than anything else, however, Thoreau's plea for Brown is built on what he takes to be Brown's moral character. In Brown, Thoreau found the man he longs for in *Civil Disobedience*, a man with a backbone who is utterly committed to principle above all else. Brown was a "transcendentalist above all, a man of ideas and principles, – that was what distinguished him."[126] He was the best of the Puritan stock, a stern and fearless hero. While many called Brown's plan at Harper's Ferry, and even he himself, insane, Thoreau suggests that such views only demonstrate the degree to which we have become corrupted by the kind of utilitarianism he dismisses in *Civil Disobedience*. A man of principle trusts that good must come from commitment to the right, that "when good seed is planted, good fruit is inevitable."[127] Unlike most of us, Brown "did not set up even a political graven image between him and his God."[128] He was animated by higher motives than is common, but this makes him easily misunderstood by the many:

> He was a superior man. He did not value his bodily life in comparison with ideal things. He did not recognize unjust human laws, but resisted them as he was bid. For once we are lifted out of the trivialness and dust of politics into the region of truth and manhood.[129]

At long last Thoreau has found an individual who embodies his ideal of the morally committed individual. He exclaims, "I rejoice that I live in this age – that I am his contemporary."[130] The enthusiasm of Thoreau's defense of Brown reflects the fact that Brown captures the moral theory Thoreau has been defending since *Civil Disobedience* was first delivered as a lecture 11 years earlier. Brown's courage and commitment to higher law make him a "superior man" to the rest of us.[131] This leads Thoreau to the extravagance of equating Brown with Christ at the end of the essay.[132] In 1844 we see Thoreau looking for his man of principle in abolitionist editor Nathaniel Rogers. Fifteen years later he has found a hero who not only embodies high principle, but has also acted dramatically on the historic stage.

This leads to one final comment about the location of *Civil Disobedience* within the broader corpus of Thoreau's writings. Remember that the intended audience of *Civil Disobedience* consists first of Thoreau's neighbors in Concord, then to fellow citizens of Massachusetts, and then, more generally, to Northern opponents of slavery. The implication is that everyone within this audience is at least potentially capable of the kind of principled acts Thoreau describes and defends. His model of moral life, however, is not a collective one. On the contrary, as we have seen, it is individualistic and personal, even private. We earlier mentioned the copy of Bunyan's *Pilgrim's Progress* in Thoreau's library, and this draws our attention to the role of pilgrimage in Thoreau's moral thinking. But the pilgrim he has in mind is not Christian, the character from Bunyan's story. Instead of a modest Christian saint, a self-sacrificing individual living to serve God and others, the model for Thoreau is the "hero," an individual of profound independence and self-confidence. The hero cares only for the highest goods and believes that preoccupation with worldly concerns and personal safety are worthy of contempt. This hero is often a literary figure in Thoreau's writings, such as Walter Raleigh or Thomas Carlyle or Nathanial Rogers, and is one who sacrifices for principle and who stands above the foolish behavior and beliefs of the many. In his 1847 essay on *Thomas Carlyle and His Works*, Thoreau writes, "To live like a philosopher, is to live, not foolishly, like other men, but wisely, and according to universal laws."[133] At the very least, these heroes avoid the pitfalls of convention. At times they rise, like John Brown, to embody principle through great historic gestures. Thoreau's audience in *Civil Disobedience* may be the democratic many, but we can see in his search for the principled man, the man with backbone, his lifelong preoccupation with rare, inspiring, and righteous individuals.

When viewed in the context of Thoreau's writings as a whole, there is a great continuity between most of the themes and ideas in *Civil Disobedience* and the rest of his work. His important later anti-slavery essays, *Slavery in Massachusetts* and *A Plea for Captain John Brown*, emphasize direct engagement with political affairs more than the earlier essay. In addition, the language of these later works is, if anything, more angry and extreme than that in *Civil Disobedience*. Despite these differences, however, we must not exaggerate the degree to which Thoreau abandoned the perspective he developed in his 1848 lectures. Personal integrity and even heroism, above all, and the insistence that political affairs be judged by principles found in the broader moral universe, are consistent themes in all three of these great political essays. Thoreau appears in the later essays to be less certain about the possibility or even the desirability of a complete disengagement from political life. Despite this one issue, however, the overall moral perspective remains quite consistent.

# NOTES

1 Henry Seidel Canby, *Thoreau* (Boston, MA: Houghton Mifflin, 1939), p. 151.
2 Ralph Waldo Emerson, *Essays and Lectures* (NY: Library of America, 1983), p. 559.
3 Ibid., p. 563.
4 Ibid., p. 567.
5 Ibid., p. 568.
6 Ibid.
7 Ibid., p. 570.
8 Canby, *Thoreau*, p. 151.
9 Daniel Walker Howe, *What Hath God Wrought: The Transformation of America, 1815–1848* (NY: Oxford University Press, 2007), p. 618.
10 Emerson, *Essays and Lectures*, p. 193.
11 Ibid., p. 195.
12 Ibid.
13 Ibid., p. 196.
14 Ibid., p. 195.
15 Ibid., p. 208.
16 Ibid., p. 1020.
17 Henry D. Thoreau, *Journal of Henry D. Thoreau*, vol. 1, Bradford Torrey and Francis H. Allen, eds., (Boston, MA: Houghton Mifflin, 1949), p. 227.
18 Gordon Wood, *Empire of Liberty* (NY: Oxford University Press, 2009), p. 706.
19 Joyce Appleby, *Liberalism and Republicanism in the Historical Imagination* (Cambridge, MA: Harvard University Press, 1992), p. 4.
20 Thomas Jefferson, *The Portable Thomas Jefferson*, Merrill D. Peterson, ed. (NY: Penguin, 1997), p. 217.
21 Letter from Jefferson to David Williams, 14 November 1803. Available at: www.monticello.org/site/jefferson/quotations-agriculture (accessed June 2014).
22 Jefferson, *Portable Thomas Jefferson*, p. 217.
23 Ibid., p. 432.
24 Emerson, *Essays and Lectures*, p. 48.
25 Harold Bloom, ed., *Henry David Thoreau* (NY: Bloom's Literary Criticism, 2008), p. 13.
26 Emerson, *Essays and Lectures*, p. 89.
27 Ibid., p. 81.
28 Ibid., p. 10.
29 George Hochfield, "Anti-Thoreau," *Sewanee Review* 96, no. 3, 1988, p. 434.
30 Taylor Stoehr, *Nay-Saying in Concord* (Hamden, CT: Archon, 1979), p. 145.
31 Ibid., p. 155.
32 Ibid.
33 Walter Harding, ed., *Thoreau: A Century of Criticism* (Dallas, TX: Southern Methodist University Press, 1954), p. 44.
34 Ibid., p. 51.
35 Sandra Harbert Petrulionis, *To Set This World Right* (Ithaca, NY and London: Cornell University Press, 2006), p. 2.

36  Walter Harding, *The Days of Henry Thoreau* (NY: Alfred A. Knopf, 1966), p. 201.

37  Petrulionis, *To Set This World Right*, p. 30.

38  William Lloyd Garrison, *Declaration of Sentiments of the American Anti-Slavery Convention* (1833). Available at: http://utc.iath.virginia.edu/abolitn/abeswlgct.html (accessed June 2014).

39  Wilfred M. McClay, "Abolition as a Master Concept," in Andrew Delbanco, *The Abolitionist Imagination* (Cambridge, MA: Harvard University Press, 2012), p. 145.

40  Richard Francis, *Transcendental Utopias* (Ithaca, NY: Cornell University Press, 1997), p. 218.

41  John C. Broderick, "Thoreau, Alcott, and the Poll Tax," *Studies in Philology* 53, no. 4, 1956, p. 616.

42  John Demos, "The Anti-Slavery Movement and the Problem of Violent Means," *New England Quarterly* 37 no. 4, 1964, p. 503.

43  Ibid., p. 517.

44  Ibid., p. 522.

45  See James Oakes, *Freedom National* (NY: W. W. Norton, 2013).

46  Petrulionis, *To Set This World Right*, p. 70.

47  Ibid., p. 40.

48  Ibid., p. 103.

49  Henry David Thoreau, *Collected Essays and Poems* (NY: Library of America, 2001), p. 160.

50  Ibid.

51  Ibid., p. 161.

52  Ibid.

53  Wendell P. Glick, "Thoreau and the 'Herald of Freedom'," *New England Quarterly* 22 no. 2, June 1949, p. 203.

54  Ibid., p. 204.

55  Amy S. Greenberg, *A Wicked War* (NY: Alfred A. Knopf, 2012), p. 274.

56  Ibid., p. 55.

57  Ibid., p. 96.

58  Ibid., p. 78.

59  Ibid., p. 106.

60  Ibid., p. 245.

61  Howe, *What Hath God Wrought*, p. 702.

62  Ibid., p. 762.

63  James M. McPherson, "America's 'Wicked War'," *New York Review of Books*, 7 February 2013, p. 33.

64  Greenberg, *A Wicked War*, p. xvii.

65  Jill Lepore, "The Force: How Much Military is Enough?," *New Yorker*, 28 January 2013, p. 75.

66  Howe, *What Hath God Wrought*, p. 771.

67  Greenberg, *A Wicked War*, p. 134.

68  Howe, *What Hath God Wrought*, p. 852.

69  Oakes, *Freedom National*, p. xiv.

70  Thoreau, *Collected Essays and Poems*, p. 226.

71  Thoreau, *Journal*, vol. 2, p. 376.
72  Henry David Thoreau, *A Week on the Concord and Merrimack Rivers; Walden, or, Life in the Woods; The Maine Woods; Cape Cod* (NY: Library of America, 1985), p. 364.
73  Ibid., p. 578.
74  Thoreau, *Collected Essays and Poems*, p. 239.
75  Ibid.
76  Thoreau, *A Week, etc.*, p. 38.
77  Ibid., p. 329.
78  Ibid., p. 327.
79  Ibid., p. 378.
80  Ibid., pp. 409–410.
81  Ibid., p. 410.
82  Ibid., p. 406.
83  Ibid., p. 583.
84  Ibid., p. 581.
85  Robert D. Richardson Jr., *Henry Thoreau: A Life of the Mind* (Berkeley, CA: University of California Press, 1986), p. 126.
86  Thoreau, *A Week, etc.*, pp. 572–573.
87  Ibid., p. 575.
88  Ibid.
89  Ibid., p. 584.
90  Thoreau, *Collected Essays and Poems*, p. 233.
91  Thoreau, *A Week, etc.*, p. 350.
92  Ibid., p. 352.
93  Ibid., p. 378.
94  Ibid., p. 377.
95  Thoreau, *Collected Essays and Poems*, p. 349.
96  Ibid., pp. 362–363.
97  Thoreau, *A Week, etc.*, p. 486.
98  Thoreau, *Collected Essays and Poems*, p. 21.
99  Ibid., p. 272.
100  Ibid., p. 266.
101  Ibid., p. 311.
102  Thoreau, *Journal*, vol. 11, p. 208.
103  Thoreau, *Collected Essays and Poems*, p. 333.
104  Ibid.
105  Ibid., p. 338.
106  Ibid.
107  Ibid., p. 342.
108  Ibid., p. 344.
109  Ibid., p. 345.
110  Ibid., p. 346.
111  Ibid.
112  Ibid., p. 343.

113  Ibid., pp. 344–345.
114  Ibid., p. 346.
115  Ibid.
116  Ibid., pp. 346–347.
117  Ibid., p. 339.
118  Thoreau, *Journal*, vol. 12, p. 331.
119  See Benjamin Quarles, *Blacks on John Brown* (Urbana, IL: University of Illinois Press, 1972).
120  Thoreau, *Collected Essays and Poems*, p. 655.
121  Ibid., p. 411.
122  Ibid., p. 410.
123  Ibid., p. 412.
124  Ibid., p. 410.
125  Ibid., p. 397.
126  Ibid., p. 399.
127  Ibid., p. 402.
128  Ibid., p. 403.
129  Ibid., p. 407.
130  Ibid.
131  Ibid.
132  Ibid., p. 416.
133  Ibid., p. 193.

# 4

## INTERPRETATIONS

The critical commentary addressing Thoreau's essay is both extensive and varied. The point of this chapter is not to provide an exhaustive survey of this secondary literature but, rather, to introduce some of the significant channels of interpretation to be found in this broad interpretive literature. Helpful examples from the secondary literature will be used to explain and illustrate points of view, but readers should not take this discussion as a thorough or complete summary of the enormous literature touching on how we might read and understand Thoreau's political views.

In what follows, interpreters are separated into four general groups: those who believe Thoreau's views are simply not relevant to serious thinking about politics; those who believe his political ideas are incoherent and therefore indefensible and possibly dangerous; those who believe Thoreau is a fundamentally undemocratic political thinker; and those who believe Thoreau contributes (coherently and importantly) to democratic theory and values in his famous essay. As we will see, there is significant variation within each of these categories, providing for lively debate even among authors sharing a general understanding of the basic thrust and meaning of Thoreau's ideas. There is huge variety in the way

Thoreau's political readers have understood his ideas, and these differences are not merely about minor issues or matters of secondary concern. It is quite remarkable how one short essay, written well over a century and a half ago, has inspired such radically different readings.

A warning is required at the outset. The extensive interpretive literature could be organized differently from how it is here. It is hoped that the set of distinctions offered in what follows is illuminating, but different distinctions could certainly be made (for example, we could compare methodological differences among interpreters rather than the different substantive conclusions they reach). In addition, the categories of interpretation described below are not mutually exclusive; any given reading of *Civil Disobedience* may actually represent, to a greater or lesser degree, one or more of the interpretive categories used here. It is possible to believe, for example, that Thoreau was both incoherent and committed to democratic values, or instead, that he is both incoherent and undemocratic. In fact, many examples from the secondary literature could be used to illustrate more than one of these positions. Keeping these points in mind, it is helpful to distinguish between these four quite different understandings of how we should understand and interpret Thoreau's political ideas.

## *CIVIL DISOBEDIENCE* AS IRRELEVANT TO CONTEMPORARY POLITICAL LIFE

More than half a century ago, one of the great American intellectual historians, Perry Miller, published an essay reflecting on "the responsibility of mind in a civilization of machines."[1] As the world becomes increasingly mechanized and technologies come to drive society in such powerful ways, how are we to maintain control of our individual lives? (Given the power of the computer, this problem may even be more difficult in our own time than when Miller was writing.) How will we manage to develop independent thoughts and ideas and opinions in the context of a society seemingly no longer controlled by individuals? Where our economies and ways of life seem more given than chosen, and the dynamism of our societies seems outside our control? Miller reflected on those writers like Thoreau in the nineteenth century who distrusted and resisted the development of "the machine," those who rejected modern commercial and industrial life and hoped to cultivate instead a pastoral simplicity and self-sufficiency. In the time since Miller published his essay in 1961, countless readers have been drawn to *Walden's* vision of an alternative and less alienating (if less affluent) economy. Miller's judgment about this vision, however, was scathing: Thoreau, he argues, was irrelevant in his own day, given the overwhelming chorus of support for the machine, and he (and likeminded writers) "provide us today with no usable programs of resistance."[2] In fact, Thoreau's writings are an example of what Miller calls a "refusal to accept what I would hopefully term adult status."[3] What so many readers think of as Thoreau's profound critique of industrial civilization, Miller characterized as a childish refusal to face facts. At the end of the day, we will have to look elsewhere if we are to find guidance for thinking about the problems of responsibility and thoughtfulness in a technological age. Rejecting the modern age outright is simply not in the cards. The only "adult" approach is to consider ways of controlling, rather than rejecting or avoiding, "the machine."

Miller's essay was addressed more to *Walden* than to *Civil Disobedience*, so he does not directly discuss the question of Thoreau's "resistance to civil government." In addition, his claim is not that people will not try to use Thoreau's ideas, but rather that the ideas will not be realistically helpful to us today. So even though Miller is not specifically discussing Thoreau's political ideas, we can imagine an argument somewhat parallel to that which he did develop in regard to Thoreau's critique of the modern economy. Might we not suggest, in the spirit of Miller's criticism, that there is little in *Civil Disobedience* to help us when we face the real political problems in the world today? The claim would not be simply that Thoreau's ideas are derivative; even if they are, he still may have expressed them in such a way as to make them more powerfully available than they were when expressed by others. The claim also is not that the arguments are incoherent, as discussed below; the point here is that even if the ideas are coherent, they may not speak effectively to our particular needs and problems. The claim certainly would not be that

Thoreau has not played, especially in the past half century or so, an important role in political life; such a claim would deny the obvious impact of *Civil Disobedience* on protest and resistance movements in the United States and around the world. Instead, the claim is that, properly understood, Thoreau's essay simply does not address political problems in such a way as to provide positive or helpful guidance for us in the twenty-first century.

Since the revival of *Civil Disobedience* during the American civil rights, student, and anti-war campaigns, interpreters have tended to be either infatuated with or infuriated by Thoreau's essay. Prior to that, few thought Thoreau's political ideas worthy of much attention. For much of the time since *Civil Disobedience* first appeared as *Resistance to Civil Government* in 1849, almost no one bothered to interpret it at all or to take Thoreau seriously as a political thinker. As we have seen, Thoreau was discovered and revived as an important literary figure in the first half of the twentieth century, but interest in *Civil Disobedience* did not grow significantly until the American civil rights and student movements of the 1950s to 70s. Just as the political use of *Civil Disobedience* becomes significant only in the second half (even the last third) of the twentieth century, so has scholarly and interpretive interest in *Civil Disobedience* only become significant and widespread in the past half century or so. One of the greatest interpreters of the broad sweep of American political thought, Louis Hartz, published his classic *The Liberal Tradition in America* in 1955.[4] It is indicative of the lack of interest in Thoreau as a political thinker in earlier generations that a scholar of Hartz's learning would not mention Thoreau at all as he walked through what he took to be the important ideas in the American political tradition. Within a decade of the appearance of Hartz's book, this indifference to Thoreau would change among scholars, just as it did for political activists; but it is important to recognize that we might think the first major interpretation of *Civil Disobedience* was simply to ignore it, thereby implying that it lacked either the intellectual merit or the impact to warrant serious scholarly and philosophical attention.

It is impossible, of course, to analyze arguments or opinions that are not explicitly expressed or explained, but we can imagine why someone might make an argument like Miller's about

Thoreau's political ideas and why someone like Hartz would not engage these ideas at all. We might say, for example, that Thoreau is simply not interested enough in political life to have significant political insights. When politics intruded on his affairs, he was invariably upset by this – violently so in *Slavery in Massachusetts*. Although he did cooperate with Underground Railroad activists, and he did make an occasional abolitionist speech or public lecture, these were the exceptions that proved the rule of Thoreau's refusal to join and regularly contribute to any organized political movement. His youthful support for the abolitionist Nathaniel Rogers grew from his admiration for a political activist who paradoxically opposed political organizations on the grounds that they violated the autonomy of individual members. Thoreau's late support for John Brown was distinctive precisely because he has virtually nothing to say about the degree to which Brown did or did not strike an effective blow against slavery; it has been observed many times that Thoreau's discussion of Brown is silent on the condition or prospects of actual slaves and that his interest seems to lie entirely with the heroic demeanor of Brown. We might argue that Thoreau is so deeply apolitical that he made it a point of moral integrity and honor to be indifferent to the outcomes of supposed virtuous acts; this is exactly the definition of what we might take to be political indifference at best, political irresponsibility at worst. We might think of this as the moral posture of a secular saint, but it does not reflect a political individual who wants to participate in public affairs and take responsibility for public choices and outcomes. We might even argue that Thoreau's concerns are too self-preoccupied and solipsistic, so overwhelmingly committed to self-cultivation, that the imaginative engagement with others required by democratic public life was stunted in him from the very start. Thoreau was the product of a millennial religious age. While he rejected conventional Protestant theology, he assumed with the religious believers of his time that the heroic or saintly individual could alter, through the sheer force of moral example, the course of human history. What the history of the abolition of slavery in America demonstrates, however, is the need for political organization, strategy, and even at times military sacrifice in order to achieve great victories over profound political injustice.

Viewed in this way, the problem with Thoreau's perspective in *Civil Disobedience* is simply that there is no reason to think that it offers serious and effective advice about how to actually address the great crimes and injustices found in the real political world. Those who take Thoreau's essay seriously may be individuals who are themselves difficult to govern, but they will never form collective organizations and institutions capable of significantly challenging tyrannical power. That is, individuals who morally fashion themselves along Thoreauvian lines cannot be expected to have the tools or inclination for prolonged and engaged and cooperative political activity. The greatest challenge we might make to Thoreau's ideas is not that they are in some way wrong or unsavory; it is that they are beside the point and a distraction from the political work they profess to engage.

This concern about relevance goes to the very heart of the argument Thoreau presents in *Civil Disobedience*. We have seen that the central moral claim of the essay is that political life must submit to principles derived from beyond the political sphere. The kind of consequentialism practiced and defended by politicians like Daniel Webster represents, for Thoreau, a kind of moral blindness, an inability to "face the facts." From this perspective, political life encourages tunnel vision, an inability to step back and apply universal moral principles to the political world. Politically engaged politicians become opportunistic negotiators, losing track of moral principles that should be guiding them. Success becomes defined by the cutting of deals, rather than standing for what is right.

It is on this critical issue that some find Thoreau's analysis least persuasive. The idea is that Thoreau was a deeply apolitical individual who thought he could assess political life without knowing very much about it. Never was he moved to think deeply about the unique dynamics, needs, and moral dilemmas generated by politics. Political naiveté, combined with a moralizing self-righteousness, are viewed by some as Thoreau's primary political legacies, and some critics go so far as to suggest that these qualities have infected and handicapped progressive forms of politics in the contemporary (especially American) world. Looking back at the New Left and protest politics of the 1960s and 70s in the U.S., one analyst suggests that the "moral absolutism" of the political stance bequeathed to us by Thoreau is "paradoxically both its greatest strength and its greatest weakness."[5] Thoreau encourages us to cultivate a strong sense of moral outrage, but he fails to provide us with anything approaching a useful political program for channeling this outrage. In fact, the form this outrage takes tends to isolate rather than unite us, insofar as it grows from a private claim to moral knowledge and integrity. Such claims depend not at all on developing evaluative judgments through conversation and debate and shared concern with others; one's private conscience alone is sufficient for evaluating and judging the world. Likewise, once the judgment is made, the moral work this produces is more private than public. Our moral work, our personal obligation, is above all to maintain our personal moral integrity. The emphasis is clearly on a private condition, rather than on promoting joint action with others to transform immoral or unjust situations. With self-reform as our ultimate concern, we may take our eye off problems of shared concern; indeed, we may actually find it hard to see and act upon such common and public issues. In one critic's biting comment, "Like Emerson, Thoreau was more concerned about the effect of reform upon the reformer than upon the reformed."[6] Instead of helping to build a strong reform politics, Thoreau's perspective "called upon others to withdraw from society and thereby become oblivious to all that is general and public."[7] In short, he "lacks any sensibility to the needs for social authority and human intercourse."[8]

It is in the light of just this kind of criticism that we find environmental theorist William Chaloupka worrying about Thoreau's legacy for the modern environmental movement. "Sanctimonious scolding is a perilous political posture," he warns.[9] While it is true that Thoreau "gave environmentalism a promising ethical model," it is one "fraught with the risk" of collapsing "into moralism" in ways that are "potentially disastrous in social and political terms."[10] What Thoreau encourages, Chaloupka suggests, is an apolitical legacy of reform, and such a legacy contains a fatal weakness at its core: our desire to right a public wrong is formulated in such a way as to subvert our ability to meaningfully and effectively address this wrong.

There are plenty of readers who find themselves annoyed, even enraged, by Thoreau's rhetorical style and moral perspective. The literary critic and democratic socialist, Irving Howe, called Thoreau's intellectual style "troubling, sometimes repellent."[11] There is no end to those who find him arrogant, pretentious, smug, self-involved, patronizing, misanthropic, humorless, priggish, and generally full of self-important but not particularly edifying hot air (see the next section for illustrations of this view). When thinking about the message of *Civil Disobedience*, many interpreters of this sort take one step beyond this type of frustration and suggest that Thoreau's political attitudes are both apolitical and politically counterproductive. The question raised by these interpretations is whether or not Thoreau represents a particular kind of pathology in the American political tradition, especially its progressive and reformist strains. In the words of one such critic, "It should be noted ... that the combination of political radicalism and self-absorption is a common trait in American culture."[12] The danger of this particular combination of qualities – political radicalism and individual self-absorption – is that it may serve to channel the radical impulse away from any meaningful political action.

One of the most prominent political theorists of the twentieth century, Hannah Arendt, provides one last example of how we might think of *Civil Disobedience* as irrelevant to our political needs, most importantly on the very topic we look to him to illuminate. The truth is, she believes, Thoreau has nothing at all useful to tell us about civil disobedience. She suggests that the idea of a civil disobedient, someone engaged in civil disobedience, is actually not addressed in Thoreau's essay "for the simple reason that he [i.e., a civil disobedient] never exists as a single individual; he can function and survive only as a member of a group."[13] Arendt's point is that engaging in civil disobedience requires appealing to a collective sensibility and experience, a shared concern and set of commitments. The power of the civil disobedient is the power of one who shares more with those she is rebelling against than the particular matter to which she is objecting. But the individual conscience that Thoreau appeals to, in Arendt's view, is not engaged with, or derived from, or reflective of a shared political life:

> It is not primarily interested in the world where the wrong is committed or in the consequences that the wrong will have for the future

course of the world. It does not say, with Jefferson, "I tremble for my country when I reflect that God is just; that His justice cannot sleep forever," because it trembles for the individual self and its integrity.[14]

At the end of the day, in this view, Thoreau can neither significantly engage nor influence public life. He may speak about politics in *Civil Disobedience*, but the paradox is that this speech can only lead, in the end, to political disengagement and irrelevance.

## CIVIL DISOBEDIENCE AS INCOHERENT

The American composer, Charles Ives, greatly admired the trans-cendentalists and wrote a piano sonata inspired by Emerson, Thoreau, the Alcotts, and Hawthorne. In an essay written to accompany this 1919 composition, Ives tells the story of an English teacher who first introduced him to Thoreau. The teacher suggested to his young students that Thoreau "was a kind of crank who styled himself a hermit-naturalist and who idled about the woods because he didn't want to work."[15] While Ives may have taken some liberties in remembering this high school lesson, his story captures a critical attitude about Thoreau that has roots reaching back to Thoreau's own lifetime. The basic idea was that Thoreau was, as Ives reports in his teacher's words, a "crank," someone of eccentric and most likely bad character, whose writings are best understood as reflections of a perverse, or at least not admirable, personality. Thoreau's contemporary, James Russell Lowell, declared in an essay published three years after Thoreau's death that Thoreau "had not a healthy mind, or he would not have been so fond of prescribing" [for others].[16] Lowell claimed that Thoreau "had no humor"[17] and that he was "not a strong thinker, but a sensitive feeler."[18] A few years later, in 1880, Robert Louis Stevenson (the Scottish novelist and author of *Treasure Island* and *The Strange Case of Dr. Jekyll and Mr. Hyde*) described Thoreau as "a prig" and "a skulker."[19] He suggests that Thoreau's was a "cold and distant personality," that he was an egotist, and that he was "dry, priggish and selfish."[20] Piling on, he claims that "In the whole man I find no trace of pity."[21] Stevenson softened his view considerably after learning more about Thoreau's biography and the ways in which he experienced real loss and sorrow. But his initial view, like Lowell's, set the stage for comments similar to those made by Ives' schoolteacher: the idea is that the best way to think about Thoreau's writings is biographically, as expressions of a damaged (and perhaps even hateful or mentally ill) individual. The implication is that Thoreau's writings are best understood as reflections of personal flaws. Given this very unfriendly perspective, voiced by some of Thoreau's earliest critics in the nineteenth century, it is not too surprising that for many years few felt the need to seriously evaluate *Civil Disobedience*, or any other Thoreau text, in terms internal to the work itself. Instead of taking the arguments at face value, and assessing them on their merits, they are dismissed as the pathologies of an unhealthy or imbalanced individual.

This attitude re-emerges in the later twentieth century when Thoreau enjoyed a critical and political revival. In 1957, one interpreter picks up and develops claims made by Lowell and Stevenson in the previous century: that Thoreau's work expresses "crass egocentricity" if not "sheer megalomania"; that he had no sense of humor; indeed, that much of what he has to say is "trivial nonsense."[22] A decade later, another scholar argues that Thoreau is an "impossible egotist," who "feels nothing but contempt" for other people.[23] In fact, the "inexcusable" element of Thoreau's writings is that he "speaks as a god," as someone so superior to his fellows that he can feel no sympathy with them whatsoever.[24] A more recent reader writes of Thoreau's "arrogant self-conceit" and "haughty aloofness," as essential elements of his writing.[25]

Arguments such as these are sometimes couched in Freudian analysis. Carl Bode, for example, explained what he took to be Thoreau's hatred of the state as an extension of an Oedipal hatred for his father.[26] C. Roland Wagner also explains Thoreau's political views as psychological pathologies:

> It is in his political essays that the infantile wishes begin to escape all civilized limits. There Thoreau's struggle for inward identity, his rage against the ideas of passive submission and apparently arbitrary authority, almost makes him lose contact with the real world and express his fantasies only.[27]

Wagner makes it clear that he does not believe Thoreau was insane,[28] but it is also clear that he believes that Thoreau's views grow from significant personal maladjustment. Over and over we find authors claiming that Thoreau is full of childish rage, is pathologically self-preoccupied and narcissistic, and is unable to view other people as fundamentally similar or equal to himself.

Much of the literature of this sort is not specifically addressed to *Civil Disobedience* or even to Thoreau's general political views. It does, however, significantly influence arguments sometimes offered to explain what are taken to be significant flaws or incoherencies in Thoreau's thinking. Such critics may begin with or share a similar distaste for Thoreau's sensibilities with critics like those mentioned above. They then develop a reading of his political views, however, that takes us from ad hominem dismissal to claims about the incoherence and dangers of the arguments themselves.

Consider in this light the analysis of Heinz Eulau, one of the most trenchant Thoreau critics from the 1960s. Eulau shares much with those who find Thoreau's political views naive, but he moves beyond the claim of irrelevance to suggest incoherence. He also shares much with those who think of Thoreau as psychologically incapable of a sensible political analysis; he speaks, for example, of Thoreau's "political immaturity."[29] This immaturity, for Eulau, allows Thoreau to mistake individual conscience and abstract principle for political responsibility: "Thoreau's whole political philosophy was based on the theoretical premise of individual conscience as the only true criterion of what is politically right and just."[30] The political world, however, is composed of many citizens with consciences. There is no assurance, or any reasonable expectation in fact, that these consciences will generate similar moral knowledge or commitments even among the most conscientious democratic citizens.

Because of this, we can see why Eulau believes Thoreau's foolish and naive moral absolutism actually promises to produce incompatible demands by comparably self-righteous individuals in the real world. This is what Eulau means when he suggests that Thoreau's "moral absolutism, being so individualized, becomes relativistic."[31] Thoreau insists upon the imperative to defend moral truth. In actual political practice, such an insistence generates a cacophony of incompatible moral demands, leaving us with no reasonable way of mediating between them. The only defense for Thoreau's view, we might say, is to assume that people of good intention, consulting their true conscience (uncorrupted by self-interest), will all reach similar moral conclusions. The problem, Thoreau might say, is not to mediate between clashing positions but, rather, to educate people and morally inspire them to pursue the good impartially. Thoreau's strategy, however, is profoundly unrealistic; it almost appears, we might suspect, to be unacquainted with living, breathing, and imperfect human beings. Real people may aspire to impartial moral evaluation, but even the best and most responsible of us never fully achieve such moral transcendence beyond our own self-interest. In truth, even good people and people of good will differ significantly in political and moral perspective. Thoreau's moral posture is that of an individual who has never taken responsibility for mediating such conflicting perspectives. It is easy to stand outside the political arena and insult all the parties involved. Such behavior does nothing to resolve the actual political conflict, however, and does little more than encourage the apolitical individual to feel self-righteous and superior to those engaged in addressing the real problems of political life. Such behavior may make us feel good about ourselves, but it does little to address the great political challenges we face.

For Eulau, then, there is a fatal incoherence at the heart of *Civil Disobedience*, which is, he believes, the "most complete theoretical statement" we have of "Thoreau's basic assumptions."[32]

> Thoreau's philosophy should warn us of the dilemma into which he fell and from which he could not escape because he returned time and again, to individual conscience as the "ultimate reality." His thought was full of ambiguity and paradox, and he did not realize sufficiently how contradictory and, in fact, dangerous the moral can be.[33]

The author of *Civil Disobedience*, in short, is at war with himself, and this conflict has produced a dangerous political doctrine.

Why dangerous? Consider the difference between two approaches to thinking about political participation. The first, represented by Thoreau, conceives of just politics as the clear, complete, and unambiguous implementation of what is morally right. When any policy fails to achieve such perfect moral integrity, it violates principle and should be resisted by conscientious individuals. The second approach, represented here by Eulau, views politics as a realm of negotiation and compromise made necessary by the inevitable conflict of interests and moral principles in any large and heterogeneous democratic political community. If we approach political life in the spirit of the first approach yet find ourselves in an environment much more closely resembling the reality assumed by the second, what do we expect the outcome to be? On the one hand, we might find some people like Thoreau simply withdrawing, but as we have already noted, this does nothing to resolve the actual problems (we might go so far as to say that such a withdrawal only allows a few individuals to literally be irresponsible, while compelling those remaining to continue to struggle toward solutions). On the other hand, those who remain in the political world while adopting Thoreau's absolutistic moral perspective will insist on the moral perfection of their own positions and refuse to compromise with their opponents whom they inevitably view as either ignorant fools or hopelessly corrupt and morally vile. The best possible outcome of such conflict would be political stalemate, "gridlock" in the current language of American politics, which, as I write, closely resembles the situation being described. Worse outcomes might eventually develop, since such uncompromising rivals could provoke conflicts resolvable only through force. Either way, the democratic mediation of conflict is replaced by political ineffectiveness or, even more insidiously, brute force.

For reasons like this, some have concluded that *Civil Disobedience* simply must not be used as a "guide to political action."[34] Thoreau is too naive about political life to be of any use, but more importantly, his essay's incoherence promises outcomes perverse from its own perspective. Thoreau's political innocence would, in practice, generate behavior significantly at odds with the values it intends to promote. Thoreau's individualistic moral absolutism is dangerously incoherent, in the end, because it fails in practice to respect the individual moral integrity it claims to cherish. For reasons such as this, some critics find a kind of intolerant political absolutism paradoxically promoted by what looks at first blush like a firm respect for individual rights, freedom, and integrity. Thoreau's views are incoherent in the deepest sense; what they profess is the opposite of what they achieve.

## CIVIL DISOBEDIENCE AS ANTI-DEMOCRATIC

It is a related but different point to argue that Thoreau's perspective is undemocratic or even anti-democratic. It is possible that Thoreau makes no good sense, or fails to understand how to achieve his own ends, but that these ends are themselves inspired by democratic values. It is also possible, however, that the moral individualism Thoreau promotes is not incoherent but simply hostile to democratic ideals and institutions. It is possible that Thoreau holds a perfectly coherent position but that this position is itself best understood as a challenge to, and perhaps a critique of, democracy. Put another way, the stress of this particular interpretation is less on what is taken to be Thoreau's political incompetence and naiveté than on what is thought to be his dangerous and explicit challenge to democratic government.

In one sense, the claim that Thoreau is an anti-democrat would seem obvious in light of certain comments in *Civil Disobedience*. After all, Thoreau has very tough criticisms of voting, and what more foundational element to democracy is there than voting? And what are we to make of his notion that a person with right on her or his side already constitutes a "majority of one"? If voting is an inappropriate form of gambling with moral principles, and if majorities are to be held in contempt when we disagree with them, it seems obvious that a person holding Thoreau's views holds the basic principles of democracy in contempt.

These observations may cause us to question Thoreau's democratic commitments, but they only set the stage for thinking about the deeper structure of Thoreau's political thinking. What leads him to make these comments about democracy? What are the broader ideas that inform his political values as a whole? Are these broader ideas of a democratic or undemocratic nature?

There are two elements we can see in *Civil Disobedience* and other writings that may lead us to think of Thoreau as more of a critic than a defender of democracy. The first of these are what many take to be his anarchist sentiments. It is important to be clear, however, that simply calling Thoreau an anarchist does not settle the question of whether or not he was a democrat. There are versions of anarchism growing from strong democratic ideals and commitments. For such anarchists, governments suppress the democratic dispositions and capabilities of common people and impose authority from above or outside. Even representative liberal democracies, from such a perspective, fail to respect the democratic participation and equality of all citizens; democratic respect can only be achieved in self-governing local communities. Anarchist theorists like Peter Kropotkin and Murray Bookchin argue that governments violate the equality and cooperation that would naturally emerge within face-to-face communities freed from the hierarchies found within even the most democratic governments (and, perhaps, also within all large-scale economic institutions). Critics of these views may find the theory of pre-political democratic social life to be unpersuasive or utopian or politically unsophistocated, but it is clear that even if these anarchist theorists have an unconvincing theory, their theory is nonetheless driven by democratic sensibilities and values.

Emma Goldman, one of the most respected and important twentieth-century anarchists, admired Thoreau and called him the "greatest American Anarchist."[35] The novelist Henry Miller also admired what he took to be the anarchist core of Thoreau's ideas, claiming that "he was not interested in politics; he was the sort of person who, if there were more of his kind, would soon cause government to become non-existent."[36] Thoreau has many such admirers, themselves sympathetic to an anarchist critique of all political power. In most cases they do not believe that Thoreau was promoting a version of anarchism that in any way put him in irresolvable conflict with those around him. Perhaps the idea of "neighborliness" that Thoreau raises in *Civil Disobedience* can be understood as the ideal and democratic relationship one might expect to emerge in a more just social order. Philosopher Edward Madden argues that Thoreau believed conscientious individuals, motivated by uncorrupted consciences, would agree on right and wrong because they have equal access to universal law.

> He believed that all civil law that covered moral concerns was an unwarranted encroachment on the rights of the individual. ... In the ideal state each individual would pattern his conduct on his own insights into Universal Truth. The result would be universal moral behavior, and there would be no need of civil government at all.[37]

When Thoreau is read as an anarchist of this sort, the claim is that at least in the future, when enough people have been reformed to produce a society of morally responsible individuals, a kind of democratic equality and civility will emerge and prevail. We may (or may not) agree with Heinz Eulau's claim that such a position is hopelessly naive, but it is nonetheless a position built upon democratic commitments.

It is a matter of dispute, however, as to whether such a harmonious vision of the future animates Thoreau's social thought. Even if Thoreau hopes for such relationships sometime in the unforeseeable future, this tells us little about the democratic nature of his recommendations for the present. To his contemporaries, Thoreau says he wishes to live aloof from the state, to stand outside the political community. This suggests a rejection of all organized authority, even democratic authority, and that he wishes, in one critic's words, to be "above law, above government, above restraint."[38] We saw in Chapter 2 that for Thoreau democracy is nothing other than a form of organized power, one form of force among many.[39] Therefore, it can never be a source of moral obligation. Our true obligations, as we have repeatedly seen, can for Thoreau grow only from non-political sources. Democratic majorities are owed respect if and only if they represent what is right, so it is the right, not democratic processes or relationships, that determines our moral commitments.

This perspective leaves Thoreau in a disturbing position. On the one hand, he suggests that individuals are bound only to laws they consent to. On the other, he demands that society bend to his particular will. Political theorist Harry Jaffa suggests that this is a paradox at the heart of Thoreau's anarchism.[40] It drives Thoreau away from the democratic process altogether and leaves him simply railing against any and all political orders. His individualism leaves him isolated, alone, claiming his right to do as he sees best, regardless of how his choices are viewed by others. Wishing to live "above restraint," Thoreau is left with no option other than to view the conscientious individual as superior to even the most democratic community. The conscientious individual, after all, would never submit her or his conscience to a majority vote. Jaffa's point is similar to Eulau's insofar as he identifies a tension (he calls it a paradox) between Thoreau's self-assertion and his professed regard for all conscientious individuals. Jaffa's conclusion from this observation is not that Thoreau is led to hopeless contradiction (as Eulau suggests). Instead, Thoreau simply must choose between self-assertion and respect for others, and clearly he choses the undemocratic option. It is not that Thoreau is forced into a position he should reject, for Jaffa. Rather, it is that he embraces the anti-democratic value when forced to choose between these competing values.

Individualistic anarchism of the sort many identify in Thoreau's writings can lead to a preoccupation with heroic personalities; after all, the position is inspired by a vision of individuals sufficiently strong to resist public opinion and even political power. This emphasis on heroism is the second element of Thoreau's thinking that leads some critics to view him as an undemocratic thinker at best, an anti-democratic thinker at worst.

The heroic elements of Thoreau's work are widely recognized, even if traced to different sources by different interpreters. Daniel Walker Howe, a distinguished historian of American intellectual and political history, traces Thoreau's conception of individual responsibility to the Protestant traditions that resonated so deeply in nineteenth-century New England. "To understand Thoreau's purpose in ... *Resistance to Civil Government*, we must see it as an example of religious perfectionism."[41] While Thoreau speaks in secular language, he is best understood as "a secularized version of a Calvinist saint."[42] Others emphasize the influence of Stoicism on Thoreau's views and suggest that ancient pagan notions of heroism are closer to capturing his position than Protestantism with its notions of saintliness. These interpreters emphasize Thoreau's worldliness, his rejection of the kind of meek and modest demeanor often associated with Christian saintliness, and note his martial arrogance and self-assertion. Thoreau is less a self-sacrificing saint, they suggest, than an aggressive combatant of the ancient heroic type. One of his favorite books, after all, was *The Iliad*, perhaps the greatest of the Western pagan chronicles of warfare, soldierly prowess, and worldly honor.

Regardless of how we trace the intellectual roots of Thoreau's conception of the heroic, it is obvious that the hero provided a fundamentally important moral type for him. One of the writers he admired was Thomas Carlyle, who wrote that "the history of the world is but the Biography of great men."[43] These great men participate in great events, but most importantly they remind us of human possibility, of our own potential, which we are often too comfortable or too timorous to embrace. This is what Carlyle means when he says that the "function of great men and teachers" is to bring us to "reality."[44] The greatest of these heroes are actually not warriors or politicians, but poets and men of letters, those who shape our character and sensibilities through the power of their writing. Thoreau's own essays and poems are full of similar sentiments, and it is clear that his own vocation as a writer was inspired by an extraordinary ambition to be influential in this way. Likewise, it is impossible to understand Thoreau's almost ecstatic defense of John Brown without understanding the importance of heroes to his entire moral perspective.

The question this raises is how we should think about the role of the hero, the great man (or woman – although Thoreau has little to say about women overall) for democracy. For some, this raises no significant problem; in the language of Carlyle quoted above, despite their unique and special role, we might think of them as paradoxically showing all of us what we might be. Their superiority to the many, we might say, is superficial and designed to inspire us to a more respectable level of equality. For others, heroic thinking is fundamentally inegalitarian and therefore insulting to one of democracy's core values. In one critic's words, Thoreau's demand for a "politics of saintliness" displays "contempt for the low, sluggish, compliant behavior of the mass of men."[45]

Michael Walzer, an influential democratic theorist, draws a distinction between what he calls "prophets" and "priests."[46] Borrowing these categories from the Old Testament and applying them to political life, he suggests that these contrasting roles provide metaphors for fundamentally different forms of political leadership. "Priests" are not democratic. They have special access to truths that are esoteric and available only to a special few. Their social role both grows from and reinforces their special and unequal access to knowledge. It also gives them responsibility to play a role in public life that is off limits to the many. A generation ago, a very pessimistic environmental theorist argued that if we are to survive the environmental crises, political power will have to be transferred away from the democratic many and placed in the hands of "ecological mandarins."[47] The people in general are both too selfish and ignorant (and always will be) to make the sacrifices required for environmental sustainability. Only a guardian class, with unchecked political power, can possibly address our environmental crisis in any meaningful way. The point here does not concern whether or not William Ophuls' environmental analysis is persuasive. Rather, it is to suggest that this is a quite useful, if extreme, illustration of the idea Walzer has in mind when he refers to revolutionary political "priests." Some may think such priests are required, but they are certainly not democratic. They stand apart from and above the many.

In contrast, Walzer suggests that "prophets" represent a kind of leadership more compatible with democracy. Prophets do not claim esoteric (secret or incomprehensible to most people) knowledge, but bring us back to ideals and truths we all share but have turned away from. They do not claim to be superior to their fellow citizens, except perhaps in the intensity of their anger over our failures to keep our promises and live up to our ideals. The prophetic weapon is the Jeremiad, a sometimes angry and passionate complaint or sermon, delivered to shame and exhort rather than to subdue and dominate. We might think of Martin Luther King's great "Letter from Birmingham Jail" as a prophetic document in Walzer's sense.[48] Addressed to liberal white clergy who had criticized King for participating in the protests in Birmingham, Alabama in 1963, King expresses both his disappointment and fellowship with these critics. He explains why he believes the protesters embody the finest of American (and human) values. Rather than cutting himself off from others, setting himself above the common ideals and purposes shared by Americans generally, King's prose is designed to show how the Birmingham protests, disruptive as they were to the social fabric of the segregated American South, actually promoted the deeper and radically more just American ideals professed even by his political opponents. In contrast to the "ecological mandarins" proposed by Ophuls, King's radicalism is grounded in an assumption of equality of social standing and shared commitments. In this sense, his leadership encourages and promotes democracy, rather than representing a challenge to it.

A great deal obviously rides on how one interprets Thoreau's heroic individuals. If we think he is appealing to capacities shared by all, we will be less inclined to think this appeal has undemocratic overtones. If, however, he holds no hope for the many, and only longs for the virtuous few, Thoreau begins to look more like one who appeals to undemocratic "great men" to shape and control, or perhaps merely to heroically defy, the many. Those who think the latter of these interpretations is more persuasive will likely view Thoreau more as an enemy than a champion of democracy.

We see then that two strains in Thoreau's thought – the anarchist and the heroic – have potentially but not necessarily undemocratic implications. These strains of Thoreau's thought are, of course, related. They represent different sides of Thoreau's commitment to personal integrity and self-cultivation. It is precisely Thoreau's independence and self-preoccupation that some interpreters believe generates a lack of concern for democracy at best, an active hostility toward it at worst. From this perspective, the most positive spin we could give to Thoreau's attitude toward democracy is that he is as hostile to it as to any other form of government. One commentator suggests that Thoreau is so alienated from group life of all kinds, let alone political institutions, that his views cannot possibly be tied to any positive set of political values. We might even think his ideas could present no serious threat to a tyrannical state, since they are "unlikely to produce more than sporadic, spontaneous rebellions with no concerted purpose."[49] Irving Howe argues that despite our habit of placing Thoreau in the American progressive and democratic tradition, there is no real anchor in his thought to any particular set of political commitments, democracy included. "Thoreau drives to an extreme a version of individualism that in later decades would lend itself to conservative bullying and radical posturing, both of which can undercut the fraternal basis of a democratic polity."[50] Thoreau can inspire cantankerous individualism of all sorts, we might say, but not a serious or important commitment to democratic life and values.

Even worse, we might suggest that Thoreau not only fails to be democracy's friend, but is in truth actively opposed to it. We saw above that Jaffa finds a paradox in Thoreau's thought, a conflict between his commitment to individual consent, on the one hand, and his insistence that the community bend to his will, on the other. Championing individual conscience, we might fear, is the flip side of radical intolerance and an imperial will. The individual who wants to simply be left alone will inevitably experience disappointment since, in the language of one critic, this ignores the real facts of social and political life, "the essential context for human life of the human community."[51] This disappointment will be more or less extreme depending on the extremity of the individualism and the degree to which one's privacy is invaded by laws and institutions one is morally appalled by. Remember that the Anthony Burns affair "interrupted" Thoreau's solitude and made his thoughts move toward murder of the state. An individual like Thoreau, we might say, has such a profound misconception of the communal elements of life that he is bound to experience grave disappointment. He is also unlikely to develop the tools required to appropriately and productively channel moral outrage over injustice. If the only options are withdrawal or murder, the potential for irresponsible and undemocratic spasms of political rebellion are real enough under certain conditions. It is this kind of logic that leads readers like Frederick Sanders to think that "the philosophical implications of *Civil Disobedience* are profoundly heretical [to constitutional and democratic government] in a way that must concern us all."[52] This conclusion grows from a fear that heroic individualists are potentially tyrants, with little in their moral arsenal to teach them restraint, or compromise, or sympathy with political opponents. Their self-confidence in their own righteousness, combined with their belief in the corruption or ignorance of the many, may make us hope that they will merely withdraw from, rather than explode upon, the political world.

## *CIVIL DISOBEDIENCE* AS A CONTRIBUTION TO DEMOCRATIC THEORY

Thoreau has very little to say, in any of his writings, about the normal mechanics and institutions of democratic governance. We know that what he does say about these matters in *Civil Disobedience* – concerning voting, democratic majorities, and political parties – suggests a deep skepticism about the moral integrity of even the most common and fundamental elements of democratic decision-making. Scattered throughout his writings, however, are passages that suggest a preference for local democracy, in contrast to a large, complex constitutional order designed to promote factional competition and representative institutions, such as that designed by the American Founders. In the previous chapter we noted his praise, in *Slavery in Massachusetts*, for small-town democratic deliberation. He also explicitly addresses many of his core writings, including *Civil Disobedience* and *Walden*, to local audiences; his political identity, such as he can be said to have one, is locally defined, extending from Concord outward to Massachusetts and New England at its furthest reaches. He says in *Walden* that "to act collectively is according to the spirit of our institutions,"[53] and as the great literary critic F. O. Matthiessen observed, this comment is found in a passage in which Thoreau is speaking in favor of the vigorous local promotion of culture and the arts.

> The context of that remark in *Walden* is where he is maintaining that the community is responsible for providing a more adequate cultural life, good libraries, distinguished lecturers at the lyceums, encouragement for the practice of all the arts. He was as opposed to the private hoarding of our spiritual resources as he was to the lust for ownership in our rapacious economy. He believed that all great values should be as public as light.[54]

Observations about these passages lead some interpreters to think of Thoreau quite differently from those critics we have considered so far. Rather than being generally opposed to political power and authority, such passages might lead us to think that Thoreau was only opposed to public life when it was separated from local participatory democracy and aimed at goods that were trivial or corrupting (such as the generation of ever-increasing wealth) rather than the cultivation of the highest human potentials. Political theorist Wilson Carey McWilliams follows these leads to suggest that Thoreau wanted not a weaker (or even nonexistent) government, but actually a stronger government in the sense of a government that was aimed at the education and cultivation of moral citizens. Thoreau's hope, McWilliams believes, was to "redirect the state and its citizens, to shift the goal of politics from the purposes of commerce and the machine to the goal of human development."[55] Far from being an anarchist, McWilliams' Thoreau is a strong supporter of a powerful, participatory, and democratic local government. The complaints he expresses in *Civil Disobedience* and elsewhere about democracy are aimed at a democracy that has lost its way, a democracy focused on the wrong values and so vast that it requires too much representation at the expense of local town-meeting democracy.

While it is true that these few passages catch the eye and suggest that Thoreau may have a sympathetic view of at least some forms of democratic life, Heinz Eulau makes a reasonable point when he observes that "The bulk of proof is, in fact, on the other side."[56] For every comment praising social cooperation or town-meeting forms of democracy, there are innumerable passages in Thoreau's writings expressing a general distaste for political life – many such passages are found in *Civil Disobedience* itself, such as the opening sentences in which he professes to desire a government that governs not at all and a late passage where he says that he has little concern for public affairs (paragraphs 1, 41). Thoreau's contribution to democratic ideas is probably not to be found in the promotion of particular political forms or institutions for organizing the daily affairs of democratic life. He had little interest in such political science and gave it little thought relative to his primary preoccupations.

Even if we find claims like Matthiessen's and McWilliams' exaggerated, they do point in a direction that can help us understand why we might find Thoreau an important thinker for all who care about the success and fate of democracy. We might think of the proper functioning of any relatively democratic regime, that is, any non-utopian democratic order, as generating two types of related problems. The first of these is simply that democratic institutions can fail in the sense that citizens can be mistaken or misled, and leaders, likewise, can be foolish or, worse, corrupt. Critics of democracy, ever since this form of government emerged in the fifth century BCE in Athens, have railed against the problem of demagogues who manipulate the many, as well as the ignorance of the people themselves, who are often portrayed, unflatteringly, as a mob. But one need not be hostile toward democracy to worry about these matters. In fact, nineteenth-century America witnessed the dramatic spread and development of public primary education, as well as the historically unprecedented growth of institutions of higher education, in large part to respond to precisely these concerns. Horace Mann, one of the great educational reformers of the era (at both the primary and the college levels) had just completed his tenure as Secretary of the Massachusetts State Board of Education and had taken a seat in the Massachusetts delegation to the U.S. House of Representatives when *Civil Disobedience* was published. Mann spoke for many in his generation when he argued that the American Founders had mistakenly failed to provide for the education of citizens and had thus placed this experiment in popular government at grave risk. Whig politicians like Mann were appalled by what they took to be the vulgar and corrupt development of Jacksonian democracy, but even Americans with fewer partisan interests opposed to the rise of the Democratic Party found themselves alarmed by the character of the newly emerging partisan newspapers, political parties, and bare-knuckled politics. Friends of democracy have at least as much reason to worry about the vices of democratic government as democracy's foes, and all the more reason to find ways to reform and control them – just recall, as an illustration of this point, our earlier discussion of the Polk administration's demagogic manipulation of some of the worst and widely shared racist attitudes in American society. Thoreau was certainly not alone in his time and place in worrying about these matters. The early years of the American republic were years of anxious experimentation, and, of course, the experiment nearly failed in the cataclysm of the Civil War just a few years after Thoreau wrote his essay. It was not at all certain in 1848 if the democratic or the radically undemocratic elements in American public life would prevail.

It is the inevitable shortfalls of democracy that we might think of as framing a first set of claims about Thoreau's positive contribution to democratic theory. In this context, we have already seen one direction that defenders of a democratic reading of Thoreau might take to interpret the message of *Civil Disobedience*: just as some view his criticisms of his contemporaries as a reflection of alienation from and contempt for his fellow citizens, others view him as taking on a more prophetic role. Sacvan Bercovitch, a distinguished literary critic, shares this view: Thoreau's "was a protest from within. ... Like a biblical prophet, he hoped to wake his countrymen up to the fact that they were desecrating their own beliefs."[57] From this perspective, Thoreau speaks as an equal to his fellow citizens. He is not attempting to impose his will upon others, but rather to bring his political community back to values it presumably shares with him in the first place. When Thoreau cries out for a "man who is a man" (paragraph 12), a man with courage, his concern is not that his fellows are ignorant of basic moral principles or that they subscribe to fundamentally mistaken political values. Rather, he appears to assume that his audience knows full well, agrees completely, that slavery is a moral abomination. The problem he addresses, we might say, is a problem of courage rather than a problem of moral knowledge. To call his fellows to defend what they already value is not an attempt to impose a superior will upon a lesser. It is, instead, a call for all citizens to live up to what they already profess. From this perspective, Thoreau's essay is less a violation of democratic principles than a call to take liberty and equality seriously. This "prophetic" Thoreau is less a revolutionary, in the sense of wanting to bring about an entirely new order of things, than a "conservative," wanting to conserve and return to what he takes to be the original principles animating the American republic.

If we think of Thoreau within what we are calling a prophetic tradition, this would lead us to think that his primary concern as a political writer was not to provide careful and detailed philosophical arguments about various components of political theory. Rather, his work would aim to inspire particular passions and dispositions, to encourage the cultivation of what Thoreau understood to be the kind of character required by individuals in a democracy. In this spirit, political theorist Jane Bennett argues that "What haunts Thoreau about civil disobedience is not, as one might expect, the question of its justification. It is, rather, the fact of its infrequency."[58] His task in *Civil Disobedience*, Bennett claims, is not to defend and explain the nature of civil disobedience – when it is legitimate, who may appropriately engage in it, and the like. Instead, he sets these questions aside and asks, why are people so unwilling to engage in "resistance to civil government"? What might we do to encourage people to be less afraid of such action? If we assume, for the moment at least, that civil disobedience is not incompatible with democracy, that it may be an important tool in the civic arsenal for keeping democracies from straying from their core commitments, then Thoreau's project might be viewed as not only compatible with democracy, but even essential to it. If it is reasonable to believe (and it certainly is) that all historical democracies have inherited undemocratic laws and institutions, and are also tempted at times to stray from their democratic commitments, then civil disobedience may very well be as important as more institutionally sanctioned forms of democratic participation such as voting and serving on juries. If the purpose of *Civil Disobedience* is less to chastise American citizens for ignorance or immoral beliefs than it is to call them to have the courage of their convictions, we might think of Thoreau as promoting behavior essential to the health of any democratic political community. We have seen that Martin Luther King Jr. says he learned and inherited from Thoreau a "legacy of creative protest." Democracy requires civic participation in the regular institutions of government by a responsible citizenry, through voting and other means, but it also requires a citizenry jealous of its liberty and equality who will use civil but extra-institutional protests, from time to time, to call the government to account. Thoreau's essay, we might say, plays a central role in the tradition of such protests.

The idea here is that Thoreau's concern in *Civil Disobedience* is less with moral argument than with the encouragement of a particular kind of character. In part, as Bennett suggests, this is the kind of character that can challenge the government when it behaves in unjust ways. But there is more to this character than simply rebelliousness. A number of political theorists have been provoked by Thoreau to consider the more general question of the character of democratic citizens not only when they resist unjust laws and authority, but how they may promote a democratic life in which such unjust events and institutions are themselves less likely. If *Civil Disobedience* asks how we might be the kind of people with characters capable of resisting injustice, some interpreters believe there is a preliminary and even more fundamental project in Thoreau's writings: how to encourage the development of independent-minded and self-sufficient individuals in the first place. For George Kateb, Thoreau (with Emerson and the poet Walt Whitman) promotes a kind of "democratic individuality" that helps to "disclose the fuller meaning of the [American] founding."[59] Without strong and independent citizens, government will overreach and expand beyond the proper limits of "expediency." What is needed, in Kateb's view, are citizens who are much too strong and independent to require an aggressive and meddlesome government, or to allow one to emerge over time. Thoreau, like Emerson and Whitman, promotes the virtues required by citizens who will demand only a limited and strictly prescribed government. For Kateb, Thoreau's individualism is democratic precisely because it defines the legitimate parameters for appropriate democratic government. While he recognizes that Emerson, Thoreau, and Whitman "are distant citizens" – and certainly we can understand, in light of *Civil Disobedience*, why Kateb would suggest that Thoreau was distant from public life – he maintains nonetheless that "we may say they remain citizens."[60] From Kateb's perspective, Thoreau encourages the kind of democratic citizenship needed to constrain and control democracy. Only a democracy limited, kept in line, by radically independent citizens can resist the diseases that inevitably develop within and threaten the health of democratic societies.

Other interpreters have different conceptions of "democratic individuality" or the appropriate limits of democratic politics from the ones Kateb has, but a lively set of interpretations has emerged that follows this pattern of viewing Thoreau's work as engaged with the essential task of promoting civic qualities required by democratic citizens. Shannon Mariotti argues that Thoreau promotes "an alternative form of democratic politics."[61] In her view, "Thoreau finds the roots of true democratic self-government in the capacity to think against conventions, to critique, to think for one's self."[62] This independence of mind is best cultivated through a "democratic withdrawal" into nature, "to recuperate the capacities that are the basis for true democracy."[63] For Mariotti, the huckleberry field at the end of *Civil Disobedience* is a "democratic space," since it teaches the essentials of a genuine democratic life.[64] Democracy requires, she believes, a critical rejection of much that we find in the modern state, which is exploitative, alienating, and frequently unjust. Thoreau's "excursions into nature are not apolitical withdrawals but alternative forms of democratically valuable political practice that aim to restore our capacity for critical negation."[65] Brian Walker argues, in similar fashion, that Thoreau provides an "alternative economics" to emerging capitalism for the purpose of "democratic cultivation."[66] The idea, again, is that materially and philosophically independent people will have the strength to resist demagogues, injustice, and the alienating conditions of modern life. Self-cultivation produces appropriately free and democratic individuals. For all their differences, Kateb, Mariotti, and Walker (as well as others arguing along similar lines) agree that Thoreau's individualism and even withdrawal from conventional political life should not mislead us into thinking that he was apolitical or uninterested in democratic values. Paradoxically, such values are best cultivated precisely through Thoreau's aloof and critical attitude toward the actual practices of our very imperfect (at best) democratic reality.

Nancy Rosenblum offers what may be the most interesting, subtle, and ambivalent version of this type of argument. Rosenblum shares with many who view Thoreau as an anti-democrat a strong sense of his frequent alienation from all forms of political life. Rather than thinking of Thoreau as trying to develop an alternative form of democratic citizenship, such as Mariotti and Walker propose, Rosenblum argues that there is an unresolved and dynamic tension in Thoreau's perspective, a struggle between his romantic desire to live outside the political world and a recognition of his own dependence on democratic forms of government.

At times he is clearly and simply disgusted with politics, as many of his critics point out, and at these moments his "heroic individualism" places him in seemingly irrevocable antagonism with virtually everyone around him. At other times he assumes a neighborly connection to his fellow citizens, a kind of equality and sympathy with others. If, on the one hand, Thoreau's romantic individualism drives him away from life shared with other people, his "democratic inhibitions" bring him back to at least a limited democratic civic sensibility.

> A dizzying internal movement jogs Thoreau's writings – romantic revulsion and self-distancing, but also backtracking from aloofness and tentative reconciliation in repeated succession. ... Torturously but decisively, democratic inhibitions recall Thoreau from imaginative flight to neighborly concern, from exceptionalism to equality.[67]

For all his hostility to politics, even democratic politics, Thoreau returns over and over again to a sense that "representative democracy is the political complement of the romantic self, where it can feel at home."[68]

What Rosenblum is describing is an ambivalence in Thoreau's views, a struggle between anti-democratic and democratic impulses, between the heroic and the neighborly. This tension defines what Rosenblum takes to be Thoreau's "democratic individualism." More than most who make claims about Thoreau's contribution to democratic thought, Rosenblum sees the promotion of heroic or romantic individualism as an inevitable challenge to democratic values and commitments. Democratic "inhibitions" may temper such individualism, making it a democratic individualism. But the tensions between these two values remain. As long as the most important values in human life are found outside political institutions and relationships, as Thoreau insists they are, democratic values are to be thought of as less essential than other important elements of human experience. Rosenblum notes that Thoreau believed that even the most democratic politics had a distinctly limited claim on a free individual's life: "The greatest interest and originality of Thoreau's political thought is precisely the way he situates democratic citizenship in the larger contours of a life well spent."[69] Placing democratic politics within this perspective helps to account for both his alienation and his appreciation for the way such politics make his private goods possible. If this suggests that democratic politics is always going to be contentious, at least when important matters are at stake, *Civil Disobedience* "successfully speaks in the voice of a conscientious democratic citizen."[70]

## NOTES

1 Perry Miller, "The Responsibility of Mind in a Civilization of Machines," *American Scholar* 31, 1961, pp. 51–69.

2 Ibid., pp. 58–59.

3 Ibid., p. 67.

4 Louis Hartz, *The Liberal Tradition in America* (NY: Harcourt, Brace and World, 1955).

5 Laraine Fergenson, "Thoreau, Daniel Berrigan, and the Problem of Transcendental Politics," *Soundings* 65, no. 1, Spring 1982, p. 113.

6 John Patrick Diggins, "Thoreau, Marx, and the 'Riddle' of Alienation," *Social Research* 39, Winter 1972, p. 596.

7 Ibid., p. 581.

8 Ibid., p. 582.

9 William Chaloupka, "Thoreau's Apolitical Legacy for American Environmentalism," in Jack Turner, ed., *A Political Companion to Henry David Thoreau* (Lexington, KY: University Press of Kentucky, 2009), p. 222.

10 Ibid.

11 Irving Howe, *The American Newness* (Cambridge, MA: Harvard University Press, 1986), p. 36.

12 Philip Abbott, *States of Perfect Freedom* (Amherst, MA: University of Massachusetts Press, 1987), p. 62.

13 Hannah Arendt, *Crisis of the Republic* (NY: Harcourt Brace Jovanovich, 1972), p. 55.

14 Ibid., pp. 60–61.

15 Charles Ives, "Essay Before a Sonata: Thoreau," 1845. Available at: http://thoreau.eserver.org/Ives.html (paragraph 13; accessed June 2014).

16 Walter Harding, ed., *Thoreau: A Century of Criticism* (Dallas, TX: Southern Methodist University Press, 1954), p. 48.

17 Ibid.

18 Ibid., p. 51.

19 Ibid., pp. 59, 60.

20 Ibid., p. 77.

21 Ibid., p. 80.

22 Vincent Buranelli, "The Case Against Thoreau," *Ethics* 67, no. 4, 1957, pp. 265, 260, 268, 266.

23 Theodore Baird, "Corn Grows in the Night," in John H. Hicks, ed., *Thoreau in Our Season* (Amherst, MA: University of Massachusetts Press, 1967), pp. 71, 77.

24  Ibid., p. 77.

25  Richard Ellis, *American Political Cultures* (NY: Oxford University Press, 1993), p. 145.

26  Carl Bode, "The Half-Hidden Thoreau," in Hicks, ed., *Thoreau in Our Season*, pp. 104–116.

27  C. Roland Wagner, "Lucky Fox at Walden," in Hicks, ed., *Thoreau in Our Season*, p. 130.

28  Ibid., p. 132.

29  Heinz Eulau, "Wayside Challenger: Some Remarks on the Politics of Henry David Thoreau," in Sherman Paul, ed., *Thoreau: A Collection of Critical Essays* (Englewood Cliffs, NJ: Prentice-Hall, 1962), p. 125.

30  Ibid., p. 118.

31  Ibid., p. 126.

32  Ibid., p. 119.

33  Ibid., p. 130.

34  C. Carroll Hollis, "Thoreau and the State," *Commonweal* 9, September 1949, p. 531.

35  Emma Goldman, *Anarchism and Other Essays* (Port Washington, NY: Kennikat Press, 1969), p. 62.

36  Harding, ed., *Thoreau*, p. 162.

37  Edward H. Madden, *Civil Disobedience and Moral Law in Nineteenth-Century American Philosophy* (Seattle, WA: University of Washington Press, 1968), p. 97.

38  Francis B. Dedmond, "Thoreau and the Ethical Concept of Government," *The Personalist* 36 no. 1, 1955, p. 46.

39  See Leigh Kathryn Jenco, "Thoreau's Critique of Democracy," in Turner, ed., *Political Companion to Henry David Thoreau*, pp. 68–96.

40  Harry V. Jaffa, "Thoreau and Lincoln," in Turner, ed., *Political Companion to Henry David Thoreau*, p. 202.

41  Daniel Walker Howe, *Making the American Self* (Oxford: Oxford University Press, 1997), p. 245.

42  Ibid., p. 249.

43  Thomas Carlyle, *Sartor Resartus and On Heroes and Hero-Worship and the Heroic in History* (London: J. M. Dent; NY: E. P. Dutton, 1910), p. 266.

44  Ibid., p. 364.

45  Myron Simon, "Thoreau's Politics," in Tibor Frank, ed., *The Origins and Originality of American Culture* (Budapest: Akademiai Kiado, 1984), p. 526.

46  Michael Walzer, *Exodus and Revolution* (NY: Basic Books, 1985), chapter 4.

47  William Ophuls, *Ecology and the Politics of Scarcity* (San Francisco, CA: W. H. Freeman, 1977).

48  Martin Luther King Jr. *Why We Can't Wait* (NY: Penguin, 1964), pp. 76–95.

49  Robert Dickens, *Thoreau* (NY: Exposition Press, 1974), p. 86.

50  Howe, *American Newness*, p. 35.

51  Frederick K. Sanders, "Mr. Thoreau's Time Bomb," *National Review*, 4 June 1968, p. 545.

52  Ibid., p. 547.

53  Henry David Thoreau, *A Week on the Concord and Merrimack Rivers; Walden, or, Life in the Woods; The Maine Woods; Cape Cod* (NY: Library of America, 1985), p. 410.

54  F. O. Matthiessen, *American Renaissance* (NY: Oxford University Press, 1941), p. 79.
55  Wilson Carey McWilliams, *The Idea of Fraternity in America* (Berkeley, CA: University of California Press, 1973), p. 296.
56  Eulau, "Wayside Challenger," p. 118.
57  Sacvan Bercovitch, *American Jeremiad* (Madison, WS: University of Wisconsin Press, 1978), p. 187.
58  Jane Bennett, "On Being a Native: Thoreau's Hermeneutics of Self," *Polity* 22, no. 4, 1990, p. 559.
59  George Kateb, "Democratic Individuality and the Claims of Politics," *Political Theory* 12, no. 3, 1984, p. 336.
60  Ibid., p. 356.
61  Shannon L. Mariotti, *Thoreau's Democratic Withdrawal* (Madison, WI: University of Wisconsin Press, 2010), p. xvii.
62  Ibid., p. 6.
63  Ibid.
64  Ibid., p. 80.
65  Ibid., p. 103.
66  Brian Walker, "Thoreau's Alternative Economics: Work, Liberty, and Democratic Cultivation," *American Political Science Review* 92, no. 4, December 1998, pp. 845–856.
67  Nancy Rosenblum, "Thoreau's Democratic Individualism," in Turner, ed., *Political Companion to Henry David Thoreau*, pp. 18, 21.
68  Ibid., p. 31.
69  Henry David Thoreau, *Thoreau: Political Writings*, Nancy L. Rosenblum, ed. (NY: Cambridge University Press, 1996), p. xxvii.
70  Ibid., p. xix.

# 5

# CIVIL DISOBEDIENCE AND POLITICAL PHILOSOPHY

Perhaps the greatest paradox of Thoreau's *Civil Disobedience* is that it offers little or nothing to help us understand and work through the theory or philosophy of what is widely understood as civil disobedience. It was pointed out in Chapter 2 that there is no evidence that Thoreau ever used the phrase "civil disobedience." The essay he published under the title *Resistance to Civil Government* was posthumously republished under the new title, *Civil Disobedience*; it is possible that he approved this change prior to his death, but we simply cannot know one way or the other. We have also seen, in Chapter 4, questions raised by Hannah Arendt about the usefulness of Thoreau's essay in thinking about problems of civil disobedience. Her claim was that civil disobedience, properly understood, is a corporate or group act, which assumes shared political commitments and moral responsibilities, and that Thoreau's appeal to individual conscience does not speak to this form of political resistance.

The comments of one of the most prominent and distinguished analysts of civil disobedience, Hugo Bedau, illustrate Thoreau's

uneasy relationship to this tradition. Bedau traces civil disobedience back to the classical Greeks (in the fictional person of
Antigone, and the historical person of Socrates) but suggests that
"it is Thoreau to whom, especially in this country [the U.S.], we
return again and again to take our bearings as we confront a
government or a law we judge to be immoral."[1] He assumes (for
reasons left unexplained) that Thoreau approved the posthumous
title of his essay,[2] and claims that "we must accept Thoreau's
refusal to pay taxes as indeed a paradigm of civil disobedience."[3]
Having placed Thoreau in this crucial historical and philosophical
role, however, Bedau finds himself undercutting his own analysis
with a comment very much capturing the position we have
already found Arendt defending: "His act was ... the solitary act
of an individual concerned about his own moral health, not the
undertaking of a social revolutionary, intent upon bringing mass
nonviolent direct action against unjust practices."[4] We know, like
Bedau, that individuals who have engaged in civil disobedience
have often turned to Thoreau for moral inspiration. Bedau leaves
us doubting, however, that what we find there can really help us
much at all in thinking about "mass nonviolent direct action
against unjust practices." Thoreau's essay may encourage a critical
attitude toward political authority, but there is little within to
help us explore the moral conditions of cooperative political
struggle of any kind. In fact, the moral position defended in the
essay appears deeply skeptical about the idea of political or protest
behavior. We also know that Thoreau writes, in *Civil Disobedience*,
that "Reform keeps many scores of newspapers in its service, but
not one man" (paragraph 21). In *Walden* he writes of reformers as
the "greatest bores of all";[5] he was never able to find a good word
for political activists.

If there are questions about Thoreau's helpfulness in thinking
about civil disobedience, however, there are other elements in his
essay, some mentioned only briefly and some developed in greater
detail, which are central to the broad tradition of political philosophy. In this chapter, a number of key philosophical themes found
in *Civil Disobedience* will be discussed in relation to classic authors
and texts in Western political theory. The intention here is not to
provide exhaustive discussions of each of these matters, but to

note the degree to which Thoreau's position resonates within a much larger tradition of political and theoretical debate and to suggest ways of framing Thoreau's views within this broader philosophical conversation. That is, readers are provided an initial set of reflections for thinking about Thoreau's views within a complex tradition of political philosophy, rather than a full-blown analysis of each idea.

In *Civil Disobedience* Thoreau touches on the following themes and ideas: the moral status of individual conscience; the role of consent in legitimate political orders; the nature and limits of political obligation; the moral claims of democratic participation; the morality of political action; alienation and individual freedom within the context of a modern economy; the role of nature in helping to focus and shape our quest for a free and just social order. While all of these themes are central to the history of political thought, it is the last, which is only hinted at in the final passages of *Civil Disobedience*, which has turned out to be Thoreau's most significant and lasting contribution to political theory.

## INDIVIDUAL CONSCIENCE

> Must the citizen ever for a moment, or in the least degree, resign his conscience to the legislator? Why has every man a conscience then?
>
> *Civil Disobedience*, paragraph 4

We saw in Chapter 2 that Thoreau was reading Sophocles' great play *Antigone* during the same period he was living at Walden Pond and writing his first book, *A Week on the Concord and Merrimack Rivers* – the time, that is, of his arrest and the development of his ideas about "resistance to civil government." It is clear that Thoreau viewed Antigone as a symbol of heroic courage and moral integrity. Readers of *Civil Disobedience* also frequently note a similarity between Thoreau and Antigone. They both refused to obey human laws they viewed as unjust. Antigone's and Thoreau's stories both suggest that responsible individuals need to summon the courage to resist capricious and unfair political authority. Both imply that the moral power of righteous individuals is greater, in the end, than the mere physical force of governments. Both figures are thus sources of encouragement and inspiration for politically and militarily powerless individuals who face tyrannical authorities or institutions. Antigone and Thoreau share a place in the hearts of all individuals who wish to speak truth to power, who view the appeal to conscience as more powerful than the appeal to arms.

Antigone's story is told as a part of Sophocles' trilogy of Theban Plays. Her father, Oedipus, the king of Thebes, famously discovers that he has unintentionally murdered his father and married his mother. Blinding himself and wandering in exile, his sons and heirs, Eteocles and Polynices, assume power and agree to share it by alternating years on the throne. After the first year, Eteocles refuses to yield to his brother. Enraged, Polynices raises an army and attacks the city. Although his army is repelled, Eteocles and Polynices slay one another in the battle. Their uncle Creon, Oedipus' brother, assumes the throne. Sophocles' *Antigone* begins in the aftermath of this war. Creon has decreed that Eteocles will be buried with honors but that Polynices' body is to be left where it fell, unburied. Antigone refuses to obey Creon's command and attempts to bury Polynices. She is bold and public in her defiance. Creon arrests her, and she hangs herself in her prison cell.

It is crucial to recognize that neither Thoreau nor Antigone think of the appeal to conscience as an appeal to their own personal impulses, desires, or private subjective realities. Both contend that their acts of disobedience are required by commitment to laws outside of themselves. Antigone speaks of the "holiest laws of heaven," and of her "duty to the dead."[6] Thoreau, as we have seen, contrasts Webster's "lawyer's truth" with the "Truth" we access through conscience (paragraph 42). The first is merely pragmatic and "expedient"; the latter deals with principles beyond the contingent and practical, and taps into realities more universal than even the Bible and the Constitution (paragraph 43). Both Antigone and Thoreau justify their rebellion by referring to higher laws than those generated by the state, and both believe such higher laws are required to evaluate and judge the political world. They contend, in short, that their rebellion is not simply a subjective choice but, rather, an objective duty. Their acts assume a moral reality beyond and greater than themselves.

Despite this similarity, there is a noticeable difference in Thoreau's and Antigone's understanding of how to think about this objective moral reality. Thoreau takes great pains to stand aloof, to disconnect himself from conventional and common ways of thinking. His posture is as an eccentric, a good neighbor but a profoundly independent and relatively solitary character. His relationship to moral truth is unmediated by personal relationships with other people or conventional social roles and customs. Antigone, in contrast, grounds her rebellion in the duties and rights of Theban women. She declares to her sister, Ismene, at the beginning of the play that Creon's decree is clearly directed against them: "It is against you and me he has made this order. Yes, against me."[7] It appears that she is wrong in this assumption, as Creon's initial speech explaining his decision not to bury Polynices is all about protecting the state and treating all traitors equally. Nonetheless, Antigone's response is revealing. Creon's order is not only "against" the sisters (or, more particularly, the elder sister Antigone) in the sense that they will most strongly feel the punishment of a member of their family. The pain Antigone suffers under this decree is not only caused by her proximity to her brother. Even more importantly, Creon's order prevents Antigone from performing her womanly duties. Sophocles says little about this, since his audience would understand the context in which Antigone acts. Women had no political standing in Greek society at this time, and their lives were generally confined to the private sphere. Certain religious functions, however, such as preparing the dead for burial, were left to them, and these duties constituted some of their greatest opportunities for participation in clearly defined and important social events and rituals. When Antigone claims she is commanded by the gods to bury her brother, she is referring to ancient cultural practices and insisting they be respected. Her rebellion is not only an assertion of the superiority of religious obligation to political edicts; it is a demand that her conventional role as a Theban woman be respected. Unlike Thoreau, Antigone gains access to the intentions of the gods by appealing to these conventional social roles and duties. It is not by distancing herself from customary relationships that she discovers her moral obligations but, rather, by embracing and cherishing these roles.

This difference aside, Thoreau and Antigone share a belief in an objective moral reality. In addition, they both appear to believe that this reality is clear to anyone willing to honestly and openly consider it. Thoreau suggests two major reasons for moral failure: a lack of courage to stand for what we know is right and a moral blindness caused by thinking too narrowly, too "politically" – that is, too consequentially and "expediently." For those who will look, he suggests that, at least concerning radical injustices such as slavery and imperial war, the moral judgment one must reach is quite clear. For these people, a much more obvious problem grows from fear of the consequences of standing up for right than from difficulty in understanding what the right is. Antigone never appears to doubt that her moral resistance to Creon is anything other than obviously justifiable. She stands, after all, on the side of the gods, and the gods trump humans, even kings. As she is taken to her prison, her certainty in her own moral judgment is unshaken: "Last daughter of your royal house go I, *his* [Creon's] prisoner, because I honoured those things to which honour truly belongs."[8] The play appears to generally agree with Antigone, as Creon ultimately admits his errors and comes to believe it was he, not his niece, who was in the wrong.

There are, however, moments of doubt about the moral certainty found in both texts. In *Antigone*, the chorus says, "glory and praise go with you, lady, to your resting-place."[9] It then claims, however, "You are the victim of your own self-will."[10] Antigone has been heroic and courageous, but also willful and stubborn. She and her uncle are both terribly sure of themselves, and they are both equally quick to fight and assume the worst of others who fail to fall in line with their views. Neither character, in fact, has the slightest understanding of the other's motivation or reasons for taking the actions they do. Antigone simply assumes that Creon has intentionally insulted her, even though Creon thinks of his actions as illustrating his willingness to put the safety and well-being of the city above his own family's interests. Creon, likewise, assumes that only individuals hoping for personal gain, and perhaps even the continued instability of the city, could possibly object to his decree. There is no way to know if the crisis in the play could have been defused with cooler minds and more willingness to talk through the issues. What is clear is that the struggle between two self-righteous individuals like Creon and Antigone will not end well. Antigone, her betrothed (and Creon's son) Haemon, and Creon's wife Eurydice are all dead at the end of the play. The less heroic figures of Ismene and Haemon, along with the prophet Teiresias and the chorus, sense the danger presented by the enraged moral certainty of the two primary antagonists. Antigone never doubts her own righteousness, and Creon only comes to doubt himself when it is too late. Teiresias counsels Creon to be more careful about the effects of his actions: "What prize outweighs the priceless worth of prudence?"[11] His advice could have applied equally well to Antigone. The tragedy of the play, in large part, grows directly from the kind of moral posture Antigone represents and has come to symbolize in Western culture. What makes Antigone so admirable, in short, is a set of traits that also make her blind to moral ambiguity and other people's perspectives. Such blindness, the story suggests, can be very dangerous.

The textual evidence for moral doubt in *Civil Disobedience* is much less significant than it is in *Antigone*. Thoreau does note that one "cannot be too much on his guard in such a case, lest his action be biased by obstinacy, or an undue regard for the opinions of men" (paragraph 38). He also recognizes that the majority of his neighbors think differently from how he does (paragraph 42). But on the whole, he is confident in his view and feels no need to soften it or to seek common ground with those he disagrees with. His opponents, he believes, are either afraid to stand up for what is right or are looking at the problem from too narrow a perspective. His point is that they have not transcended the context of politics in forming their moral views (his comments in the remainder of paragraph 42 are about politicians and lawyers), and they would presumably come to agreement with him if they learned to reason morally, and not merely politically. So *Civil Disobedience* does not provide much material to encourage us to question our own moral certainty. Thoreau appears quite confident about our ability to reach obviously correct moral understandings, at least concerning issues as morally outrageous as slavery and imperial war. We might note, however, that Thoreau's biography would seem to suggest the difficulty even people of good will have in coming to agreement about difficult and significant political conflict. His forebears had divided over the American Revolution. His paternal grandfather served in the Revolution under Paul Revere, while his maternal grandmother's family had Tory sympathies (this grandmother actually helped her brothers escape to Loyalist Canada).[12] One might think his family history could suggest to Thoreau the difficulty even conscientious people have in coming to moral agreement at moments of crisis. This suggestion echoes only faintly in Thoreau's essay, however.

In contrast to Thoreau and Antigone, consider these two possible positions we might take on the existence and certainty of universal and timeless moral truths. First, we might simply deny the existence of the kind of universal moral principles Antigone and Thoreau assume to be real. In Book 1 of Plato's *Republic*, the character Thrasymachus famously argues, against Socrates, that justice is nothing other than the "interest of the stronger." That is, when we make moral claims, such as that this law or act is "just," what we are really doing is providing a euphemistic defense of the interests of those in power. More than 2,000 years later, Karl Marx suggested, along similar lines, that both moral and legal codes reflect and legitimate the interests of the ruling class. Although many of us would reject Thrasymachus' deep cynicism about moral discourse, or would not be comfortable with a strict Marxist class analysis about moral principles and values, many of us would be comfortable thinking of moral codes and commitments as culturally created and bounded. From this perspective, there is little to be said when comparing one cultural moral code with another, other than that each human community seems to require a moral code of some sort. The idea that there are universal moral principles that transcend our historical or cultural contexts is an idea that meets with a great deal of skepticism in modern society.

Second, even if we are sympathetic to the idea of universal moral law, there are still reasons to be wary of the message Thoreau and Antigone deliver. Let us assume, for the sake of argument, that for matters of great moral importance, there is in principle a correct (and only one correct) moral position. Even if this is true, an obvious difficulty presents itself: how are we to know, with confidence, that we have discovered the right or correct answer?

In real political life, we know that people disagree significantly about public policy, even about ultimate political goals; we know, for example, that Abraham Lincoln shared with Thoreau an abhorrence of slavery, yet these men disagreed profoundly about the moral importance of defending the Constitution and maintaining the unity of the nation. If disagreement is a commonplace of democratic politics (and it certainly is), what then are we to do when people simply disagree? Sometimes, no doubt, disagreement grows from blunt self-interest, at least on one side of a political debate. But a significant amount of political disagreement is to be expected among people incapable of knowing for certain that they understand or have direct access to the moral truth about a political issue, policy, or situation. As we have seen, a number of critics attack Thoreau's moral position along lines similar to this.

The existence of moral truth, then, does not settle the issue of moral certainty in a contentious political world populated by imperfect individuals. The more we emphasize the uncertainty of our (and others') moral evaluation, the more we may come to view compromise and submission to legitimate political authority as politically virtuous rather than morally lazy, cowardly, or a violation of the obligation to honor our conscience. At its extreme, we might be led to a position similar to that held by seventeenth-century political theorist Thomas Hobbes, who argued that we are morally obliged to consent to any political authority we find ourselves governed by. The alternative, in his view, is moral and political chaos. The slaughter of the English Civil War, which he witnessed, suggested to him the profound danger of encouraging self-righteous individuals to follow their consciences; after all, people on both sides of that terrible conflict were sure they had God and moral truth on their side. We might reject the extreme nature of Hobbes' political absolutism, however, and still feel that in a democratic political order, minorities are obliged to obey majorities precisely because there is no way outside of a fair political process for settling disputes between people who *all* believe themselves to be right. We might hold a commitment to democratic processes as a moral obligation growing not from moral skepticism (that is, skepticism about the existence of moral truths), but from the realistic expectation that imperfect citizens will inevitably disagree about the content of moral reality.

How we feel about Thoreau's appeal to individual conscience against political authority (including the authority of democratic majorities) depends a great deal on our retrospective evaluation of the substantive content of the position he conscientiously defended. That is, our approval of Thoreau's appeal to conscience is at least in part contingent on our evaluation that his conscience in this case pointed to the substantively correct moral position. In Thoreau's case, this seems easy: we may be confident today that both slavery and imperial war are morally indefensible. We should note, however, that such evaluations are always more certain in retrospect than they are in the heat of political controversy. At the very least we might recognize the dangers of appealing to conscience, and the degree to which such appeals should probably be reserved for only the most extreme political contexts. After all, such an appeal raises dangers that are themselves potentially extreme (as Thomas Hobbes observed). There is no rule for knowing when such an appeal might be appropriate. For all its ambiguity and imprecision, however, the message of Antigone might provide something of a counterweight to Thoreau's moral confidence; perhaps all appeals to conscience must be tempered by both the doubts and prudence taught by Sophocles as a counterforce to Antigone's and Creon's moral arrogance. Such a teaching leaves us uncertain about when appeals to conscience are appropriate. But this uncertainty may be helpful in taming the potential arrogance of supremely self-confident, but possibly mistaken, conscientious moral individuals.

## CONSENT

> The authority of government, even such as I am willing to submit to ... is still an impure one: to be strictly just, it must have the sanction and consent of the governed.
>
> *Civil Disobedience*, paragraph 45

Given Thoreau's emphasis on individual conscience, it is not surprising that he also stresses, in the final paragraph of *Civil Disobedience*, the importance of consent for just government. If we are morally obliged to listen to the dictates of our conscience, it would seem that political authority must be in harmony with our conscience in order for it to be justifiable. In this way, the idea of consent suggests that legitimate political authority reflects the agreement or active recognition by the citizen of the compatibility of the political order with her or his conscience. If a conscientious citizen would agree to abide by a law or recognize the legitimacy of a political order, we can say this law or political order is justified by the consent of the citizen. Individual conscience and the political value of consent thus both grow from a commitment to respecting individuals as the ultimate arbiters of moral (and therefore political) authority. In the language of seventeenth-century political theorist John Locke, "*Every man* being ... *naturally free*, and nothing being able to put him into subjection to any earthly power, but only his own *consent*."[13]

This idea obviously plays a central role in Thoreau's political theory. The first paragraph of *Civil Disobedience*, like the last, mentions consent and uses the idea to criticize President Polk's manipulation of American diplomatic, political, and military authority to pursue war with Mexico. The war, Thoreau holds, is the "work of comparatively a few individuals using the standing government as their tool; for, in the outset, the people would not have consented to this measure" (paragraph 1). In a similar vein, we have seen Thoreau brag about refusing to pay a tax to support the clergy, whose church he did not attend. The idea of consent is taken to an extreme at the end of this passage, when Thoreau writes: "If I had known how to name them, I should then have signed off in detail from all the societies which I never signed on to; but I did not know where to find a complete list" (paragraph 25). The conscientious individual seems to find him or herself, in Thoreau's view, unjustly imposed upon by any number of institutions with political authority.

Hints of the importance of consent are found as early in the tradition of Western political philosophy as Plato's *Crito*, where Socrates is imaginatively interrogated by the laws of Athens and asked if he objects to them. (We will return to this text in the next section.) He does not; the implication is that his lack of objection indicates, along with his lifelong willingness to remain in Athens, consent to abide by the laws. However, it is not until modern social contract theory in the seventeenth and eighteenth centuries, in the work of theorists like Thomas Hobbes, John Locke, and Jean-Jacques Rousseau, that the notion of consent becomes a standard tool for explaining the origin and nature of just government. This early liberal political theory deeply influenced political ideas in the British American colonies. The revolution leading to the creation of the United States, in fact, is often thought of as a uniquely Lockean political event. Thoreau came by the language of consent quite naturally; he self-consciously appeals to the ideology of revolution and individual rights that was widely accepted among his local, regional, and national audience.

If we return to the paragraph of Locke's *Second Treatise of Government* quoted briefly above, we see that immediately after asserting that all legitimate government grows from the consent of the governed, Locke introduces a crucial distinction between what he calls "express" and "tacit" consent. Express consent seems an easy case to Locke, since if we find a situation where an individual explicitly – "expressly" – and clearly states his consent, through an oath or a recited pledge for example, it seems obvious and clear that that individual is bound by an overt promise: "No body doubts but an express *consent*, of any man entering into any society, makes him a perfect member of that society, a subject of that government."[14] When we are thinking about naturalized citizens, for example, or perhaps of members of the armed forces or civil servants who take oaths to uphold and protect the laws of a nation, it seems unobjectionable to suggest that their consent is both clear and morally binding.

The difficulty arises, however, when we think about all the people living in a political community who have not made such a clear and unambiguous gesture of consent. What about all those people who find themselves living under a government simply due to the fact that they were born within the boundaries of a particular nation? Many of these citizens may have never expressly stated their consent to the laws. Locke recognizes that this is a more difficult case:

> The difficulty is, what ought to be looked upon as a *tacit consent*, and how far it binds, i.e. how far any one shall be looked on to have

consented, and thereby submitted to any government, where he has made no expressions of it at all.[15]

Although less obvious than express consent, a tacit consent – a consent we may *assume* simply from the context of the situation, even if no express statements are made – seems to Locke an almost equally powerful idea:

I say, that every man, that hath any possessions, or enjoyment, of any part of the dominions of any government, doth thereby give his *tacit consent*, and is as far forth obliged to obedience to the laws of that government, during such enjoyment, as any one under it; whether this his possession be of land, to him and his heirs for ever, or a lodging only for a week; or whether it be barely travelling freely on the highway; and in effect, it reaches as far as the very being of any one within the territories of that government.[16]

The logical thrust of this statement is both clear and remarkable. Locke begins by suggesting that when we enjoy the security of our property by living under a government, this suggests an acceptance, a consent, to the laws of that government. This is true, however, not just for those who have chosen to live their lives within a particular nation. Even those who visit temporarily can be assumed to consent to the laws governing the territory. In fact, even travelers, or anyone finding themselves within the territorial boundaries of a government, can be assumed to have tacitly consented to that government as long as they have freely chosen to be within the territory.

For Locke, then, tacit consent grows from our uncoerced acceptance of the benefits provided by government. As long as we benefit from being within a particular political jurisdiction, and as long as this benefit can be assumed to be welcomed by us since we are not being held within this jurisdiction against our will, our consent to the government can be assumed. If it has been our choice to be there, this choice itself indicates a consensual act to abide by the laws of the jurisdiction. Locke's view that everyone freely within the territory of a government for any amount of time can be assumed to have consented to that government is remarkable because it has moved us from a quite limited understanding of consent to an extremely expansive one. A moral idea that originates in observing the power of explicit promises grows, in Locke's hands, to encompass a wide range of much less clear or self-conscious relationships. (It is worth noting that the philosopher David Hume objected to Locke's argument on the ground that it is comparable to suggesting that someone tacitly consents to obey a ship's captain "though he was carried on board while asleep and must leap into the ocean and perish the moment he leaves her."[17])

Contemporary theorists have removed the idea of consent even one more step from the explicit promise that inspired the idea in the first place. The notion of "hypothetical consent" has been proposed as a way of retaining the power of the idea of consent but separating it from any particular act, express or tacit, of the citizen. The moral question was originally, what have I done to signal my acceptance of the government? From the perspective of hypothetical consent the question becomes, would a rational and informed individual give his or her consent to this particular law or regime? While tacit consent, for Locke, still retains some meaningful relationship to the free actions of real individuals, hypothetical consent can be evaluated independently of any actions of particular people. The justice of a government can be determined not by the acts of citizens, in this case, but by analyzing the degree to which the government conforms to general principles of justice.

Moving from express to tacit to hypothetical consent is a move, conceptually, from an emphasis on individual choice to an emphasis on substantive moral evaluation. The conceptual power of express consent grows from the promise, the expressed will, of the citizen: what counts morally is the choice of the individuals involved in a particular political context. With hypothetical consent, the will of individuals has been removed almost entirely from sight (it remains not as an actual event, but only as a hypothetical). From this perspective, moral obligation is assumed to grow not from any particular act of will but, rather, from the moral qualities of the political institutions under consideration. With hypothetical consent, the actual choice of real political actors does not constitute the critical moral fact; what matters, instead, is how the political situation measures up to some independent moral standard. Consent originates as an idea focusing on the free choice of political subjects. In its "hypothetical" form, consent has been transformed into the substantive evaluation of the government. The neutral philosopher, rather than the living citizen, becomes the appropriate judge of our obligation to a particular government.

Thoreau's use of consent appears to be almost as varied as the ways in which it has been used in liberal political theory since at least Locke's time. He begins and ends with a very robust understanding, comparable to Locke's idea of express consent. In fact, when discussing his withdrawal from church membership, he seems to take this idea so literally as to suggest that he would like to find a full list of the human associations claiming him as a member so that he could clarify whether he was or was not willing to clearly and explicitly consent to such membership.

We find only hints that Thoreau may have found some power in the idea of tacit consent. His discussion of voting, for example, suggests that his refusal to participate grows in part from his concern that he not be implicated in the outcome of majority rule; he seems to fear that voting gives tacit consent or approval to the outcome of elections, which would be inappropriate in the event that the outcome violates moral law. There is also the suggestion that by not resisting the current government, many American citizens are in fact lending their support to it: "Those who, while they disapprove of the character and measures of a government, yield to it their allegiance and support, are undoubtedly its most conscientious supporters, and so frequently the most serious obstacles to reform" (paragraph 14). Thoreau's charge might be interpreted to suggest that these citizens have granted an inappropriate tacit consent to the government.

Aside from these cases, however, when Thoreau appeals to consent he seems to want to limit it to its most demanding (and morally powerful) form – and for good reason. If Locke is right, after all, that voluntarily dwelling within the borders of a nation is sufficient to indicate our tacit consent, Thoreau would be much more implicated in the American government than he admits. Does he not accept, tacitly, the civil order and protection provided by local, state, and federal government? He claims he does not need such protection, mainly because he has little wealth to be protected. He also claims, in the opening of *Civil Disobedience*, that the achievements of the American people owe little or nothing to the government: "The character inherent in the American people has done all that has been accomplished; and it would have done somewhat more, if the government had not sometimes got in its way" (paragraph 2). In these ways, Thoreau denies the benefits provided by the government, both for him and for the society at large. To the degree we find this persuasive, we may find little power in the idea of tacit consent, at least as far as Thoreau's case is concerned; he cannot be thought to be signaling consent when there are no services he is accepting from the government. Then again, the degree to which we do *not* find Thoreau's claim to be persuasive – that is, the degree to which we think he *does* accept important goods and services from the government, his protests to the contrary notwithstanding – is the degree to which we may think Thoreau is more bound by tacit consent than he admits.

We mentioned above that Thoreau criticizes his fellows for implicitly lending their support to unjust institutions. We may think of this as a criticism of the tacit consent given by many Americans, even those who claim to oppose them, to slavery and imperialism. There is thus good reason to believe that Thoreau is not fully committed to the will of citizens as the final arbiters of moral legitimacy; after all, giving consent to these institutions is not sufficient to establish their justice or legitimacy. We saw in the previous section that Thoreau's vigorous appeal to individual conscience grows from his commitment to universal moral law. Likewise, the core of his criticism of the American government, and the reason he believes conscientious individuals should refuse to be associated with it lest they share in its disgrace, is not primarily that it violates the consent of citizens. Ultimately, the problem is that it violates fundamental moral principles by protecting slavery and pursuing imperial war. Even if citizens consent to these, even if overwhelming majorities consent to them, Thoreau would never find them justifiable. They are simply incompatible with justice, in his view, regardless of what people may or may not consent to. In this sense, Thoreau's understanding of consent begins to look "hypothetical": the emphasis is on what individuals with access to moral principle would consent to, rather than what actual individuals in the real political world do in fact consent to. Thoreau's evaluation of the justice of government rests much more on the degree to which he believes it conforms to or departs from moral law than on whether or not citizens consent to it. From Thoreau's perspective, only in a hypothetically perfect citizen, one who has both an unshakable commitment to moral truth and an unambiguous access to it, would consent to the government prove its justice. Even then, the compatibility of such a government with moral law, not the consenting wills of its citizens, is the critical and decisive issue.

We have seen elsewhere that Thoreau assumes in *Civil Disobedience* that the main problem with which to confront his audience is its unwillingness to do what is right, not its inability to understand what is right. Thoreau is actually quite optimistic about the ability of most individuals to be conscientious in the full sense of the word – to be both committed to the moral truth and to understand what this truth is and demands of us. It is clear, then, that a set of concerns can be raised about Thoreau's understanding of consent that are similar to those we have already discussed concerning his defense of individual conscience. Both conscience and consent, for Thoreau, are powerful ideas only to the degree that they are subordinated to an independent moral truth. As such, neither is particularly helpful for thinking about how to contend with deep moral disagreement between imperfect people of good will, people for whom access to such moral truths is uncertain. Thoreau's use of the language of consent cannot resolve this critical issue any more than his promotion of individual conscience can. The appeals to consent at the beginning and end of the essay, in truth, look more rhetorical than substantive.

## OBLIGATION

> [T]he government does not concern me much, and I shall bestow the fewest possible thoughts on it. It is not many moments that I live under a government, even in this world.
>
> *Civil Disobedience*, paragraph 41

We have seen clearly in previous sections that Thoreau believes himself bound to moral laws beyond the laws of the state and the constitutional order. There is no need to reinvestigate that point here, but it may be helpful to contrast it with a foundational text of the Western political canon, Plato's *Crito*. Socrates, in Plato's account, offers a view that first appears diametrically opposed to Thoreau's understanding of his moral relationship to the political community. When pushed a little further, however, we find that Plato offers not so much an opposing view as a significantly more nuanced perspective.

In the *Apology*, Plato provides an account of Socrates' defense at his trial, which resulted from an indictment accusing him of "criminal meddling, in that he inquires into things below the earth and in the sky, and makes the weaker argument defeat the stronger, and teaches others to follow his example."[18] The two key elements of this indictment charge Socrates with violating the conventions of Athenian religion and with corrupting his young followers through these teachings. We need not be concerned here with the details of Socrates's defense, other than to note that he professes his innocence.

*Crito* takes place after Socrates' conviction. The dialogue opens in Socrates' jail cell just days before his scheduled execution. His friend, Crito, has bribed a guard in order to enter the prison. He has also made arrangements for Socrates to escape to a neighboring city and has come to persuade Socrates to flee. Socrates resists, and the dialogue recounts the discussion in which Socrates eventually persuades Crito that it would be unjust for him to escape.

For our purposes, the most interesting arguments in *Crito* are found in its final passage. Socrates imagines that the Laws of Athens are personified and speak with him. The Laws, Socrates suggests, view the planned escape as a direct attack on them, a potential willingness on Socrates' part to overthrow lawful institutions "because the State wronged me by passing a faulty judgment" at the trial.[19] Part of the argument the Laws provide against Crito's plan is worth quoting at length:

> "... Come now, what charge do you bring against us and the State, that you are trying to destroy us? Did we not give you life in the first place? Was it not through us that your father married your mother and begot you? Tell us, have you any complaint against those of us Laws

that deal with marriage?" "No, none," I should say. "Well, have you any against the Laws which deal with children's upbringing and education, such as you had yourself? Are you not grateful to those of us Laws which were instituted for this end, for requiring your father to give you a cultural and physical education?" "Yes," I should say. "Very good. Then since you have been born and brought up and educated, can you deny, in the first place, that you were our child and servant, both you and your ancestors? And if this is so, do you imagine that what is right for us is equally right for you, and that whatever we try to do to you, you are justified in retaliating?"[20]

These claims appear audacious, especially if we are sympathetic to Thoreau's perspective. While Thoreau brags of having little to do with the government, of living much of his life outside the reach of the state and its laws, Socrates is suggesting that he owes his very life to Athens – "did we not give you life in the first place?" The political community regulates marriage, families, and the education of the young to one degree or another. Law provides the stability, guidance, and context in which even our private lives are experienced. This political context is of primary importance, as it allows all lesser associations to flourish. In fact, the individual Socrates has become would be unimaginable except within this Athenian context. While Thoreau argues that the government does not concern him much, Socrates seems to believe the opposite, that the political community nurtured him to be the man he is, and therefore the laws are like a parent or master to him. Government is, at best, an "expedient" for Thoreau, a servant to the people. For Socrates, it seems a superior moral force, essential for giving form to society.

There is one obvious reason why the Laws' argument might have seemed more plausible to Socrates than we would expect it to sound to Thoreau. Athens in the fifth century BCE was a small independent city-state. The political community was close at hand and easy to recognize. As a participatory democracy, the government was immediate, local, and accessible, an arm of the local community. The decisions made by the political community regarding both domestic and foreign affairs had clear and easily recognized effects on the citizenry. The United States in the mid-nineteenth century, in contrast, was a sprawling republic with millions of citizens. While still a far cry from the massive and bureaucratic government of the twenty-first century, the political world within which Thoreau lived was relatively impersonal and removed from citizens' daily life, at least in comparison with ancient Athens. Thoreau lived in a world in which it was much easier to imagine onerself independent of the political community than it was in Socrates' political environment.

Be that as it may, Socrates makes a point to which Thoreau is particularly tone deaf, at least in *Civil Disobedience*. While politics may have been further removed from his daily life than it was for Socrates, it is true nonetheless that Thoreau received significantly more from the government, at all levels, than he is willing to admit. Like Socrates, Thoreau lived in a political environment that provided security, built essential infrastructure, and defined essential institutions – such as families – that shaped and nurtured him. Thoreau declares that the government "never of itself furthered any enterprise, but by the alacrity with which it got out of its way" (paragraph 2). His rhetoric, however, is excessive, if not willfully blind to reality. He thought a great deal about the fate of American Indians, so he was well aware of the role the American military played in waging war against the Indian nations in order to conquer land for European expansion (President Jackson had been particularly aggressive on this front during Thoreau's early adulthood). As a former schoolteacher and a graduate of Harvard University, Thoreau could hardly have been unaware of the degree to which education, both primary and higher, had been tied to law and political decision-making from the earliest years of settlement in New England; Harvard had been established by a vote of the Great and General Court of the Massachusetts Bay Company in 1636, and laws had also been passed as early as that century requiring parents in Massachusetts to provide their children with literacy minimally sufficient for reading and understanding the Bible. Thoreau may not have been as intimately connected to his political community as Socrates was in fifth-century Athens, but he was certainly more influenced and shaped by that community than he claims.

A first reading of *Crito* seems to suggest that due respect for law and government requires subordination of our own judgment to the command of government. If this were true, Socrates would be defending a view profoundly incompatible with Thoreau's. In fact, however, Socrates' view of personal responsibility is much closer to Thoreau's than the above discussion might lead us to believe. The laws Socrates evaluates in *Crito* are laws to which he has no objection. But what if Socrates had been confronted with a law or a political command he believed to be unjust? We know from the *Apology* that Socrates was willing to resist government when he was confident it was in the wrong. He boasts about how he had once been ordered by the political authorities to help arrest an individual for execution. He believed the order violated Athenian law (properly understood), so he refused to obey. This suggests that despite his respect for the political community, Socrates reserved the right to judge for himself the justice of any particular political act, policy, or law. He even considers the possibility, when addressing the jury during his trial, that he might be offered acquittal on condition that he cease his religious and philosophical pilgrimage. "I should reply," he says,

> Gentlemen, I am your very grateful and devoted servant, but I owe a greater obedience to God than to you; and so long as I draw breath and have my faculties, I shall never stop practicing philosophy and exhorting you and elucidating the truth for everyone that I meet.[21]

Socrates, we can see, was perfectly capable of "resisting civil government." He insists on his right to do so, in fact, whenever higher goods and laws are at stake. In this sense, Socrates shares with Thoreau a belief in a moral law that is greater than any political law, and a deep sense of the responsibility individuals have to follow the highest principles at stake in any given situation.

This philosophical commitment leads Socrates, like Thoreau, to refrain from conventional political participation. He admits, in the *Apology*, that he has self-consciously avoided active political life: "you may be quite sure, gentlemen, that if I had tried long ago to engage in politics, I should long ago have lost my life, without doing any good either to you or to myself."[22] Neither Socrates nor Thoreau believed that normal political life, as preoccupied as it is with power and interests, was likely to support the moral seriousness and honesty they both valued.

Yet Socrates combines his philosophical commitments with a much richer sense of communal obligation than we find in *Civil Disobedience*. Compared with Socrates, Thoreau is detached and militantly individualistic. Socrates reminds us, at the very least, of the depth of our obligation to that which is just in our political community. These obligations by no means override higher goods and obligations, but they are real and substantial nonetheless. If we forget them, we may be tempted to think we can simply wash our hands of the injustices in our society and look after our own moral purity as a completely private and personal affair. Thoreau never entirely succumbs to this temptation in *Civil Disobedience*. He insists on speaking as a citizen (paragraph 3), for example, and implies that he gives himself more "entirely to his fellow-men" than others who give themselves partially and are pronounced benefactors and philanthropists (paragraph 6). The overwhelming thrust of Thoreau's discussion, however, suggests that he seeks privacy and independence more than integration into his political community. The obligation he owes to his government, however, may be more significant and complex than he admits.

## THE MORAL CLAIMS OF DEMOCRATIC PARTICIPATION

> All voting is a sort of gaming ...
>
> *Civil Disobedience*, paragraph 11

> ... any man more right than his neighbors constitutes a majority of one already.
>
> *Civil Disobedience*, paragraph 20

Thoreau's moral posture in *Civil Disobedience* obviously generates a significant skepticism toward democratic decision-making. If there is a natural or universal moral law, knowable to conscientious individuals, the decisions of democratic majorities can never be authoritative. A conscientious individual, for Thoreau, should never take the decisions of majorities at face value. Instead, he or she should always evaluate such decisions in terms of their relationship to higher law or moral principle. The authority of democratic decisions can only derive from their compatibility with such laws or principles. From this moral perspective, the democratic process is itself relatively unimportant. It is the substance of a decision or a law, not the process by which it is derived, that determines its moral integrity. The contemporary philosopher Robert Paul Wolff uses different language from Thoreau, but his point is the same. We are obligated as free individuals to evaluate and regulate our actions in the light of moral principle. Such behavior reflects what Wolff calls our autonomy, and we are obliged, as free and moral people, to assert our autonomy in the face of any demand for obedience by authorities of any kind – even democratic authorities.

> It is out of the question to give up the commitment to moral autonomy. Men are no better than children if they not only accept the rule of others from force of necessity, but embrace it willingly and forfeit their duty unceasingly to weigh the merits of the actions which they perform. When I place myself in the hands of another, and permit him to determine the principles by which I shall guide my behavior, I repudiate the freedom and reason which give me dignity.[23]

For Wolff, as for Thoreau, moral law compels us to view all political authority, even democratic political authority, with skepticism. We have seen that Thoreau suggests (paraphrasing John Knox), "any man more right than his neighbors constitutes a majority of one already" (paragraph 20). To put any stock in the outcome of elections is comparable, for Thoreau, to merely hoping that one's view prevails, rather than insisting on the rightness of this view regardless of majority opinion.

We earlier noted that the existence of moral law does much less to settle differences of opinion concerning its content than we might hope. Now we should consider the possibility that there is no reason to believe in the existence of such moral principles at all. Philosopher Richard Rorty has praised Walt Whitman for his belief that "there was no reason to be curious about God because there is no standard, not even a divine one, against which the decisions of a free people can be measured."[24] John Dewey is likewise praised by Rorty for his "systematic attempt to temporalize everything, to leave nothing fixed."[25] There are no fixed standards, including moral standards, to which humans must submit. Instead, Rorty believes that Dewey shares Whitman's contention that we human beings "are the greatest poem because we put ourselves in the place of God."[26] In Rorty's view, democracy grows from a conviction that there is no principle or law above the will of human beings. He reveres Whitman and Dewey as the prophets of American democracy because of their thoroughgoing humanism, their belief that

> the terms "America" and "democracy" are shorthand for a new conception of what it is to be human – a conception which has no room for obedience to a nonhuman authority, and in which nothing save freely achieved consensus among human beings has any authority at all.[27]

While Rorty draws specifically on American sources for his understanding of democracy, the ideas he taps grow from a broader democratic tradition. Consider the arguments of eighteenth-century philosopher Jean-Jacques Rousseau in his greatest political work, *On The Social Contract*. Like his British predecessor John Locke (among many others), Rousseau thinks about political society as growing out of a "state of nature" in which there is no political organization. Rousseau imagined these pre-political "natural" men and women as living instinctive lives similar to other animals. As described in another work, the *Discourse on the Origin of Inequality*, these natural people were solitary, cared only about their very simple needs and desires, and were generally peaceable and happy. They were not, however, capable of the kind of relationships that would allow them to become either moral or immoral beings. They were pre-moral creatures, driven by the simple instinctive impulses that helped them preserve their lives in the most basic sense.

The movement from the state of nature to civil society is transformative for Rousseau: "This passage from the state of nature to the civil state produces quite a remarkable change in man, for it substitutes justice for instinct in his behavior and gives his actions a moral quality they previously lacked."[28] The human changes from "a stupid, limited animal into an intelligent being and a man."[29]

Nature gave us the freedom to pursue our instinctive lives. Society allows for the development of intelligence and choice. The natural individual responds to the environment and his or her own internal impulses. The civilized person has the capacity to choose how she or he will live. In Rousseau's language, "the acquisition in the civil state of moral liberty" is what "makes man truly the master of himself. For to be driven by appetite alone is slavery, and obedience to the law one has prescribed for oneself is liberty."[30] Civilization, that is, creates the possibility for a new kind of freedom. We may assert our wills and decide what kind of people we wish to become. Instead of submitting to natural impulse, we learn the freedom of thinking and choosing, of deciding what a satisfying and admirable life might look like.

Like Thoreau in the next century, Rousseau is deeply dissatisfied with the injustices and lack of freedom in the world around him – he begins the first chapter of *On the Social Contract* with the famous declaration that "Man is born free, and everywhere he is in chains."[31] The cure for the injustices and lack of freedom in our world, however, is not to be found in nature or in any laws beyond our own wills. For Rousseau, democracy is the key to freedom once the "state of nature" has been left far behind. The question is this: is it possible to imagine a process by which a group of individuals is able to make laws for themselves, but also live together? In Rousseau's words, can we find "a form of association which defends and protects with all common forces the person and goods of each associate, and by means of which each one, while uniting with all, nevertheless obeys only himself and remains as free as before?"[32] He believes the answer is, yes. This "form of association," for Rousseau, is democracy. If the laws that govern have been for-mulated and agreed to by the governed, political authority does not violate the freedom of individual citizens.

For Rousseau, this process requires all those who live under laws to participate in making these laws. For this reason, he was very skeptical about the legitimacy of democratic representation, of selecting others to make laws for us (how, after all, can their decisions be our own?). But Thoreau's concern does not focus on this problem.

Instead, he worries about the degree to which minorities are bound by majorities and the possibility that the decisions of majorities may violate higher laws. On both these matters, Rousseau gives reasons to doubt Thoreau's concerns and claims.

Let us begin with the broader issue, the idea that democratic decisions may violate higher laws. Rousseau very provocatively suggests, on the contrary, that democratic decisions – he calls such decisions an expression of the "general will" – can never be mistaken: "The general will is always right, but the judgment that guides it is not always enlightened."[33] He means that if a decision is genuinely democratic, there are no legitimate external standards with which to criticize it. It is possible that people are mistaken about the best way to achieve the goods they desire, so it is possible they will pursue foolish policies or design their laws poorly in regard to the goals they profess, and even their goals may prove less satisfactory than they hope. This is different, however, from suggesting that democratically designed laws could violate some external standards of morality. At best, they might not live up to their own assumed values or goals. For Rousseau, the democratic process gives legitimacy to law. This process alone is what uncovers the public good.

As for Thoreau's claim that voting is a kind of gambling, Rousseau suggests, on the contrary, that voting is the process through which we discover the will of the group. There is "but one law," he argues, "that by its nature requires unanimous consent. This is the social compact."[34] Once the political community is established, we can assume that all who participate agree to abide by the majority decisions of all votes. "Aside from this primitive contract, the vote of the majority always obligates all the others. This is a consequence of the contract itself."[35] Rousseau's language, again, is provocative:

> The citizen consents to all the laws, even to those that pass in spite of his opposition, and even to those that punish him when he dares violate any of them. ... When a law is proposed in the people's assembly, what is asked of them is not precisely whether they approve or reject, but whether or not it conforms to the general will that is theirs. Each man, in giving his vote, states his opinion on this matter, and the declaration of the general will is drawn from the counting of votes. When, therefore, the opinion contrary to mine prevails, this

proves merely that I was in error, and that what I took to be the
general will was not so.[36]

Rousseau has in mind the idea that all those who participate can
be thought to have agreed, beforehand, to the outcome of all
votes – even if they vote in the minority. When we are voting,
we are giving our best individual judgment about what would be
best for the group. The final judgment, however, is agreed before
the vote to be determined by majority rule. So, paradoxically,
minorities are bound to the majority decisions just as strongly as if
they had voted the opposite way. Participation in the voting process indicates willingness to both express one's opinion and to view
the outcome of the vote as a final expression of your own will.

This is a difficult point to understand, particularly if one is
sympathetic to Thoreau's perspective. Submitting to a majority
decision contrary to your own vote may (at least in some cases) grow
from the recognition of the fairness of an electoral process, we might
think, and a virtuous acceptance of the decision for the sake of peace
and political stability. But why should we believe that the majority
vote we opposed has actually declared our own will? Remember that
Rousseau rejects the idea that there is a correct answer to political
questions, considered from any perspective other than that of a fair
political process. So, we have no grounds upon which to object to
the outcome of a vote from some external or philosophical principle. All that makes a law legitimate is that it expresses the will
of the group, and the group has determined (by the original social
compact) that the way to discover the will of the group is by
majority will. So, once the vote is taken, it expresses the view not
just of the winning majority, but also of the group as a whole.
Something like this seems to be what Rousseau has in mind with
his provocative and paradoxical comments.

We have only touched on a number of claims in Rousseau's
complex and difficult political theory. Given the prominent role of
representation in U.S. politics, to speak nothing of the enslavement
and disenfranchisement of huge numbers of African Americans,
we can be certain that Rousseau would not have argued that
Thoreau was rebelling against a genuinely democratic political
order. A significant element of Thoreau's objection to the American

political order, however, was precisely on the grounds that it *was* democratic and that democracy threatened and potentially degraded his moral autonomy. The challenge of Rousseau (and of much democratic theory) to Thoreau's position, however, lies in the suggestion that the problem in antebellum U.S. politics was an insufficiency rather than a surplus of democracy. Majority rule is not the threat to our freedom so much as is the inability of so many inhabitants of the American republic to participate meaningfully in the democratic process. The democratic challenge to Thoreau is less about the appeal to timeless moral principles than it is about promoting political processes that will fully and fairly integrate the widest number of voices into the civic conversation about law and public policy. The democrat deeply distrusts Thoreau's appeal to principles that override the decisions of free men and women. Thoreau, in contrast, distrusts any attempt to unleash even the most democratic political process; for him, our obligation is to look not only for what we will or wish, but also for what is right and morally necessary.

## THE MORALITY OF POLITICAL ACTION

> This people must cease to hold slaves, and to make war on Mexico, though it cost them their existence as a people.
>
> *Civil Disobedience*, paragraph 9

In *The Prince*, Niccolo Machiavelli's famous (some would say infamous) little book, one of the remarkable stories concerns Cesare Borgia, called by his followers Duke Valentino. This particular story, Machiavelli tells us, is "worthy of special note, and of imitation by others," so he refuses to "pass lightly over it." Machiavelli's narrative is worth considering at length:

> When the duke took over the Romagna, he found it had been controlled by impotent masters, who instead of ruling their subjects had plundered them, and had given them more reason for strife than unity, so that the whole province was full of robbers, feuds, and lawlessness of every description. To establish peace and reduce the land to obedience, he decided good government was needed; and he named Messer Remirro

de Orco, a cruel and vigorous man, to whom he gave absolute powers. In short order this man pacified and unified the whole district, winning thereby great renown. But then the duke decided such excessive authority was no longer necessary, and feared it might become odious; so he set up a civil court in the middle of the province, with an excellent judge and a representative from each city. And because he knew that the recent harshness had generated some hatred, in order to clear the minds of the people and gain them over to his cause completely, he determined to make plain that whatever cruelty had occurred had come, not from him, but from the brutal character of the minister. Taking a proper occasion, therefore, he had him placed on the public square of Cesena one morning, in two pieces, with a piece of wood beside him and a bloody knife. The ferocity of this scene left the people at once stunned and satisfied.[37]

In some ways, this is obviously an appalling story. Borgia appoints a "cruel and vigorous man" to do his dirty work, which is successfully accomplished. Orco's reward is to be (literally!) cut in half, both because of his growing power (a possible challenge to Borgia's authority) and because of the cruelty that has caused many to hate the new regime. Borgia successfully deflects criticism from himself by putting Orco on trial for doing what in truth he had been asked to do. Prior to judgment he is murdered and displayed to the citizens, both to satisfy and intimidate them. The dirty work gets done, and Borgia has found his "fall guy." Machiavelli tells the story with such gusto precisely because he knows there is plenty of morally alarming material here to catch our attention.

Once he has received our attention, however, Machiavelli is clear: he thinks there is an important and positive message to be gleaned from Borgia's example. The Romagna, we must not forget, was poorly governed. In fact, Machiavelli equates the "impotence" of the previous rulers with tyranny – their desire to plunder, rather than properly govern, the citizens. This bad government leads to terrible disorder, lawlessness, and criminality. Borgia's decision to give the region good government requires both vigor and cruelty; good government, he is suggesting, can only be established out of political disorder by skillfully deploying violence and intimidation. Machiavelli uses this story as an example of cruelty well used, since it leads to the creation of civic peace and political order. Borgia uses hypocrisy, deceit, and brutality, but he does so in order to build a new political environment with obvious and significant advantages over the previous condition. Machiavelli explains elsewhere in *The Prince* that anyone intending to establish a new regime is engaged in a perilous and uncertain business: "it is worth noting that nothing is harder to manage, more risky in the undertaking, or more doubtful of success than to set up as the introducer of a new order."[38] In fact, "new orders" can only be established and maintained if a prince is willing to use evil means. Machiavelli refuses to sugar-coat this. We live in a world populated with bad people, and to succeed in establishing good government, princes "must learn how not to be good, and use that knowledge, or refrain from using it, as necessity requires."[39] One must not use cruelty indiscriminately. One must instead be prudent. How do we know if a prince has used cruelty well? Presumably by the establishment of the kind of good government Machiavelli implies in his discussion of Borgia and Orco. "In the actions of all men, and especially of princes who are not subject to a court of appeal, we must always look to the end."[40] The means used by a prince, even evil means, can only be evaluated in the final analysis by their relationship to the ends achieved.

Machiavelli's moral perspective, of course, could not be further from Thoreau's. When Thoreau argues that the United States must "cease to hold slaves, and to make war on Mexico, though it cost them their existence as a people" (paragraph 9), he is suggesting that moral principle is known not by its outcomes or consequences but, rather, through (and only through) its compatibility with the highest laws. We know that the utilitarianism of thinkers like Paley appalls Thoreau; he believes such consequentialism inevitably leads to self-interested rationalizations, the very opposite of moral integrity. Sometimes, as he says, it is necessary to allow another individual to cling to a plank, even though it may lead to our own drowning (paragraph 9). Doing the right thing may require giving up "our existence as a people." A moral individual acts from principle uncontaminated with concern for outcomes. If the proper moral response to slavery and imperialism could lead to the dissolution of the nation, so be it.

How are we to think about the choice between these two competing ethical stances? Is Machiavelli simply a political opportunist, apologizing for (perhaps even glorifying) brutal power, violence, and political gamesmanship, or is his pragmatic realism the only responsible way to influence political events, in the end, for the good? Is Thoreau a political naïf, more concerned with his own moral purity than with actually doing something meaningful to address the terrible injustices in the world, or is his unbending principle an admirable and necessary response to injustice? Which of these political ethics is more attractive for anyone seriously outraged by political wrongs? Put bluntly, was Thoreau's moral attitude an appropriate response to the crime of slavery, or was a more consequentialist ethic called for?

When we look at the actual history of abolition in the United States, from the growth of the radical abolitionists in the 1830s through the destruction of slavery during and following the Civil War, the moral lesson is far from clear. In one telling, Lincoln and the Republican Party are generally hostile to slavery but committed, above all, to the maintenance of the Constitution and the Union. Their commitment to abolition is tepid and vaguely focused on the distant future. They cannot imagine a post-abolition America that includes black citizens – they support, instead, plans for colonization of former slaves in Africa or elsewhere. Their discomfort with slavery does not necessarily suggest an egalitarian view of human beings, or an explicit rejection of racism. The common implication of such interpretations is that mainstream Republican politicians like Lincoln were pushed, reluctantly and over time, in the moral direction pioneered by radical abolitionists. As historian Manisha Sinha writes, "Far from being naïve religious reformers with no plans for a post-emancipation society, the abolitionist movement championed the idea of an interracial democracy long before the enactment of emancipation."[41] For Sinha and many others, abolitionists (like Thoreau), with their absolutist political ethics, led the way for the rest of American society. They were the visionaries who exerted a moral authority that over time became clear and increasingly powerful. Practical politicians were pulled along, but only grudgingly. The moral heroes, from this perspective, were abolitionists who shared with

Thoreau a deep commitment to uncompromising personal integrity. Eric Foner, one of the most distinguished scholars of nineteenth-century U.S. history, suggests that abolitionists made it possible to imagine a just society that until then had been unimaginable in American society: "their agitation helped to establish the context within which politicians like Lincoln operated."[42] Indeed, Foner concludes that Lincoln's experience during the war led him to "abandon or modify many of his previous beliefs," bringing him into close harmony with the views articulated and defended by abolitionists for a generation.[43] The abolitionists were the moral pioneers who staked out the territory that mainstream politicians like Lincoln would only come to over time.

Historian James Oakes offers a very different reading of events building to the Civil War. He argues that the Republicans (including Lincoln) shared with abolitionists a hatred of slavery but, unlike the abolitionists, had a practical (and ultimately successful) political strategy for actually attacking it. For Republicans, the U.S. Constitution was an anti-slavery document, in which slavery was given only local (not national) status. While recognition of the local reality of slavery was a compromise necessary for the establishment of the Union, an understanding of the Constitution developed as early as the 1830s (along with the growth of abolition generally) suggesting that the Constitution treats slavery as incompatible with its own values (for example, slaves were referred to, pointedly, as "persons"). On this reading, a proper respect for the Constitution required isolating slavery as an anomalous local institution, refusing to respect slavery as a national property right (this view, of course, was exactly the opposite of the Supreme Court's infamous Dred Scott decision of 1857, which established the "property rights" of slaveholders, even when traveling with their slaves in free states). The Republican strategy was to confine slavery within the slave states and hope that eventually, by preventing slavery's spread into the territories and refusing to recognize the right of property in slaves within the national context (in both the territories and the free states), the institution would wither and die.

In Oakes' view, the Southern slave states were exactly right to feel threatened by Lincoln's election and to insist that succession was their only option for protecting the institution of slavery.[44] The doctrine of "freedom national" developed by the Republicans made slavery impossible in the long run – assuming their political success, and the survival of the Union. In Oakes' view, this legal and political strategy ultimately forced the South to choose between submission and succession. It chose the latter, of course, making the Civil War, with its 750,000 dead,[45] the necessary final stage in the terrible history of American slavery. The hero in this account is the Republican Party. Over time, the perfectionist abolitionists were of increasingly marginal political importance. In 1880, Frederick Douglass looked back on the events of the previous half century and noted, "Men are important, but parties are incomparably more important."[46] The implication, of course, was that precisely the kind of political organization, compromise, and strategic action that abolitionists like Thoreau found so corrupt and threatening to personal integrity turned out to be exactly what was required to bring an end to slavery.

Lincoln and the Republican Party were obviously not as cynical and blunt as Machiavelli, but they do represent a significantly more "Machiavellian" position than Thoreau. Responsible political action must be evaluated, from this perspective, as Machiavelli suggests, by the ends attempted and achieved. It is not unusual for significant political successes to require equally significant compromises, strategic behavior, and political organization. We might even argue that such an approach is exactly what we mean when we talk about responsible political action.

This is not the place to settle matters concerning the interpretation of the history of abolition in the United States. It is important to recognize, however, that even if we are more sympathetic to the first than the second reading of the history leading up to the U.S. Civil War, there remains a strong challenge to the perspective we find in *Civil Disobedience*. It may be true that moral absolutists like Thoreau drove mainstream politicians to an abolition position they would not have come to without such pressure. It is also true, however, that once driven in that direction, real political (and then military) action needed to be pursued to finally destroy slavery. Thoreau, however, has little or nothing to say about either the practical or ethical elements of such political work.

Because his political strategy is to altogether withdraw his support from politics, he has little light to shed on the moral qualities of defensible – even necessary – political action.

## CAPITALISM AND ALIENATION

> Absolutely speaking, the more money, the less virtue; for money comes between a man and his objects ...
>
> *Civil Disobedience*, paragraph 23

The year 1848, when *Civil Disobedience* was delivered as a lecture, was the year that also saw the publication of Marx and Engel's *Communist Manifesto*. In many ways, these are radically different documents: Thoreau defends moral individualism while Marx and Engels promote cooperative political action; Thoreau's moral theory was ahistorical, built on the idea of timeless moral truths and realities, while the *Manifesto* develops a theory of history in which ideas (including moral ideals) derive from and reflect contingent historical conditions and social class interests; perhaps most obviously, Marx and Engels were professional revolutionaries, while Thoreau thought of himself primarily as a literary figure drawn, against his intention and will, into the political conflicts of his time. Despite these differences, and regardless of the fact that there is no reason to think Thoreau and Marx were in any way aware of one another, Thoreau shares with Marx a deep distrust of modern capitalism. For both thinkers, industrialism and market economies distort and corrupt the relationship workers have with the conditions under which they labor.

This element of Thoreau's views is only hinted at in *Civil Disobedience*, in his claims about the morally corrupting nature of wealth, but it is well developed in *Walden* and elsewhere in his writings. We saw in Chapter 3 that he scathingly criticizes the American economy, suggesting that the "luxury of one class is counterbalanced by the indigence of another."[47] Even those who are not exploiting others "lead lives of quiet desperation."[48] As the economy develops, it becomes increasingly technologically sophisticated, generates vast quantities of new wealth, and becomes a monster seemingly beyond human control: we saw earlier his fear that men "have become the tools of their tools."[49] We find ourselves baffled, disoriented, and corrupted by this modern economy.

> Most men, even in this comparatively free country, through mere ignorance and mistake, are so occupied with the factitious cares and superfluously course labors of life that its finer fruits cannot be plucked by them. Their fingers, from excessive toil, are too clumsy and tremble too much for that. Actually, the laboring man has not leisure for a true integrity day by day; he cannot afford to sustain the manliest relations to men; his labor would be depreciated in the market. He has not time to be any thing but a machine.[50]

The modern economy, Thoreau suggests, dehumanizes the worker, even while producing radical inequality and significant human unhappiness.

This economic critique shares a great deal with Marx's analysis of capitalist economic relationships. In the *Economic and Philosophical Manuscripts of 1844*, Marx, like Thoreau, suggests that capitalist economic relationships dehumanize workers and turn the productive process into a form of exploitation and disorientation. Workers, Marx writes, become "alienated" in a number of ways. Labor, which is potentially an individual's most basic creative power, becomes something separate from the worker, something sold on the market to the capitalist who comes to control it. As such, one's own labor is lost as a source of personal self-expression and satisfaction:

> labour is *external* to the worker, i.e., it does not belong to his essential being; ... in his work, therefore, he does not affirm himself but denies himself, does not feel content but unhappy, does not develop freely his physical and mental energy but mortifies his body and ruins his mind.[51]

Under ideal conditions, Marx seems to suggest, we could experience our own capacities for work as liberating, as expressions of our greatest capacities and most admirable personality. When we sell our labor to a capitalist, however, we lose control of these capacities. Instead of enjoying the exercise of our powers, we experience work as drudgery and something to be avoided.

Marx's analysis of "estranged labor" suggests that workers in a capitalist economy become alienated not only from their own capacities for creative work, but also from the products they manufacture, as well as from their own human nature and the people they live with and around. The objects workers produce are manufactured with tools and machinery owned by the capitalist, and the manufactured product is owned not by those who make it but by the capitalist who has hired the worker for a wage. This process of wage labor therefore separates the worker from control of his own labor, the products of his labor, and his own nature as a creative creature. Because she must compete with other workers for jobs, and submit to the authority of the capitalist, she becomes divided from other people. The process Marx describes is one in which the worker is exploited, confused, isolated, and degraded as an object to be deployed in this productive system without concern for her or his fundamental humanity.

The details of Thoreau's and Marx's critique of work in a capitalist economy are not exactly the same, of course. They draw on quite different literary and philosophical traditions to develop their ideas. It is nonetheless remarkable to see the degree to which both, within a few years of one another, were thinking about the modern economy as a kind of deformation of human experience. For both, the central facts of this economic system include individual confusion and unhappiness, systemic inequality, and a lack of freedom. Capitalist economies are productive to an unprecedented degree, but for both Thoreau and Marx, this productivity comes at the cost of human freedom and happiness.

Despite the similarity of their critiques, however, Marx and Thoreau come to very different conclusions about how to address the problems created by capitalist economies. Marx became the greatest theorist of Communist revolution, committed to cooperative revolutionary activity by the industrial working class. Thoreau, in contrast, counseled personal reform: "Simplicity, simplicity, simplicity! I say, let your affairs be as two or three, and not a hundred or a thousand."[52] For Marx, only with the destruction of private property, and thereby the elimination of the bourgeoisie or capitalist class, will the proletariat be able to create a Communist society. This, for Marx, constituted winning the "battle of democracy," since the vast majority of people, the immediate economic producers, would now be in a position to organize and administer their own society without an exploitative social class preventing them from controlling their own labor. Thoreau, in contrast, suggests that by choosing to live simply and independently, individuals can reclaim their freedom: "In short, I am convinced, both by faith and experience, that to maintain one's self on this earth is not a hardship but a pastime, if we will live simply and wisely."[53] Marx's vision was political, cooperative, and aimed toward a future built upon the full development, and then the destruction of, capitalist society. Thoreau's vision was individualistic, stressed the degree to which a freer life was immediately available to all who would see it, and required rejecting the seductions of the modern division of labor and the promises of great wealth in favor of simpler forms of self-sufficiency.

Yet despite their very different proposals for liberating individuals from what they take to be the pathologies of capitalist economics, Thoreau shares with Marx one more significant idea. When Thoreau comments, in the opening paragraph of *Civil Disobedience*, that government "is best but an expedient" (paragraph 1), he seems to be suggesting that an ideal government would be a neutral or nonpartisan form of public administration. Most governments today are "inexpedient," and all known governments are at least sometimes inexpedient. By this, Thoreau means that instead of delivering services equitably and without bias, powerful individuals, groups, or even majorities manipulate governments for the sake of their narrow interests. Instead of being "only the mode which the people have chosen to execute their will," the government "is equally liable to be abused and perverted before the people can act through it" (paragraph 1). Throughout the essay, Thoreau continually accuses political authority of being corrupt precisely because it has shaped political power to serve narrow or partial interests. Just government serves the public as a whole. The American government has been corrupted by slavery and the pursuit of wealth to such a degree that it fails to be the "better government" Thoreau demands (paragraph 3).

Marx shares with Thoreau a contempt for political power used to pursue partial interests. In the *Communist Manifesto* he writes, "The executive of the modern State is but a committee for managing the common affairs of the whole bourgeoisie."[54] In fact, the term politics always indicates, for Marx, what Thoreau calls "inexpedient" politics; that is, politics corrupted by social class interests. For Marx, there is no politics exempt from such corruption: "Political power, properly so called, is merely the organized power of one class for oppressing another."[55] Because capitalist society is shaped by social class interests and conflicts (as are all historical forms of society), government and politics always reflect the interests of the ruling class.

A Communist revolution, however, promises an unprecedented departure from this pattern. For the first time in history, the revolutionary class is made up of the vast majority of people, and this class need not exploit any other class in order to pursue its interests. With the abolition of private property, the bourgeoisie disappears, leaving only the proletariat. Since there is only one social class, society loses its class character; social class struggle disappears. At this point, Marx suggests, politics dissolves as well: "When, in the course of human development, class distinctions have disappeared, and all production has been concentrated in the hands of a vast association of the whole nation, the public power will lose its political character."[56] This does not mean that there is no "public power" anymore. The working class will still need to organize itself for the purposes of planning, administration, and social coordination – presumably it will need public authorities to build roads and schools and sewers, to say nothing of managing economic life more generally. But Marx believes that such organization will no longer have a "political" character since it will aim to serve the good of the whole rather than some partial class interest. The idea seems to be that since there are no longer social class interests in conflict with one another, there is no longer any important force to distort and corrupt the "public power."

What Marx shares with Thoreau is a vision of politics in which particular or partial interests have dissolved and government serves and respects the interests of each individual. This is a vision of a society in which politics is no longer an arena in which conflicting interests compete for political power and, if forced by constitutional and institutional arrangements, need to compromise with one another. In *Federalist 10*, James Madison defended the proposed U.S. Constitution, then being debated for ratification, on the grounds that it allowed for the freedom of factions, or interests, to form, yet controlled these factions through the institutions of federalism and the division of power between the executive, legislative, and judicial branches of government. Free government, for Madison, requires an acceptance of "faction" as a fact of life in free societies. Constitutional mechanisms are designed to tame and control, rather than eliminate, these conflicting interests. For Marx, such a constitution could never be anything other than a façade for class rule. For Thoreau, factional competition always represents a kind of political (and moral) corruption. For both, just governance may only be found in a society in which competing interests have either dissolved (Marx) or individuals have developed the moral character to transcend them (Thoreau). While Marx and Thoreau share a powerful set of insights into the confusion and unhappiness produced by capitalist economies, they also share a utopian conception of political authority. We might even say that in the final analysis Thoreau and Marx share an apolitical, seemingly technocratic, conception of just government.

## NATURE

> When I was let out the next morning, I proceeded to finish my errand, and having put on my mended shoe, joined a huckleberry party, who were impatient to put themselves under my conduct; and in half an hour, – for the horse was soon tackled, – was in the midst of a huckleberry field, on one of our highest hills, two miles off, and then the State was nowhere to be seen.
>
> *Civil Disobedience*, paragraph 34

We have seen in this chapter that Thoreau draws on conventional themes and ideas in political theory – from concerns about consent, the morality of political action, the nature and obligations of democracy and political authority more generally, to claims about the nature of freedom and independence in a modern capitalist economy – in order to develop his argument in *Civil Disobedience*. In all these cases, Thoreau participates in important ongoing conversations about significant philosophical issues. Regarding these themes, however, Thoreau does not break significantly new ground or contribute a new and widely influential conceptual move that redefines or significantly reshapes the form these debates would take in the wake of his writings.

There is a hint, and only a hint, in *Civil Disobedience*, however, of the one set of ideas around which Thoreau would become one of the most influential American figures. In Chapter 3 we noted that the huckleberry party Thoreau joins after being released from jail represents for him an alternative America to that which he has been confronting over slavery, imperialism, and taxes. He tells us very little in this essay about this alternative world, but the hints are clear: he finds in this gathering outside of Concord village a form of association more free and neighborly, more just and consensual, than that found in our conventional political and economic life.

Recall that in *Civil Disobedience* Thoreau claims: "Statesmen and legislators, standing so completely within the institution, never distinctly and nakedly behold it. They speak of moving society, but have no resting-place without it" (paragraph 42). His thought is that serious moral reflection requires us to find a way to get outside our conventional ways of thinking, our common sense, beyond the traditions and habits that shape our daily lives. If we are to "nakedly behold," that is, truly understand and evaluate, our society and its institutions, we need a way of claiming some moral independence from their assumptions and prejudices. Without such independence, we have no way to evaluate the moral qualities of the status quo; we are left with no possible alternative to our society with its values and practices and commitments. With no imaginable alternatives, no alternative perspective to draw on, the world as it currently presents itself assumes an incontestable quality. What *is* comes to look like what *must be*.

We know that in *Walden* (and many of his essays) Thoreau develops the idea hinted at in *Civil Disobedience*, the idea that nature allows us the kind of moral distance we need for living morally serious lives. Walden Pond is within easy walking distance of Concord village, and it was not even close to being untouched wilderness in Thoreau's lifetime; a railroad ran past one end of the pond and Thoreau's account makes clear that loggers, fishermen, ice harvesters, and many other visitors frequented the area. Nonetheless, it was far enough from the village to represent, for Thoreau, a kind of moral distance from daily life. It was just far enough from the village to offer the opportunity to live in much closer contact with the natural world, even while maintaining a connection to and concern for social and political life.

In an opening passage of *Walden*, as we have mentioned before, Thoreau claims that the "mass of men live lives of quiet desperation."[57] Thoreau offers his own experiences as reason to hope that all people might overcome this desperation and unhappiness. Such success, however, requires that we overcome the narrowness of our own sense of possibility, our conventional beliefs about what the options for our lives really are. "Public opinion is a weak tyrant compared with our own private opinion."[58] Remember that the central metaphor in *Walden* is of awakening, which symbolizes for Thoreau the reflection and self-consciousness required for overcoming this tyrannical "private opinion." Thoreau famously says, "I do not propose to write an ode to dejection, but to brag as lustily as chanticleer in the morning, standing on his roost, if only to wake my neighbors up."[59] This project is moral in the deepest sense of the word: it aims to teach us how to properly live and enjoy our lives. "Morning is when I am awake and there is a dawn in me. Moral reform is the effort to throw off sleep. ... I have never yet met a man who was quite awake. How could I have looked him in the face?"[60] *Walden* chronicles a year at Walden Pond (for the sake of literary simplicity, Thoreau collapses his own stay of more than two years into one annual cycle). It builds to the "awakening" of Walden in the spring, the thawing of the pond and renewal of life. The final sentences of the book are: "Only that day dawns to which we are awake. There is more day to dawn. The sun is but a morning star."[61] Thoreau is suggesting that the cycle of the seasons can inspire moral renewal in our lives if we only learn to pay appropriate attention.

This project of learning to be awake, of being fully alive, is the project of being free and responsible – of becoming, in fact, the kind of person capable of "resisting civil government." Thoreau developed impressive scientific habits of observation and record keeping over the course of his career, but he was above all a poet and philosopher. He believed that if we learn to closely observe and experience nature, as he illustrates for us in *Walden* and other writings, we learn a kind of modesty and simplicity, our imaginations are stimulated, and we become aware of a much wider world than our narrow experiences and concerns commonly cause us to become preoccupied with.

> The earth is not a mere fragment of dead history, stratum upon stratum like the leaves of a book, to be studied by geologists and antiquaries chiefly, but living poetry like the leaves of a tree, which precede flowers and fruit, – not a fossil earth, but a living earth; compared with whose great central life all animal and vegetable life is merely parasitic.[62]

In passages like this, we see Thoreau encouraging us to be provoked by the poetry he believes we can find in nature. We can be the "flowers and fruit" that the earth brings forth if we learn to take our cues from nature rather than social convention. To become fully human, we must recognize that we are merely a part of the greater natural environment. To learn this is both humbling and inspiring. "In proportion as he simplifies his life, the laws of the universe will appear less complex, and solitude will not be solitude, nor poverty poverty, nor weakness weakness."[63] The simplicity encouraged by nature actually stimulates the independence that allows us to be free and responsible individuals. Something along these lines is what he has in mind when he suggests, "Our village life would stagnate if it were not for the unexplored forests and meadows which surround it. We need the tonic of wildness."[64]

Thoreau's respect for nature and his belief that attending more to the natural world can offer us moral and not merely material benefits have helped make him a central figure in the modern environmental movement. As a keen observer of the natural environment, he is deeply aware of the human dependence and impact on nature. He also has a strong sense of the intrinsic moral value of other living things and natural processes. Above all, he has an extraordinary sense of the moral and aesthetic value of nature, of the degree to which sensitivity to nature can positively shape our characters, dispositions, values, and relationships. He is both a scientist and a poet-philosopher. Modern environmental thinkers have drawn on both of these dispositions to defend environmental sensibilities, perspectives, and values.

It is impossible to provide a history of modern environmentalism here, but it is worth noting that while this is a profoundly varied, complex, and diverse movement, there are two widely recognizable elements of great importance. Perhaps most importantly, we find environmentalism growing out of the science of ecology and the alarm many scientists have felt (and continue to feel) about the human impact on the environment. Early environmental heroes in the United States, for example, were often biologists like Rachel Carson and Paul Ehrlich: Carson's *Silent Spring*, published in 1962, raised serious concerns about modern chemical pesticides such as DDT, helping to pave the way for a growing wave of concern about environmental pollution; Ehrlich's *Population Bomb* appeared a few years later, in 1968, and questioned the earth's capacity to feed a dramatically growing human population. To this day, as we see most importantly with contemporary concerns about climate change and global warming, a prominent (indeed, probably the most prominent) form of environmentalism grows from scientific concern about the human impact on the environment, how this threatens our own health and well-being, and how it harms other elements of the natural world.

Although Thoreau's legacy as a naturalist contributes modestly to this dominant strain of contemporary environmentalism, his greatest contribution is to another important, if somewhat less prominent, tradition of environmental thought. We have seen that Thoreau's interest in nature is ultimately moral. He promoted the view that lives lived modestly and in close contact with the natural world are valuable not, primarily, because they produced less ecological stress on nature, but because such lives (he believes) are more satisfying and free. His claim is that if we take seriously the ideas of liberty and personal responsibility, we must resist the temptations of ever-increasing wealth. We have seen (in Chapter 3) that he comments in *Walden* that his "greatest skill has been to want but little."[65] Thoreau's fear was that American society was becoming frantically preoccupied with the endless pursuit of wealth and luxury. This preoccupation produced growing interdependency, dissatisfaction, overwork, and too little cultivation of the arts of reflection. Even more grotesquely, it produced the kind of greed and thoughtlessness that rationalized an acceptance of slavery and the willingness to brutally attack our neighbors for frankly selfish gain. If we could learn to be satisfied with less, we could live more independently, more happily, more self-consciously, and more justly. Political crimes growing from the lust for wealth and power would become unnecessary, even unthinkable. For Thoreau, nature held the key to a more humane, free, equitable, and neighborly life. He notes that he went to live at Walden Pond on July 4;[66] he makes clear, in this way, that his project of learning to live closer to nature is a project aimed at fulfilling what he takes to be the true promise of American independence.

Here we find Thoreau's most lasting legacy and ongoing influence as a political thinker. Other great environmental writers, from Aldo Leopold in the first half of the twentieth century to Bill McKibben in the first half of the twenty-first, follow Thoreau in important ways. They, too, promote a close attention to the natural world as well as the belief that such attention can lead not only to a safer world, but to a simpler, more satisfying, and ultimately more democratic human experience. Writers ranging from economist E. F. Schumacher (who argues that "small is beautiful") to food writer Michael Pollan (who promotes local food systems) continue to promote small-scale, locally based industry and agriculture on the grounds both of health and satisfaction. These writers and many more, from organic farmers to alternative energy and local economy advocates, continue in the tradition pioneered, at least in the American vernacular, by Thoreau. Concerns about health and safety are present in this tradition, but they are subordinate to matters of human justice and fulfillment. For these environmentalists, as for Thoreau, life lived more closely with nature is a life more satisfying, responsible, and just than lives committed to ever-increasing wealth and artificiality.

Even though this argument is not fully developed in *Civil Disobedience*, the reference to the huckleberry party in paragraph 34 reminds us that Thoreau's commitment to nature had moral and political elements we must not ignore. The animating question of *Civil Disobedience* is, how do we become the kind of people capable of resisting terrible injustice? The answer, in part, relies on the ways in which Thoreau believes nature can help us morally reorient ourselves and discover the kind of strength and independence required for such resistance. Thoreau will always be a central figure for anyone exploring the political traditions growing out of such claims.

## NOTES

1 Hugo Adam Bedau, ed., *Civil Disobedience* (Indianapolis, IN: Pegasus, 1969), p. 15.

2 Ibid., p. 18.

3 Ibid.

4 Ibid., p. 52.

5 Henry David Thoreau, *A Week on the Concord and Merrimack Rivers; Walden, or, Life in the Woods; The Maine Woods; Cape Cod* (NY: Library of America, 1985), p. 445.

6 Sophocles, *Theban Plays* (NY: Penguin, 1982), pp. 128, 140.

7 Ibid., p. 127.

8 Ibid., p. 151.

9 Ibid., p. 148.

10 Ibid., p. 149.

11 Ibid., p. 154.

12 Walter Harding, *The Days of Henry Thoreau* (NY: Alfred A. Knopf, 1966), pp. 4, 6.

13 John Locke, *Second Treatise of Government* (Indianapolis, IN and Cambridge: Hackett, 1980), p. 63.

14 Ibid., pp. 63–64.

15 Ibid., p. 64.

16 Ibid.

17 David Hume, *Of the Original Contract*, 1748. Available at: www.constitution. org/dh/origcont.htm (accessed June 2014).

18 Plato, *Last Days of Socrates* (Baltimore, MD: Penguin, 1969), p. 47.

19 Ibid., p. 90.

20 Ibid.

21 Ibid., p. 61.

22 Ibid., p. 64.

23 Robert Paul Wolff, *In Defense of Anarchism* (NY: Harper and Row, 1976), pp. 71–72.

24 Richard Rorty, *Achieving Our Country* (Cambridge, MA: Harvard University Press, 1998), p. 16.

25 Ibid., p. 20.

26 Ibid., p. 22.

27 Ibid., p. 18.

28 Jean-Jacques Rousseau, *Basic Political Writings* (Indianapolis, IN and Cambridge: Hackett, 1987), p. 150.

29  Ibid., p. 151.
30  Ibid.
31  Ibid., p. 141.
32  Ibid., p. 148.
33  Ibid., p. 162.
34  Ibid., p. 205.
35  Ibid., p. 206.
36  Ibid.
37  Niccolo Machiavelli, *The Prince* (NY and London: W. W. Norton, 1977), p. 21.
38  Ibid., p. 17.
39  Ibid., p. 42.
40  Ibid., p. 49.
41  Manisha Sinha, "Did the Abolitionists Cause the Civil War?," in Andrew Delbanco, *The Abolitionist Imagination* (Cambridge, MA: Harvard University Press, 2012), p. 95.
42  Eric Foner, *The Fiery Trial: Abraham Lincoln and American Slavery* (NY: W. W. Norton, 2010), p. xix.
43  Ibid., p. 249.
44  James Oakes, *Freedom National* (NY: W. W. Norton, 2013), p. xii.
45  This is Oakes' estimate. Ibid, p. xiv.
46  Ibid., p. xix.
47  Thoreau, *A Week, etc.*, p. 350.
48  Ibid., p. 329.
49  Ibid., p. 352.
50  Ibid., p. 327.
51  Karl Marx and Friedrich Engels, *The Marx-Engels Reader*, Robert Tucker, ed., (NY and London: W. W. Norton, 1978), p. 74.
52  Thoreau, *A Week, etc.*, p. 395.
53  Ibid., p. 378.
54  Marx, *Marx-Engels Reader*, p. 475.
55  Ibid., p. 490.
56  Ibid.
57  Thoreau, *A Week, etc.*, p. 329.
58  Ibid., p. 328.
59  Ibid., p. 389.
60  Ibid., p. 394.
61  Ibid., p. 587.
62  Ibid., p. 568.
63  Ibid., p. 580.
64  Ibid., p. 575.
65  Ibid., p. 377.
66  Ibid., p. 358.

# 6

---

# POSTSCRIPT

In the last chapter we mentioned that in *The Apology*, Plato's account of Socrates' speech at his trial, Socrates brags about not participating in public life. He claims, in fact, that for a person committed to the truth above all else, participation in democratic politics is a dangerous proposition.

> No man on earth who conscientiously opposes either you or any other organized democracy ... can possibly escape with his life. The true champion of justice, if he intends to survive even for a short time, must necessarily confine himself to private life and leave politics alone.[1]

So Socrates has avoided not only lawsuits and the courts (he mentions that this trial constitutes his first appearance in an Athenian court, at age 70),[2] but also all the conventional forms of democratic participation. Yet he also suggests, much as Thoreau does in *Civil Disobedience*, that despite his withdrawal from conventional political life, his private philosophical pursuits have paradoxically allowed him to be the best citizen of his city. While he has clearly angered many fellow citizens, this anger blinds others to the service he provides the political community:

> it is my belief that no greater good has ever befallen you in this city
> than my service to my God; for I spend all my time going about trying
> to persuade you, young and old, to make your first and chief concern
> not for your bodies nor for your possessions, but for the highest
> welfare of your souls.[3]

Athens, Socrates suggests, is like a lazy horse that needs to be roused, and he is like "some stinging fly" who provides this service.[4] He seems annoying, of course, since he insists on calling into question so much of what his neighbors take for granted. The annoyance is necessary, however, if the horse is to be aroused from its (moral) lethargy. Socrates is far from being a serious threat or danger to the community. The anger unleashed at him, eventually resulting in his conviction and execution, is a wild overreaction to whatever discomfort he has caused by provoking Athenian citizens to give greater critical scrutiny to their opinions, prejudices, and conventional ways of living. From Socrates' perspective, most people become preoccupied with matters (having to do with the body and with possessions) that should properly be subordinate to higher goods (the welfare of our souls). They also take offense when accused of this, even though in calmer moments many would be sympathetic to the claim that health and wealth, while good and important things, are not the greatest goods a person should cultivate (such as, for example, love, a commitment to the truth, and a willingness to sacrifice for others).

Similar themes appear in striking force in Thoreau's writings. In 1850, a year after the publication of *Resistance to Civil Government*, Thoreau wrote in his *Journal*, "I do not think much of the actual. It is something which we have long since done with. It is a sort of vomit in which the unclean love to wallow."[5] This is a strong and even ugly statement, but it gives us insight into the way Thoreau thought about the world around him and his relationship to it. Thoreau's transcendentalist roots taught him that the world we experience with our senses is, in itself, illusory. It is changeable and impermanent; as soon as we think we know it, it changes, evolves, develops in new and unpredictable ways. In the words of the great novelist Philip Roth, this is "a place where nothing keeps its promise and everything is perishable."[6] For Thoreau, this is the world of "the actual," and it is a world of flux and instability. Individuals are born, grow, age, and die. History crashes in on private lives, upsetting them in terrible and unforeseen ways. Nothing is fixed and nothing is permanent save change itself. In his dark comment, Thoreau expresses his contempt for the world of experience and the people who are (in his view) foolish enough to "wallow" in it, who are mistakenly committed to the idea that such a world constitutes reality itself. People like this live lives shaped primarily by concern with jobs, business, and the pleasures of the body, with what Thoreau sometimes refers to as "affairs." These individuals are equally prone to being obsessed with safety, with sensual goods and the pleasures these bring, and with the pain and fear and death that are the inevitable flip side of the life and pleasures of the body. Lives lived in "the actual" are as unfixed and changeable as the goods to which they are committed. A character from a recent novel broods rather depressingly on this point: "For humans – trapped in biology – there was no mercy: we lived a while, we fussed around for a bit and died, we rotted in the ground like garbage. Time destroyed us all soon enough."[7] Thoreau's comment is equally depressing, suggesting that he feels nothing but disgust and contempt for this dimension of life, which he equates with filth.

What is the alternative to a life lived in "the actual"? During the period in which Thoreau wrote the above comment he reflects repeatedly on this matter. He notes that "You might say of a philosopher that he was in this world as a spectator."[8] Again, he writes, "The philosopher contemplates human affairs as calmly and from as great a remoteness as he does natural phenomena."[9] It is the reality behind the changeable, which he believes is permanent and universal, that interests the philosopher. From this perspective, the world of social and political life takes on a very different cast from that composed of men and women living in "the actual": "To the philosopher all sects, all nations, are alike."[10] The philosopher, that is, sees the patterns and universal truths that underlie all the superficial differences in the experienced world. Pursuing thoughts along these lines, Thoreau writes of his own life as being significantly different from those lived by his neighbors. Unlike them, he is committed to understanding not the world of the actual but the deeper reality to which nature points. We have seen that the transcendentalists believed that the changeable world actually directs us to a world of timeless reality, of law, of permanence. In Emerson's language, nature is "emblematic," a metaphor for the stable and permanent truths accessible to the human mind.[11] Nature leads us to this deeper reality, of which Thoreau's "actual" is a mere shadow.

It is in this spirit that Thoreau sets himself apart from his fellows:

> We are enabled to criticize others only when we are different from, and in a given particular superior to, them ourselves. By our aloofness from men and their affairs we are enabled to overlook and criticize them. There are but few men who stand on the hills by the roadside. I am sane only when I have risen above my common sense, when I do not take the foolish view of things which is commonly taken, when I do not live for the low ends for which men commonly live. Wisdom is not common. To what purposes have I senses, if I am thus absorbed in affairs? My pulse must beat with Nature.[12]

Common sense is both shaped and misled by the chaos of daily experiences; philosophy steps away and finds deeper truths. In *Life Without Principle*, Thoreau advises: "Read not the Times. Read the Eternities. Conventionalities are at length as bad as impurities."[13] When we live in the actual, we come to believe that the events in the newspapers represent the whole of what there is to know and care for. We come to think of our affairs as the only matters to be attended to. "Conventionalities" mislead and direct us away from the deeper laws and truths that constitute not the daily flux of the world, but "the Eternities." The degree to which we find ourselves misled in this way is the degree to which we fail to understand and commit ourselves to the most important elements of human life.

There are other times in the *Journal* when Thoreau speaks of "the poet" rather than "the philosopher." "The true poet," he writes in 1854, "will ever live aloof from society, wild to it, as the finest singer is the woodthrush, a forest bird."[14] Three years later, he comments: "Is not the poet bound to write his own biography? Is there any other work for him but a good journal? We do not wish to know how his imaginary hero, but how he, the actual hero, lived from day to day."[15] Not only does Thoreau's ideal require that he set himself apart from other people; the record of this life apart becomes the subject for his pen. Again we see Thoreau's aspiration, his sense that his life has heroic qualities to the degree that he records a life most people ignore or even fail to imagine. If it is true that "All men sympathize by their lower natures; the few, only, by their higher,"[16] the task for the philosopher or poet, as he sees it, is to bring the higher potentials to our attention. Thoreau's work as a writer is to demonstrate that a human life can be practically engaged with a reality above and beyond the world of affairs:

> My work is writing, and I do not hesitate, though I know that no subject is too trivial for me, tried by ordinary standards; for, ye fools, the theme is nothing, the life is everything. All that interests the reader is the depth and intensity of the life excited.[17]

Indeed, for Thoreau the writer (as he aspires to be) is the most heroic human figure. "The thinker, he who is serene and self-possessed, is the brave, not the desperate soldier."[18] "There is no more Herculean task than to think a thought about this life and then get it expressed."[19]

Holding these views places Thoreau in an idealist philosophical tradition with roots reaching back to Socrates and Plato. In order to cultivate the true and the timeless, philosophers (or, perhaps in Thoreau's terms, "poets") step away from the bustle and concerns of daily affairs to cultivate an understanding of the reality underlying this experience. This is not a choice made by many; indeed, it is not a choice sympathized with by many. To most people, such philosophers and poets look like impractical dreamers. Even worse, they look arrogant and snobby. At its worst, as in the case of Socrates, they look as though they represent significant threats to democracy itself. The passages from the *Journal* we have looked at above confirm our suspicions that Thoreau's philosophical and artistic views tempt him with a genuine feeling of contempt for others. He is blunt about his own feeling of superiority. After all, he contemplates the eternities while his neighbors are absorbed with the newspaper. There are good reasons for Thoreau to be suspicious of the wisdom of public opinion, and for us to be sympathetic with Thoreau's project of trying to get beyond the platitudes and biases of common sense. There are also good reasons to be wary of his alienated feeling of self-confidence and moral superiority, and to understand why his neighbors (or his readers) may distrust his moral indignation and eccentricity.

Thoreau was well aware that the pursuit of truth could produce its own vices. Most common among these are self-righteousness and an attitude of intellectual imperiousness. During the same period when he expresses such contempt for others, he also writes more critically of the dangers of self-righteousness. We have noted the observation in his *Journal* (in 1852) that "My countrymen are to me foreigners."[20] He also writes (1851), however, "Let us not have a rabid virtue that will be revenged on society."[21] He appears to hope; that is, not to allow his own desire to get beyond "the actual" to turn him into a potential tyrant toward the many. In *A Week on the Concord and Merrimack Rivers*, he reflects on the dangers of the conscience he champions in *Civil Disobedience*:

> The conscience really does not, and ought not to monopolize the whole of our lives, any more than the heart or the head. It is as liable to disease as any other part. I have seen some whose consciences, owing undoubtedly to former indulgence, had grown to be as irritable as spoilt children, and at length gave them no peace. They did not know when to swallow their cud, and their lives of course yielded no milk.[22]

This comment may surprise readers of *Civil Disobedience*. But Thoreau was well aware that arrogant self-righteousness could be as unattractive and counterproductive as moral sloth. When he was still relatively young he had commented in his *Journal*, "I don't like people who are too good for this world."[23] He often sounds as though he is, in fact, one of these people who are "too good for this world." Yet, it is also clear that he recognized this temptation and the dangers it posed.

We are now in a position to appreciate how this theme illuminates Thoreau's political ideas. In Chapter 1 we mentioned a comment by Sherman Paul, one of Thoreau's most thoughtful biographers, to the effect that Thoreau's only political weapons were persuasion and his own example. Listen, again, to Paul's observation (in slightly expanded form from what is quoted in the Introduction):

> As far as other reformers went Thoreau was aware of the danger of legislating one's dyspepsia into law, and what saved Thoreau from this predicament was his refusal to use coercion in behalf of his ideals. He was not a reformer in this sense: persuasion and example were his only weapons.[24]

Paul's point helps clarify what it is about Thoreau's writing that sets him apart from other reformers. He was uninterested in actually wielding political power or directly guiding those who do. He aspired to be a poet, a philosopher, a writer, rather than a reformer in the conventional sense. His aspiration, however, was not without a profound ambition. His hope was to present himself and his journeys, in his writing, as emblematic of a morally serious life. He understood that such a project tempted "dyspepsia" – precisely the kind of "heartburn" with the rest of the world that he does, in fact, express frequently in his writings. It was essential for him, then, to confine himself to what he imagines as a "glorious private life," the life of a writer and thinker.[25] The degree to which he influenced others would depend entirely upon the degree to which readers were persuaded by the example of "Henry David Thoreau" they find in Thoreau's literary work. He would refrain from all attempts to use other forms of power to bring the public around to his position. He, like Socrates, would be a "stinging fly" to the community around him. He would take care to prevent his own mistakes, his own vices, from becoming grave threats by refusing conventional forms of authority and political power. His art as a writer was the only tool he cultivated for bringing his audience around to the most important moral commitments.

This does not mean that Thoreau is unimportant for thinking about political matters. But it does mean that we need to be careful about how we understand what it is that Thoreau has to offer. It is simply not the case that he tells us much about conventional democratic participation or about conventional forms of protest and reform politics – all of which he was terribly uninterested in if not actively hostile to. There is nothing here about how to lobby political elites, how to organize a protest movement, or how to run for political office. There is nothing about political strategy at all. As we have seen repeatedly, Thoreau is counseling a withdrawal from political life, not a conventional or straightforward political engagement.

This also means that we must be careful about exaggerating the dangers of "Thoreauvian" politics, at least in part because there is no politics here at all, at least not in any literal sense. We have seen that some interpreters are deeply suspicious of what they take to be the undemocratic or even potentially tyrannical elements of Thoreau's ideas. Thoreau, however, was not attempting to control or govern others. Instead, as he puts it in *Walden*, he was determined to "brag as lustily as chanticleer in the morning, standing on his roost, if only to wake my neighbors up."[26] He was persuaded that most people suffer more from a weak commitment (or even attention) to moral seriousness than from a lack of moral knowledge. He presents his own example, in *Walden* and in all of his writings, as a rebuke to our moral laziness, not as an attempt to tyrannize us. His model is of a rooster crowing to rouse us from our slumber, not of a leader governing.

So, what, then, does Thoreau have to offer our political community? Like Socrates, Thoreau has withdrawn from political participation (he even refused to vote). Like Socrates, however, he also suggests, paradoxically, that he is among the best of citizens (his friend Alcott exaggerates this point, effusing that Thoreau "seemed ... the best republican citizen in the world").[27] His intention is to reorient individual citizens, to encourage them to become the kind of morally serious individuals capable of seeing moral principles and committing to them. Recall that Jane Bennett suggests that what disturbs Thoreau about civil disobedience is not its justification but, rather, its infrequency. How do we become the kind of people who are morally serious? How do we commit ourselves to principles rather than to comfort and pleasure, to truth beyond our narrow economic interests, to a thoughtful moral independence rather than a thoughtless conformity? Thoreau's writings aim to force us to look beneath the surface of our affairs – personal, economic, and political – in the search for bedrock principle. He hopes, as well, to goad us into screwing up the courage to stand by our considered moral convictions.

Thoreau's role as a writer is, therefore, less as a political activist than as a tutor to our character. His project has more in common with the teachings of his Puritan forebears than with those of more explicitly political thinkers or reformers. He believes there is moral work to do prior to just and effective political engagement. Like his friend Emerson, he thinks that if this work is done well politics will become much less important, perhaps even beside the point. Readers looking for guidance in how to use political power, in any of its forms or incarnations, to reform or perhaps even transform citizens and society, will need to look to more conventional political thinkers than Thoreau. Paul's observation that Thoreau's only weapon was the example of his own life as conveyed through the art of his writing reminds us that for Thoreau, all reform begins with individuals, not with political communities.

## NOTES

1 Plato, *Last Days of Socrates* (Baltimore, MD: Penguin, 1969), p. 64.

2 Ibid., p. 45.

3 Ibid., p. 62.

4 Ibid., p. 63.

5 Henry D. Thoreau, *Journal of Henry D. Thoreau*, vol. 2, Bradford Torrey and Francis H. Allen, eds. (Boston, MA: Houghton Mifflin, 1949), p. 44.

6 Philip Roth, interviewed by Daniel Sandstrom, *New York Times*, 2 March 2014. Available at: www.nytimes.com/2014/03/16/books/review/my-life-as-a-writer.html?_r=0 (accessed June 2014).

7 Donna Tartt, *The Goldfinch* (NY: Little, Brown, 2013), p. 695.

8 Thoreau, *Journal*, vol. 2, p. 83.

9 Ibid., p. 193.

10 Ibid., p. 4.

11 Ralph Waldo Emerson, *Essays and Lectures* (NY: Library of America, 1983), p. 24.

12 Thoreau, *Journal*, vol. 2, pp. 267–268.

13 Henry David Thoreau, *Collected Essays and Poems* (NY: Library of America, 2001), p. 362.

14 Thoreau, *Journal*, vol. 6, p. 257.

15 Ibid., vol. 10, p. 115.

16 Ibid., vol. 12, p. 370.

17 Ibid., vol. 9, p. 121.

18 Ibid., vol. 10, p. 404.

19 Ibid., p. 405.

20 Ibid., vol. 3, p. 194.

21 Ibid., vol. 2, p. 333.

22 Henry David Thoreau, *A Week on the Concord and Merrimack Rivers; Walden, or, Life in the Woods; The Maine Woods; Cape Cod* (NY: Library of America, 1985), pp. 60–61.

23 Henry David Thoreau, *Consciousness in Concord*, Perry Miller, ed. (Boston, MA: Houghton Mifflin, 1958), p. 211.

24 Sherman Paul, *The Shores of America* (Urbana, IL: University of Illinois Press, 1958), p. 246.

25 Henry David Thoreau, *Familiar Letters of Henry David Thoreau*, F. B. Sanborn, ed. (Boston, MA and NY: Houghton Mifflin, 1894), p. 297.

26 Thoreau, *A Week, etc.*, p. 389.

27 Harold Bloom, ed., *Henry David Thoreau* (NY: Bloom's Literary Criticism, 2008), p. 125.

# APPENDIX

## *CIVIL DISOBEDIENCE* BY HENRY DAVID THOREAU[1]

**1.**

I heartily accept the motto, – "That government is best which governs least";[2] and I should like to see it acted up to more rapidly and systematically. Carried out, it finally amounts to this, which also I believe, – "That government is best which governs not at all"; and when men are prepared for it, that will be the kind of government which they will have. Government is at best but an expedient; but most governments are usually, and all governments are sometimes, inexpedient. The objections which have been brought against a standing army, and they are many and weighty, and deserve to prevail, may also at last be brought against a standing government. The standing army is only an arm of the standing government. The government itself, which is only the mode which the people have chosen to execute their will, is equally liable to be abused and perverted before the people can act through it. Witness the present Mexican war, the work of comparatively a few individuals using the standing government as their tool; for, in the outset, the people would not have consented to this measure.

**2.**

This American government, – what is it but a tradition, though a recent one, endeavoring to transmit itself unimpaired to posterity, but each instant losing some of its integrity? It has not the vitality and force of a single living man; for a single man can bend it to his will. It is a sort of wooden gun to the people themselves.[3] But it is not the less necessary for this; for the people must have some complicated machinery or other, and hear its din, to satisfy that idea of government which they have. Governments show thus how successfully men can be imposed on, even impose on themselves, for their own advantage. It is excellent, we must all allow. Yet this government never of itself furthered any enterprise, but by the alacrity with which it got out of its way. *It* does not keep the country free. *It* does not settle the West. *It* does not educate. The character inherent in the American people has done all that has been accomplished; and it would have done somewhat more, if the government had not sometimes got in its way. For government is an expedient by which men would fain succeed in letting one another alone; and, as has been said, when it is most expedient, the governed are most let alone by it. Trade and commerce, if they were not made of India-rubber, would never manage to bounce over the obstacles which legislators are continually putting in their way; and, if one were to judge these men wholly by the effects of their actions and not partly by their intentions, they would deserve to be classed and punished with those mischievous persons who put obstructions on the railroads.

**3.**

But, to speak practically and as a citizen, unlike those who call themselves no-government men, I ask for, not at once no government, but *at once* a better government. Let every man make known what kind of government would command his respect, and that will be one step toward obtaining it.

**4.**

After all, the practical reason why, when the power is once in the hands of the people, a majority are permitted, and for a long period continue, to rule, is not because they are most likely to be in the right, nor because this seems fairest to the minority, but because they are physically the strongest. But a government in which the majority rule in all cases cannot be based on justice, even as far as men understand it. Can there not be a government in which majorities do not virtually decide right and wrong, but conscience? – in which majorities decide only those questions to which the rule of expediency is applicable? Must the citizen ever for a moment, or in the least degree, resign his conscience to the legislator? Why has every man a conscience, then? I think that we should be men first, and subjects afterward. It is not desirable to cultivate a respect for the law, so much as for the right. The only obligation which I have a right to assume, is to do at any time what I think right. It is truly enough said, that a corporation has no conscience; but a corporation of conscientious men is a corporation *with* a conscience. Law never made men a whit more just; and, by means of their respect for it, even the well-disposed are daily made the agents of injustice. A common and natural result of an undue respect for law is, that you may see a file of soldiers, colonel, captain, corporal, privates, powder-monkeys,[4] and all, marching in admirable order over hill and dale to the wars, against their wills, ay, against their common sense and consciences, which makes it very steep marching indeed, and produces a palpitation of the heart. They have no doubt that it is a damnable business in which they are concerned; they are all peaceably inclined. Now, what are they? Men at all? or small movable forts and magazines, at the service of some unscrupulous man in power? Visit the Navy-Yard, and behold a marine, such a man as an American government can make, or such as it can make a man with its black arts, – a mere shadow and reminiscence of humanity, a man laid out alive and standing, and already, as one may say, buried under arms with funeral accompaniments, though it may be, –

"Not a drum was heard, not[5] a funeral note,
As his corse to the rampart[6] we hurried;
Not a soldier discharged his farewell shot
O'er the grave where our hero we buried."[7]

**5.**

The mass of men serve the state thus, not as men mainly, but as machines, with their bodies. They are the standing army, and the militia, jailers, constables, posse comitatus, &c. In most cases there is no free exercise whatever of the judgment or of the moral sense; but they put themselves on a level with wood and earth and stones; and wooden men can perhaps be manufactured that will serve the purpose as well. Such command no more respect than men of straw or a lump of dirt. They have the same sort of worth only as horses and dogs. Yet such as these even are commonly esteemed good citizens. Others, – as most legislators, politicians, lawyers, ministers, and office-holders, – serve the state chiefly with their heads; and, as they rarely make any moral distinctions, they are as likely to serve the Devil, without *intending* it, as God. A very few, as heroes, patriots, martyrs, reformers in the great sense, and *men*, serve the state with their consciences also, and so necessarily resist it for the most part; and they are commonly treated as enemies by it. A wise man will only be useful as a man, and will not submit to be "clay," and "stop a hole to keep the wind away," but leave that office to his dust at least:[8] –

> "I am too high-born to be propertied,
> To be a secondary at control,
> Or useful serving-man and instrument
> To any sovereign state throughout the world."[9]

**6.**

He who gives himself entirely to his fellow-men appears to them useless and selfish; but he who gives himself partially to them is pronounced a benefactor and philanthropist.

**7.**

How does it become a man to behave toward this American government to-day? I answer, that he cannot without disgrace be associated with it. I cannot for an instant recognize that political organization as *my* government which is the *slave's* government also.

## 8.

All men recognize the right of revolution; that is, the right to refuse allegiance to, and to resist, the government, when its tyranny or its inefficiency are great and unendurable. But almost all say that such is not the case now. But such was the case, they think, in the Revolution of '75.[10] If one were to tell me that this was a bad government because it taxed certain foreign commodities brought to its ports, it is most probable that I should not make an ado about it, for I can do without them. All machines have their friction; and possibly this does enough good to counterbalance the evil. At any rate, it is a great evil to make a stir about it. But when the friction comes to have its machine, and oppression and robbery are organized, I say, let us not have such a machine any longer. In other words, when a sixth of the population of a nation which has undertaken to be the refuge of liberty are slaves, and a whole country is unjustly overrun and conquered by a foreign army, and subjected to military law, I think that it is not too soon for honest men to rebel and revolutionize. What makes this duty the more urgent is the fact, that the country so overrun is not our own, but ours is the invading army.

## 9.

Paley, a common authority with many on moral questions, in his chapter on the "Duty of Submission to Civil Government," resolves all civil obligation into expediency; and he proceeds to say, "that so long as the interest of the whole society requires it, that is, so long as the established government cannot be resisted or changed without public inconveniency, it is the will of God that the established government be obeyed, and no longer. ... This principle being admitted, the justice of every particular case of resistance is reduced to a computation of the quantity of the danger and grievance on the one side, and of the probability and expense of redressing it on the other." Of this, he says, every man shall judge for himself. But Paley appears never to have con-templated those cases to which the rule of expediency does not apply, in which a people, as well as an individual, must do justice, cost what it may. If I have unjustly wrested a plank from a drowning man, I must restore it to him though I drown myself.[11] This, according to Paley, would be inconvenient. But he that would save his life, in such a case, shall lose it.[12] This people must cease to hold slaves, and to make war on Mexico, though it cost them their existence as a people.

## 10.

In their practice, nations agree with Paley; but does anyone think that Massachusetts does exactly what is right at the present crisis?

> A drab of state, a cloth-o'-silver slut,
> To have her train borne up, and her soul trail in the dirt.[13]

Practically speaking, the opponents to a reform in Massachusetts are not a hundred thousand politicians at the South, but a hundred thousand merchants and farmers here, who are more interested in commerce and agriculture than they are in humanity, and are not prepared to do justice to the slave and to Mexico, *cost what it may.* I quarrel not with far-off foes, but with those who, near at home, co-operate with, and do the bidding of, those far away, and without whom the latter would be harmless. We are accustomed to say, that the mass of men are unprepared; but improvement is slow, because the few are not materially wiser or better than the many. It is not so important that many should be as good as you, as that there be some absolute goodness somewhere; for that will leaven the whole lump.[14] There are thousands who are *in opinion* opposed to slavery and to the war, who yet in effect do nothing to put an end to them; who, esteeming themselves children of Washington and Franklin, sit down with their hands in their pockets, and say that they know not what to do, and do nothing; who even postpone the question of freedom to the question of free-trade, and quietly read the prices-current along with the latest advices from Mexico, after dinner, and, it may be, fall asleep over them both. What is the price-current of an honest man and patriot to-day? They hesitate, and they regret, and sometimes they petition; but they do nothing in earnest and with effect. They will wait, well disposed, for others to remedy the evil, that they may no longer have it to regret. At most, they give only a cheap vote, and a feeble countenance and God-speed, to the right, as it goes by them. There are nine hundred and ninety-nine patrons of virtue to one virtuous man. But it is easier to deal with the real possessor of a thing than with the temporary guardian of it.

## 11.

All voting is a sort of gaming, like checkers or backgammon, with a slight moral tinge to it, a playing with right and wrong, with moral questions; and betting naturally accompanies it. The character of the voters is not staked. I cast my vote, perchance, as I think right; but I am not vitally concerned that that right should prevail. I am willing to leave it to the majority. Its obligation, therefore, never exceeds that of expediency. Even voting *for the right* is *doing* nothing for it. It is only expressing to men feebly your desire that it should prevail. A wise man will not leave the right to the mercy of chance, nor wish it to prevail through the power of the majority. There is but little virtue in the action of masses of men. When the majority shall at length vote for the abolition of slavery, it will be because they are indifferent to slavery, or because there is but little slavery left to be abolished by their vote. *They* will then be the only slaves. Only *his* vote can hasten the abolition of slavery who asserts his own freedom by his vote.

## 12.

I hear of a convention to be held at Baltimore,[15] or elsewhere, for the selection of a candidate for the Presidency, made up chiefly of editors, and men who are politicians by profession; but I think, what is it to any independent, intelligent, and respectable man what decision they may come to? Shall we not have the advantage of his wisdom and honesty, nevertheless? Can we not count upon some independent votes? Are there not many individuals in the country who do not attend conventions? But no: I find that the respectable man, so called, has immediately drifted from his position, and despairs of his country, when his country has more reason to despair of him. He forthwith adopts one of the candidates thus selected as the only *available* one, thus proving that he is himself *available* for any purposes of the demagogue. His vote is of no more worth than that of any unprincipled foreigner or hireling native, who may have been bought. O for a man who is a *man*, and, as my neighbor says, has a bone in his back which you cannot pass your hand through! Our statistics are at fault: the population has been returned too large. How many *men* are there to a square thousand miles in this country? Hardly one. Does not America offer any inducement for men to settle here? The American has dwindled into an Odd Fellow,[16] – one who may be known by the development of his organ of gregariousness, and a manifest lack of intellect and cheerful self-reliance; whose first and chief concern, on coming into the world, is to see that the Almshouses are in good repair; and, before yet he has lawfully donned the virile garb,[17] to collect a fund for the support of the widows and orphans that may be; who, in short, ventures to live only by the aid of the Mutual Insurance company, which has promised to bury him decently.

## 13.

It is not a man's duty, as a matter of course, to devote himself to the eradication of any, even the most enormous wrong; he may still properly have other concerns to engage him; but it is his duty, at least, to wash his hands of it, and, if he gives it no thought longer, not to give it practically his support. If I devote myself to other pursuits and contemplations, I must first see, at least, that I do not pursue them sitting upon another man's shoulders. I must get off him first, that he may pursue his contemplations too. See what gross inconsistency is tolerated. I have heard some of my townsmen say, "I should like to have them order me out to help put down an insurrection of the slaves, or to march to Mexico; – see if I would go"; and yet these very men have each, directly by their allegiance, and so indirectly, at least, by their money, furnished a substitute. The soldier is applauded who refuses to serve in an unjust war by those who do not refuse to sustain the unjust government which makes the war; is applauded by those whose own act and authority he disregards and sets at naught; as if the State were penitent to that degree that it hired one to scourge it while it sinned, but not to that degree that it left off sinning for a moment. Thus, under the name of Order and Civil Government, we are all made at last to pay homage to and support our own meanness. After the first blush of sin comes its indifference; and from immoral it becomes, as it were, *un*moral, and not quite unnecessary to that life which we have made.

### 14.

The broadest and most prevalent error requires the most disinterested virtue to sustain it. The slight reproach to which the virtue of patriotism is commonly liable, the noble are most likely to incur. Those who, while they disapprove of the character and measures of a government, yield to it their allegiance and support, are undoubtedly its most conscientious supporters, and so frequently the most serious obstacles to reform. Some are petitioning the State to dissolve the Union, to disregard the requisitions of the President.[18] Why do they not dissolve it themselves, – the union between themselves and the State, – and refuse to pay their quota into its treasury? Do not they stand in the same relation to the State, that the State does to the Union? And have not the same reasons prevented the State from resisting the Union, which have prevented them from resisting the State?

### 15.

How can a man be satisfied to entertain an opinion merely, and enjoy *it*? Is there any enjoyment in it, if his opinion is that he is aggrieved? If you are cheated out of a single dollar by your neighbor, you do not rest satisfied with knowing that you are cheated, or with saying that you are cheated, or even with petitioning him to pay you your due; but you take effectual steps at once to obtain the full amount, and see that you are never cheated again. Action from principle, the perception and the performance of right, changes things and relations; it is essentially revolutionary, and does not consist wholly with anything which was. It not only divides states and churches, it divides families; ay, it divides the *individual*, separating the diabolical in him from the divine.

### 16.

Unjust laws exist: shall we be content to obey them, or shall we endeavor to amend them, and obey them until we have succeeded, or shall we transgress them at once? Men generally, under such a government as this, think that they ought to wait until they have persuaded the majority to alter them. They think that, if they should resist, the remedy would be worse than the evil. But it is the fault of the government itself that the remedy *is* worse than the evil. *It* makes it worse. Why is it not more apt to anticipate and provide for reform? Why does it not cherish its wise minority? Why does it cry and resist before it is hurt? Why does it not encourage its citizens to be on the alert to point out its faults, and *do* better than it would have them? Why does it always crucify Christ, and excommunicate Copernicus and Luther, and pronounce Washington and Franklin rebels?

### 17.

One would think, that a deliberate and practical denial of its authority was the only offense never contemplated by government; else, why has it not assigned its definite, its suitable and proportionate penalty? If a man who has no property refuses but once to earn nine shillings for the State,[19] he is put in prison for a period unlimited by any law that I know, and determined only by the discretion of those who placed him there; but if he should steal ninety times nine shillings from the State, he is soon permitted to go at large again.

### 18.

If the injustice is part of the necessary friction of the machine of government, let it go, let it go: perchance it will wear smooth, — certainly the machine will wear out. If the injustice has a spring, or a pulley, or a rope, or a crank, exclusively for itself, then perhaps you may consider whether the remedy will not be worse than the evil; but if it is of such a nature that it requires you to be the agent of injustice to another, then, I say, break the law. Let your life be a counter friction to stop the machine. What I have to do is to see, at any rate, that I do not lend myself to the wrong which I condemn.

## 19.

As for adopting the ways which the State has provided for reme- dying the evil, I know not of such ways. They take too much time, and a man's life will be gone. I have other affairs to attend to. I came into this world, not chiefly to make this a good place to live in, but to live in it, be it good or bad. A man has not everything to do, but something; and because he[20] cannot do *everything*, it is not necessary that he should do *something* wrong. It is not my business to be petitioning the Governor or the Legislature any more than it is theirs to petition me; and, if they should not hear my petition, what should I do then? But in this case the State has provided no way: its very Constitution is the evil. This may seem to be harsh and stubborn and unconciliatory; but it is to treat with the utmost kindness and consideration the only spirit that can appreciate or deserves it. So is all change for the better, like birth and death, which convulse the body.

## 20.

I do not hesitate to say, that those who call themselves Abolitionists should at once effectually withdraw their support, both in person and property, from the government of Massachusetts, and not wait till they constitute a majority of one, before they suffer the right to prevail through them. I think that it is enough if they have God on their side, without waiting for that other one. Moreover, any man more right than his neighbors constitutes a majority of one already.[21]

## 21.

I meet this American government, or its representative, the State government, directly, and face to face, once a year – no more – in the person of its tax-gatherer; this is the only mode in which a man situated as I am necessarily meets it; and it then says distinctly, Recognize me; and the simplest, the most effectual, and, in the present posture of affairs, the indispensablest mode of treating with it on this head, of expressing your little satisfaction with and love for it, is to deny it then. My civil neighbor, the tax-gatherer,[22] is the very man I have to deal with, – for it is, after all, with men and not with parchment that I quarrel, – and he has voluntarily chosen to be an agent of the government. How shall he ever know well what he is and does as an officer of the government, or as a man, until he is obliged to consider whether he shall treat me, his neighbor, for whom he has respect, as a neighbor and well-disposed man, or as a maniac and disturber of the peace, and see if he can get over this obstruction to his neighborliness without a ruder and more impetuous thought or speech corresponding with his action. I know this well, that if one thousand, if one hundred, if ten men whom I could name, – if ten *honest* men only, – ay, if *one* HONEST man, in this State of Massachusetts, *ceasing to hold slaves*, were actually to withdraw from this copartnership, and be locked up in the county jail therefor, it would be the abolition of slavery in America. For it matters not how small the beginning may seem to be: what is once well done is done forever. But we love better to talk about it: that we say is our mission. Reform keeps many scores of newspapers in its service, but not one man. If my esteemed neighbor, the State's ambassador,[23] who will devote his days to the settlement of the question of human rights in the Council Chamber, instead of being threatened with the prisons of Carolina, were to sit down the prisoner of Massachusetts, that State which is so anxious to foist the sin of slavery upon her sister, – though at present she can discover only an act of inhospitality to be the ground of a quarrel with her, – the Legislature would not wholly waive the subject the following winter.

## 22.

Under a government which imprisons any unjustly, the true place for a just man is also a prison. The proper place to-day, the only place which Massachusetts has provided for her freer and less desponding spirits, is in her prisons, to be put out and locked out of the State by her own act, as they have already put themselves out by their principles. It is there that the fugitive slave, and the Mexican prisoner on parole, and the Indian come to plead the wrongs of his race, should find them; on that separate, but more free and honorable ground, where the State places those who are not *with* her, but *against* her, – the only house in a slave State in which a free man can abide with honor. If any think that their influence would be lost there, and their voices no longer afflict the ear of the State, that they would not be as an enemy within its walls, they do not know by how much truth is stronger than error, nor how much more eloquently and effectively he can combat injustice who has experienced a little in his own person. Cast your whole vote, not a strip of paper merely, but your whole influence. A minority is powerless while it conforms to the majority; it is not even a minority then; but it is irresistible when it clogs by its whole weight. If the alternative is to keep all just men in prison, or give up war and slavery, the State will not hesitate which to choose. If a thousand men were not to pay their tax-bills this year, that would not be a violent and bloody measure, as it would be to pay them, and enable the State to commit violence and shed innocent blood. This is, in fact, the definition of a peaceable revolution, if any such is possible. If the tax-gatherer, or any other public officer, asks me, as one has done, "But what shall I do?" my answer is, "If you really wish to do anything, resign your office." When the subject has refused allegiance, and the officer has resigned his office, then the revolution is accomplished. But even suppose blood should flow. Is there not a sort of blood shed when the conscience is wounded? Through this wound a man's real manhood and immortality flow out, and he bleeds to an everlasting death. I see this blood flowing now.

## 23.

I have contemplated the imprisonment of the offender, rather than the seizure of his goods, – though both will serve the same purpose, – because they who assert the purest right, and consequently are most dangerous to a corrupt State, commonly have not spent much time in accumulating property. To such the State renders comparatively small service, and a slight tax is wont to appear exorbitant, particularly if they are obliged to earn it by special labor with their hands. If there were one who lived wholly without the use of money, the State itself would hesitate to demand it of him. But the rich man, – not to make any invidious comparison, – is always sold to the institution which makes him rich. Absolutely speaking, the more money, the less virtue; for money comes between a man and his objects, and obtains them for him; and it was certainly no great virtue to obtain it. It puts to rest many questions which he would otherwise be taxed to answer; while the only new question which it puts is the hard but superfluous one, how to spend it. Thus his moral ground is taken from under his feet. The opportunities of living are diminished in proportion as what are called the "means" are increased. The best thing a man can do for his culture when he is rich is to endeavor to carry out those schemes which he entertained when he was poor. Christ answered the Herodians according to their condition. "Show me the tribute-money," said he; – and one took a penny out of his pocket; – if you use money which has the image of Caesar on it, and which he has made current and valuable, that is, *if you are men of the State*, and gladly enjoy the advantages of Caesar's government, then pay him back some of his own when he demands it; "Render therefore to Caesar that which is Caesar's, and to God those things which are God's," – leaving them no wiser than before as to which was which; for they did not wish to know.[24]

## 24.

When I converse with the freest of my neighbors, I perceive that, whatever they may say about the magnitude and seriousness of the question, and their regard for the public tranquillity, the long and the short of the matter is, that they cannot spare the protection of the existing government, and they dread the consequences to their property and families of disobedience to it. For my own part, I should not like to think that I ever rely on the protection of the State. But, if I deny the authority of the State when it presents its tax-bill, it will soon take and waste all my property, and so harass me and my children without end. This is hard. This makes it impossible for a man to live honestly, and at the same time comfortably, in outward respects. It will not be worth the while to accumulate property; that would be sure to go again. You must hire or squat somewhere, and raise but a small crop, and eat that soon. You must live within yourself, and depend upon yourself always tucked up and ready for a start, and not have many affairs. A man may grow rich in Turkey even, if he will be in all respects a good subject of the Turkish government. Confucius said: "If a state is governed by the principles of reason, poverty and misery are subjects of shame; if a state is not governed by the principles of reason, riches and honors are the subjects of shame."[25] No: until I want the protection of Massachusetts to be extended to me in some distant Southern port, where my liberty is endangered, or until I am bent solely on building up an estate at home by peaceful enterprise, I can afford to refuse allegiance to Massachusetts, and her right to my property and life. It costs me less in every sense to incur the penalty of disobedience to the State, than it would to obey. I should feel as if I were worth less in that case.

## 25.

Some years ago, the State met me in behalf of the Church, and commanded me to pay a certain sum toward the support of a clergyman whose preaching my father attended, but never I myself. "Pay," it said, "or be locked up in the jail." I declined to pay. But, unfortunately, another man saw fit to pay it.[26] I did not see why the schoolmaster should be taxed to support the priest, and not the priest the schoolmaster; for I was not the State's schoolmaster, but I supported myself by voluntary subscription. I did not see why the lyceum should not present its tax-bill, and have the State to back its demand, as well as the Church. However, at the request of the selectmen, I condescended to make some such statement as this in writing: – "Know all men by these presents, that I, Henry Thoreau, do not wish to be regarded as a member of any incorporated society which I have not joined."[27] This I gave to the town clerk; and he has it. The State, having thus learned that I did not wish to be regarded as a member of that church, has never made a like demand on me since; though it said that it must adhere to its original presumption that time. If I had known how to name them, I should then have signed off in detail from all the societies which I never signed on to; but I did not know where to find a complete list.

## 26.

I have paid no poll-tax for six years. I was put into a jail once on this account, for one night; and, as I stood considering the walls of solid stone, two or three feet thick, the door of wood and iron, a foot thick, and the iron grating which strained the light, I could not help being struck with the foolishness of that institution which treated me as if I were mere flesh and blood and bones, to be locked up. I wondered that it should have concluded at length that this was the best use it could put me to, and had never thought to avail itself of my services in some way. I saw that, if there was a wall of stone between me and my townsmen, there was a still more difficult one to climb or break through, before they could get to be as free as I was. I did not for a moment feel confined, and the walls seemed a great waste of stone and mortar. I felt as if I alone of all my townsmen had paid my tax. They plainly did not know how to treat me, but behaved like persons who are underbred. In every threat and in every compliment there was a blunder; for they thought that my chief desire was to stand the other side of that stone wall. I could not but smile to see how industriously they locked the door on my meditations, which followed them out again without let or hindrance, and *they* were really all that was dangerous. As they could not reach me, they had resolved to punish my body; just as boys, if they cannot come at some person against whom they have a spite, will abuse his dog. I saw that the State was half-witted, that it was timid as a lone woman with her silver spoons, and that it did not know its friends from its foes, and I lost all my remaining respect for it, and pitied it.

## 27.

Thus the State never intentionally confronts a man's sense, intellectual or moral, but only his body, his senses. It is not armed with superior wit or honesty, but with superior physical strength. I was not born to be forced. I will breathe after my own fashion. Let us see who is the strongest. What force has a multitude? They only can force me who obey a higher law than I. They force me to become like themselves. I do not hear of *men* being *forced* to live this way or that by masses of men. What sort of life were that to live? When I meet a government which says to me, "Your money or your life," why should I be in haste to give it my money? It may be in a great strait, and not know what to do: I cannot help that. It must help itself; do as I do. It is not worth the while to snivel about it. I am not responsible for the successful working of the machinery of society. I am not the son of the engineer. I perceive that, when an acorn and a chestnut fall side by side, the one does not remain inert to make way for the other, but both obey their own laws, and spring and grow and flourish as best they can, till one, perchance, overshadows and destroys the other. If a plant cannot live according to its nature, it dies; and so a man.

## 28.

The night in prison was novel and interesting enough. The prisoners in their shirt-sleeves were enjoying a chat and the evening air in the doorway, when I entered. But the jailer said, "Come, boys, it is time to lock up"; and so they dispersed, and I heard the sound of their steps returning into the hollow apartments. My room-mate was introduced to me by the jailer, as "a first-rate fellow and a clever man." When the door was locked, he showed me where to hang my hat, and how he managed matters there. The rooms were whitewashed once a month; and this one, at least, was the whitest, most simply furnished, and probably the neatest apartment in the town. He naturally wanted to know where I came from, and what brought me there; and, when I had told him, I asked him in my turn how he came there, presuming him to be an honest man, of course; and, as the world goes, I believe he was. "Why," said he, "they accuse me of burning a barn; but I never did it." As near as I could discover, he had probably gone to bed in a barn when drunk, and smoked his pipe there; and so a barn was burnt. He had the reputation of being a clever man, had been there some three months waiting for his trial to come on, and would have to wait as much longer; but he was quite domesticated and contented, since he got his board for nothing, and thought that he was well treated.

### 29.

He occupied one window, and I the other; and I saw, that, if one stayed there long, his principal business would be to look out the window. I had soon read all the tracts that were left there, and examined where former prisoners had broken out, and where a grate had been sawed off, and heard the history of the various occupants of that room; for I found that even here there was a history and a gossip which never circulated beyond the walls of the jail. Probably this is the only house in the town where verses are composed, which are afterward printed in a circular form, but not published. I was shown quite a long list of verses which were composed by some young men who had been detected in an attempt to escape, who avenged themselves by singing them.

### 30.

I pumped my fellow-prisoner as dry as I could, for fear I should never see him again; but at length he showed me which was my bed, and left me to blow out the lamp.

### 31.

It was like travelling into a far country, such as I had never expected to behold, to lie there for one night. It seemed to me that I never had heard the town-clock strike before, nor the evening sounds of the village; for we slept with the windows open, which were inside the grating. It was to see my native village in the light of the Middle Ages, and our Concord was turned into a Rhine stream, and visions of knights and castles passed before me. They were the voices of old burghers that I heard in the streets. I was an involuntary spectator and auditor of whatever was done and said in the kitchen of the adjacent village-inn, – a wholly new and rare experience to me. It was a closer view of my native town. I was fairly inside of it. I never had seen its institutions before. This is one of its peculiar institutions; for it is a shire town.[28] I began to comprehend what its inhabitants were about.

### 32.

In the morning, our breakfasts were put through the hole in the door, in small oblong-square tin pans, made to fit, and holding a pint of chocolate, with brown bread, and an iron spoon. When they called for the vessels again, I was green enough to return what bread I had left; but my comrade seized it, and said that I should lay that up for lunch or dinner. Soon after he was let out to work at haying in a neighboring field, whither he went every day, and would not be back till noon; so he bade me good-day, saying that he doubted if he should see me again.

### 33.

When I came out of prison, – for some one interfered, and paid that tax,[29] – I did not perceive that great changes had taken place on the common, such as he observed who went in a youth, and emerged a tottering and gray-headed man; and yet a change had to my eyes come over the scene, – the town, and State, and country, – greater than any that mere time could effect. I saw yet more distinctly the State in which I lived. I saw to what extent the people among whom I lived could be trusted as good neighbors and friends; that their friendship was for summer weather only; that they did not greatly propose to do right; that they were a distinct race from me by their prejudices and superstitions, as the Chinamen and Malays are; that, in their sacrifices to humanity, they ran no risks, not even to their property; that, after all, they were not so noble but they treated the thief as he had treated them, and hoped, by a certain outward observance and a few prayers, and by walking in a particular straight though useless path from time to time, to save their souls. This may be to judge my neighbors harshly; for I believe that many of them are not aware that they have such an institution as the jail in their village.

**34.**

It was formerly the custom in our village, when a poor debtor came out of jail, for his acquaintances to salute him, looking through their fingers, which were crossed to represent the grating of a jail window, "How do ye do?" My neighbors did not thus salute me, but first looked at me, and then at one another, as if I had returned from a long journey. I was put into jail as I was going to the shoemaker's to get a shoe which was mended. When I was let out the next morning, I proceeded to finish my errand, and having put on my mended shoe, joined a huckleberry party, who were impatient to put themselves under my conduct; and in half an hour, – for the horse was soon tackled, – was in the midst of a huckleberry field, on one of our highest hills, two miles off, and then the State was nowhere to be seen.

**35.**

This is the whole history of "My Prisons."[30]

**36.**

I have never declined paying the highway tax, because I am as desirous of being a good neighbor as I am of being a bad subject; and, as for supporting schools, I am doing my part to educate my fellow-countrymen now. It is for no particular item in the tax-bill that I refuse to pay it. I simply wish to refuse allegiance to the State, to withdraw and stand aloof from it effectually. I do not care to trace the course of my dollar, if I could, till it buys a man or a musket to shoot one with, – the dollar is innocent, – but I am concerned to trace the effects of my allegiance. In fact, I quietly declare war with the State, after my fashion, though I will still make what use and get what advantage of her I can, as is usual in such cases.

**37.**

If others pay the tax which is demanded of me, from a sympathy with the State, they do but what they have already done in their own case, or rather they abet injustice to a greater extent than the State requires. If they pay the tax from a mistaken interest in the individual taxed, to save his property, or prevent his going to jail, it is because they have not considered wisely how far they let their private feelings interfere with the public good.

## 38.

This, then, is my position at present. But one cannot be too much on his guard in such a case, lest his action be biassed by obstinacy, or an undue regard for the opinions of men. Let him see that he does only what belongs to himself and to the hour.

## 39.

I think sometimes, Why, this people mean well; they are only ignorant; they would do better if they knew how: why give your neighbors this pain to treat you as they are not inclined to? But I think again, this is no reason why I should do as they do, or permit others to suffer much greater pain of a different kind. Again, I sometimes say to myself, When many millions of men, without heat, without ill will, without personal feeling of any kind, demand of you a few shillings only, without the possibility, such is their constitution, of retracting or altering their present demand, and without the possibility, on your side, of appeal to any other millions, why expose yourself to this overwhelming brute force? You do not resist cold and hunger, the winds and the waves, thus obstinately; you quietly submit to a thousand similar necessities. You do not put your head into the fire. But just in proportion as I regard this as not wholly a brute force, but partly a human force, and consider that I have relations to those millions as to so many millions of men, and not of mere brute or inanimate things, I see that appeal is possible, first and instantaneously, from them to the Maker of them, and, secondly, from them to themselves. But, if I put my head deliberately into the fire, there is no appeal to fire or to the Maker of fire, and I have only myself to blame. If I could convince myself that I have any right to be satisfied with men as they are, and to treat them accordingly, and not according, in some respects, to my requisitions and expectations of what they and I ought to be, then, like a good Mussulman[31] and fatalist, I should endeavor to be satisfied with things as they are, and say it is the will of God. And, above all, there is this difference between resisting this and a purely brute or natural force, that I can resist this with some effect; but I cannot expect like Orpheus,[32] to change the nature of the rocks and trees and beasts.

### 40.

I do not wish to quarrel with any man or nation. I do not wish to split hairs, to make fine distinctions, or set myself up as better than my neighbors. I seek rather, I may say, even an excuse for conforming to the laws of the land. I am but too ready to conform to them. Indeed, I have reason to suspect myself on this head; and each year, as the tax-gatherer comes round, I find myself disposed to review the acts and position of the general and State governments, and the spirit of the people, to discover a pretext for conformity.

> We must affect our country as our parents
> And if at any time we alienate
> Our love or industry from doing it honor,
> We must respect effects and teach the soul
> Matter of conscience and religion,
> And not desire of rule or benefit.[33]

I believe that the State will soon be able to take all my work of this sort out of my hands, and then I shall be no better a patriot than my fellow-countrymen. Seen from a lower point of view, the Constitution, with all its faults, is very good; the law and the courts are very respectable; even this State and this American government are, in many respects, very admirable and rare things, to be thankful for, such as a great many have described them; but seen from a point of view a little higher, they are what I have described them; seen from a higher still, and the highest, who shall say what they are, or that they are worth looking at or thinking of at all?

## 41.

However, the government does not concern me much, and I shall bestow the fewest possible thoughts on it. It is not many moments that I live under a government, even in this world. If a man is thought-free, fancy-free, imagination-free, that which *is not* never for a long time appearing *to be* to him, unwise rulers or reformers cannot fatally interrupt him.

## 42.

I know that most men think differently from myself; but those whose lives are by profession devoted to the study of these or kindred subjects, content me as little as any. Statesmen and legislators, standing so completely within the institution, never distinctly and nakedly behold it. They speak of moving society, but have no resting-place without it. They may be men of a certain experience and discrimination, and have no doubt invented ingenious and even useful systems, for which we sincerely thank them; but all their wit and usefulness lie within certain not very wide limits. They are wont to forget that the world is not governed by policy and expediency. Webster never goes behind government, and so cannot speak with authority about it. His words are wisdom to those legislators who contemplate no essential reform in the existing government; but for thinkers, and those who legislate for all time, he never once glances at the subject. I know of those whose serene and wise speculations on this theme would soon reveal the limits of his mind's range and hospitality. Yet, compared with the cheap professions of most reformers, and the still cheaper wisdom and eloquence of politicians in general, his are almost the only sensible and valuable words, and we thank Heaven for him. Comparatively, he is always strong, original, and, above all, practical. Still his quality is not wisdom, but prudence. The lawyer's truth is not Truth, but consistency, or a consistent expediency. Truth is always in harmony with herself, and is not concerned chiefly to reveal the justice that may consist with wrong-doing. He well deserves to be called, as he has been called, the Defender of the Constitution. There are really no blows to be given by him but defensive ones. He is not a leader, but a follower. His leaders are the men of '87.[34] "I have never made an effort," he says, "and never propose to make an effort; I have never countenanced an effort, and never mean to countenance an effort, to disturb the arrangement as originally made, by which the various States came into the Union." Still thinking of the sanction which the Constitution gives to slavery, he says, "Because it was a part of the original compact, – let it stand." Notwithstanding his special acuteness and ability, he is unable to take a fact out of its merely political relations, and behold it as it lies absolutely to be disposed of by the intellect, – what, for instance, it behooves a man to do here in America to-day with regard to slavery, but ventures, or is driven, to make some such desperate answer as the following, while professing to speak absolutely, and as a private man, – from which what new and singular code of social duties might be inferred? "The manner," says he, "in which the governments[35] of those States where slavery exists are to regulate it, is for their own considera-tion, under their responsibility to their constituents, to the gen-eral laws of propriety, humanity, and justice, and to God. Associations formed elsewhere, springing from a feeling of humanity, or any other cause, have nothing whatever to do with it. They have never received any encouragement from me, and they never will."[36]

### 43.

They who know of no purer sources of truth, who have traced up its stream no higher, stand, and wisely stand, by the Bible and the Constitution, and drink at it there with reverence and humi-lity; but they who behold where it comes trickling into this lake or that pool, gird up their loins once more, and continue their pilgrimage toward its fountain-head.

### 44.

No man with a genius for legislation has appeared in America. They are rare in the history of the world. There are orators, politicians, and eloquent men, by the thousand; but the speaker has not yet opened his mouth to speak, who is capable of settling the much-vexed questions of the day. We love eloquence for its own sake, and not for any truth which it may utter, or any heroism it may inspire. Our legislators have not yet learned the comparative value of free-trade and of freedom, of union, and of rectitude, to a nation. They have no genius or talent for comparatively humble questions of taxation and finance, commerce and manufactures and agriculture. If we were left solely to the wordy wit of legislators in Congress for our guidance, uncorrected by the seasonable experience and the effectual complaints of the people, America would not long retain her rank among the nations. For eighteen hundred years, though perchance I have no right to say it, the New Testament has been written; yet where is the legislator who has wisdom and practical talent enough to avail himself of the light which it sheds on the science of legislation?

## 45.

The authority of government, even such as I am willing to submit to, – for I will cheerfully obey those who know and can do better than I, and in many things even those who neither know nor can do so well, – is still an impure one: to be strictly just, it must have the sanction and consent of the governed. It can have no pure right over my person and property but what I concede to it. The progress from an absolute to a limited monarchy, from a limited monarchy to a democracy, is a progress toward a true respect for the individual. Even the Chinese philosopher[37] was wise enough to regard the individual as the basis of the empire.[38] Is a democracy, such as we know it, the last improvement possible in government? Is it not possible to take a step further towards recognizing and organizing the rights of man? There will never be a really free and enlightened State, until the State comes to recognize the individual as a higher and independent power, from which all its own power and authority are derived, and treats him accordingly. I please myself with imagining a State at last which can afford to be just to all men, and to treat the individual with respect as a neighbor; which even would not think it inconsistent with its own repose, if a few were to live aloof from it, not meddling with it, nor embraced by it, who fulfilled all the duties of neighbors and fellow-men. A State which bore this kind of fruit, and suffered it to drop off as fast as it ripened, would prepare the way for a still more perfect and glorious State, which also I have imagined, but not yet anywhere seen.

## NOTES

1  When this essay was first published in 1849, its title was *Resistance to Civil Government* (in Elizabeth P. Peabody, ed., *Aesthetic Papers*, Boston, MA and NY: G. P. Putnam, 1849, pp. 189–211). Later editions sometimes bore the title *On the Duty of Civil Disobedience* or *On Civil Disobedience*. The lecture upon which the essay was based was delivered in Concord Lyceum, 26 January and 16 February 1848. The text reproduced here (including the title *Civil Disobedience*) is based on the posthumous edition of the essay in Henry D. Thoreau, *A Yankee in Canada, with Anti-Slavery and Reform Papers* (Boston, MA: Ticknor and Fields, 1866, pp. 123–151). In addition to the change in title, there are three other substantive changes in the 1866 edition. I have noted each of these below. Numerous editorial differences between the two editions (mainly, but not only, concerning punctuation) have been ignored; style and editorial decisions from 1866 are reproduced here. Paragraphs have been separated and numbered for convenience of study.

2  This motto appeared on the masthead of the *Democratic Review*. Thoreau had published an essay in this widely read magazine in 1843.

3  This sentence appeared in a longer form in the 1849 edition of the essay: "It is a sort of wooden gun to the people themselves; and, if ever they should use it in earnest as a real one against each other, it will surely split."

4  Boys used by the army to carry gunpowder from the storehouses to the guns.

5  Incorrectly written "nor" in 1849 edition.

6  Incorrectly written "ramparts" in 1849 edition.

7  Poem by Charles Wolfe (died 1823), remembering British General Sir John Moore, killed in battle in 1809.

8  Shakespeare, *Hamlet*, 5:i. This line refers to Hamlet's observation that Alexander died and turned to dust (like any man), and "Imperious Caesar, dead and turn'd to clay, Might stop a hole to keep the wind away. O, that that earth, which kept the world in awe, Should patch a wall to expel winter's flaw."

9  Shakespeare, *King John*, 5:ii.

10  The Battle of Lexington and Concord was fought in 1775.

11  Cicero, *De Officiis*, III:xxiii: "If a fool should snatch a plank from a wreck, shall a wise man wrest it from him if he is able?"

12  Luke 9:24: "For whoever would save his life will lose it; and whoever loses his life for my sake, he will save it."

13  Cyril Tourneur, *The Revenger's Tragedy* (1607). Verse should read: "A drab of State, a cloath, a silver slut."

14  1 Corinthians 5:6: "Know ye not that a little leaven leaveneth the whole lump?"

15  The Democratic Party convention of 1848, which nominated Lewis Cass for President. Cass was defeated in the general election by the Whig candidate, Zachary Taylor.

16  The Odd Fellows was a "Friendly Society," a fraternal and mutual aid organization originating in Great Britain and dating from the first half of the eighteenth century.

17  Adult clothing a Roman boy was allowed to wear at age 14.

18  President Polk had requisitioned volunteer troops for the war with Mexico from the various states.

19  A shilling was a sixth of a dollar. Nine shillings, therefore, was $1.50 – the value of Thoreau's annual poll tax.

20  Corrected from "be" in the 1849 edition.

21  John Knox (died 1572) held that, "One man with God is always in the majority."

22  Sam Staples.

23  Former Congressman Samuel Hoar.

24  Matthew 22:15–22.

25  *Analects*, Book 8:13.

26  Who paid this tax is unknown.

27  Note preserved in the Concord Public Library reads: "Mr Clerk Concord Jan 6th 1841. I do not wish to be considered a member of the First Parish in this town. Henry D. Thoreau."

28  Concord was the county seat.

29  The best guess is that Thoreau's Aunt Maria Thoreau paid the tax.

30  Reference is to *Le Mie Prigioni* by Silvio Pellico (1832). English translation, *My Prisons*, appeared in 1836.

31  Muslim.

32  Orpheus could charm all of nature, including inanimate objects, with his music.

33  George Peele, *The Battle of Alcazar* (1594). This verse did not appear in the 1849 edition. Line 4 should read, "It must respect effects and touch the soul."

34  The U.S. Constitution was drafted in the summer of 1787.

35  Corrected from the original "government."

36  These extracts have been inserted since the Lecture was read. [Thoreau's note.]

37  Confucius.

38  Sentence added to 1866 edition.

# Bibliography

Abbott, Philip. *States of Perfect Freedom*. Amherst, MA: University of Massachusetts Press, 1987.

Appleby, Joyce. *Liberalism and Republicanism in the Historical Imagination*. Cambridge, MA: Harvard University Press, 1992.

Arendt, Hannah. *Crisis of the Republic*. NY: Harcourt Brace Jovanovich, 1972.

Bedau, Hugo Adam, ed. *Civil Disobedience*. Indianapolis, IN: Pegasus, 1969.

Bennett, Jane. "On Being a Native: Thoreau's Hermeneutics of Self." *Polity* 22, no. 4 (1990): 559–580.

Bercovitch, Sacvan. *American Jeremiad*. Madison, WS: University of Wisconsin Press, 1978.

Bloom, Harold, ed. *Henry David Thoreau*. NY: Bloom's Literary Criticism, 2008.

Broderick, John C. "Thoreau, Alcott, and the Poll Tax." *Studies in Philology* 53, no. 4 (1956): 612–626.

Buranelli, Vincent. "The Case Against Thoreau." *Ethics* 67, no. 4 (1957): 257–268.

Canby, Henry Seidel. *Thoreau*. Boston, MA: Houghton Mifflin, 1939.

Carlyle, Thomas. *Sartor Resartus and On Heroes and Hero-Worship and the Heroic in History*. London: J. M. Dent; NY: E. P. Dutton, 1910.

Daily Kos. "The Banning of Mexican American Authors in Tucson." 16 January 2012. Available at: www.dailykos.com/story/2012/01/16/1055318/-The-Banning-of-Mexican-American-authors-in-Tucson# (accessed June 2014).

Dedmond, Francis B. "Thoreau and the Ethical Concept of Government." *The Personalist* 36, no. 1 (1955): 36–46.

Delbanco, Andrew. *The Abolitionist Imagination*. Cambridge, MA: Harvard University Press, 2012.

Demos, John. "The Anti-Slavery Movement and the Problem of Violent Means." *New England Quarterly* 37, no. 4 (1964): 501–526.

Dickens, Robert. *Thoreau.* NY: Exposition Press, 1974.

Diggins, John Patrick. "Thoreau, Marx, and the 'Riddle' of Alienation." *Social Research* 39, no. 4 (Winter 1972): 571–598.

Ellis, Richard. *American Political Cultures.* NY: Oxford University Press, 1993.

Emerson, Ralph Waldo. *Essays and Lectures.* NY: Library of America, 1983.

Fergenson, Laraine. "Thoreau, Daniel Berrigan, and the Problem of Transcendental Politics." *Soundings* 65, no. 1 (Spring 1982): 103–122.

Foner, Eric. *The Fiery Trial: Abraham Lincoln and American Slavery.* NY: W. W. Norton, 2010.

Francis, Richard. *Transcendental Utopias.* Ithaca, NY: Cornell University Press, 1997.

Frank, Tibor, ed. *The Origins and Originality of American Culture.* Budapest: Akademiai Kiado, 1984: 525–550.

Garrison, William Lloyd. *Declaration of Sentiments of the American Anti-Slavery Convention* (1833). Available at: http://utc.iath.virginia.edu/abolitn/abeswlgct.html (accessed June 2014).

Glick, Wendell P. "Thoreau and the 'Herald of Freedom.'" *New England Quarterly* 22, no. 2 (June 1949): 193–204.

Goldman, Emma. *Anarchism and Other Essays.* Port Washington, NY: Kennikat Press, 1969.

Greenberg, Amy S. *A Wicked War: Polk, Clay, Lincoln, and the 1846 Invasion of Mexico.* NY: Alfred A. Knopf, 2012.

Harding, Walter, ed. *Thoreau: A Century of Criticism.* Dallas, TX: Southern Methodist University Press, 1954.

Harding, Walter, ed. *The Thoreau Centennial.* Albany, NY: The State University of New York Press, 1962.

Harding, Walter. *The Days of Henry Thoreau.* NY: Alfred A. Knopf, 1966.

Harding, Walter and Michael Meyer. *The New Thoreau Handbook.* NY: New York University Press, 1980.

Hartz, Louis. *The Liberal Tradition in America.* NY: Harcourt, Brace and World, 1955.

Hicks, John, ed. *Thoreau in Our Season.* Amherst, MA: University of Massachusetts Press, 1967.

Hochfield, George. "Anti-Thoreau." *Sewannee Review* 96, no. 3 (1988): 433–443.

Hollis, Carroll C. "Thoreau and the State." *The Commonweal* 9 (September 1949): 530–533.

Howe, Daniel Walker. *Making the American Self.* Oxford: Oxford University Press, 1997.

Howe, Daniel Walker. *What Hath God Wrought: The Transformation of America, 1815–1848.* NY: Oxford University Press, 2007.

Howe, Irving. *The American Newness.* Cambridge, MA: Harvard University Press, 1986.

Hume, David. *Of the Original Contract,* 1748. Available at: www.constitution.org/dh/origcont.htm (accessed June 2014).

Ives, Charles. "Essay Before a Sonata: Thoreau," 1845. Available at: http://thoreau.eserver.org/Ives.html (paragraph 13, accessed June 2014).

Jefferson, Thomas. Letter to David Williams, 14 November 1803. Available at: www.monticello.org/site/jefferson/quotations-agriculture (accessed June 2014).

Jefferson, Thomas. *The Portable Thomas Jefferson*. Merrill D. Peterson, ed. NY: Penguin, 1997.

Kateb, George. "Democratic Individuality and the Claims of Politics." *Political Theory* 12, no. 3 (1984): 331–360.

King, Martin Luther. *Why We Can't Wait*. NY: Penguin, 1964.

Kritzberg, Barry. "Thoreau, Slavery, and Resistance to Civil Government." *Massachusetts Review* 30, no. 4 (1989): 535–565.

Lawrence, Jerome and Robert E. Lee. *The Night Thoreau Spent in Jail*. NY: Hill and Wang, 1970.

Lepore, Jill. "The Force: How Much Military is Enough?" *New Yorker* (28 January 2013): 70–76.

Lewis, John. "Veteran Civil Rights Leader: Snowden Acted in Tradition of Civil Disobedience." *The Guardian*, 7 August 2013. Available at: www.theguardian.com/world/2013/aug/07/john-lewis-civil-rights-edward-snowden (accessed June 2014).

Locke, John. *Second Treatise of Government*. Indianapolis, IN and Cambridge: Hackett, 1980.

Lynd, Staughton. *From Here to There*. Oakland, CA: PM Press, 2010.

Machiavelli, Niccolo. *The Prince*. NY and London: W. W. Norton, 1977.

Madden, Edward H. *Civil Disobedience and Moral Law in Nineteenth-Century American Philosophy*. Seattle, WA: University of Washington Press, 1968.

Mariotti, Shannon L. *Thoreau's Democratic Withdrawal*. Madison, WI: University of Wisconsin Press, 2010.

Marx, Karl and Friedrich Engels, *The Marx-Engels Reader*. Robert Tucker, ed. NY and London: W. W. Norton, 1978.

Matthiessen, F. O. *American Renaissance*. NY: Oxford University Press, 1941.

McPherson, James M. "America's 'Wicked War'." *New York Review of Books* (7 February 2013): 32–33.

McWilliams, Wilson Carey. *The Idea of Fraternity in America*. Berkeley, CA: University of California Press, 1973.

Meyer, Michael. *Several More Lives to Live: Thoreau's Political Reputation in America*. Westport, CT: Greenwood Press, 1977.

Miller, Perry. "The Responsibility of Mind in a Civilization of Machines." *American Scholar* 31, no. 1 (1961): 51–69.

Oakes, James. *Freedom National*. NY: W. W. Norton, 2013.

Ophuls, William. *Ecology and the Politics of Scarcity*. San Francisco, CA: W. H. Freeman, 1977.

Paley, William. *The Principles of Moral and Political Philosophy*. London: printed for F. C. and J. Rivington, 1822.

Paul, Sherman. *The Shores of America: Thoreau's Inward Exploration*. Urbana, IL: University of Illinois Press, 1958.

Paul, Sherman, ed. *Thoreau: A Collection of Critical Essays*. Englewood Cliffs, NJ: Prentice-Hall, 1962.

Peabody, Elizabeth P., ed. *Aesthetic Papers*. Boston, MA and New York, NY: G. P. Putnam, 1849.

Petrulionis, Sandra Habert. *To Set This World Right: The Anti-Slavery Movement in Thoreau's Concord*. Ithaca, NY and London: Cornell University Press, 2006.

Plato. *Last Days of Socrates*. Baltimore, MD: Penguin, 1969.

Quarles, Benjamin. *Blacks on John Brown*. Urbana, IL: University of Illinois Press, 1972.

Richardson, Robert D. *Henry Thoreau: A Life of the Mind*. Berkeley, CA: University of California Press, 1986.

Richardson, Robert D. *Emerson: The Mind on Fire*. Berkeley, CA: University of California Press, 1996.

Rorty, Richard. *Achieving Our Country*. Cambridge, MA: Harvard University Press, 1998.

Roth, Philip. Interviewed by Daniel Sandstrom. *New York Times* (2 March 2014). Available at: www.nytimes.com/2014/03/16/books/review/my-life-as-a-writer. html?_r=0 (accessed June 2014).

Rousseau, Jean-Jacques. *Basic Political Writings*. Indianapolis, IN and Cambridge: Hackett, 1987.

Sanders, Frederick K. "Mr. Thoreau's Time Bomb." *National Review* 4 (June 1968): 541–547.

Sims, Michael. *The Adventures of Henry Thoreau*. NY, London, New Delhi, Sydney: Bloomsbury, 2014.

Sophocles. *Theban Plays*. NY: Penguin, 1982.

Stoehr, Taylor. *Nay-Saying in Concord*. Hamden, CT: Archon, 1979.

Sweet, John Wood. "The Liberal Dilemma and the Demise of the Town Church: Ezra Ripley's Pastorate in Concord, 1778o-1841." *Proceedings of the Massachusetts Historical Society* 104 (1992): 73–109.

Tartt, Donna. *The Goldfinch*. NY: Little, Brown, 2013.

Thoreau, Henry David. *Familiar Letters of Henry David Thoreau*. F. B. Sanborn, ed. Boston, MA and NY: Houghton Mifflin, 1894.

Thoreau, Henry David. *Journal of Henry D. Thoreau*. Bradford Torrey and Francis H. Allen, eds. Boston, MA: Houghton Mifflin, 1949, 14 vols.

Thoreau, Henry David. *Consciousness in Concord*. Perry Miller, ed. Boston, MA: Houghton Mifflin, 1958.

Thoreau, Henry David. *The Variorum "Walden" and the Variorum "Civil Disobedience."* Walter Harding, ed. NY: Washington Square Press, 1968.

Thoreau, Henry David. *A Week on the Concord and Merrimack Rivers; Walden, or, Life in the Woods; The Maine Woods; Cape Cod*. NY: Library of America, 1985.

Thoreau, Henry David. *Thoreau: Political Writings*. Nancy L. Rosenblum, ed. NY: Cambridge University Press, 1996.

Thoreau, Henry David. *Collected Essays and Poems*. NY: Library of America, 2001.

Thoreau, Henry D. *Essays*. Jeffrey S. Cramer, ed. New Haven, CT and London: Yale University Press, 2013.

Thoreau, Henry David. *A Yankee in Canada, with Anti-Slavery and Reform Papers*. Boston, MA: Ticknor and Fields, 1866.

Timpe, Eugene F., ed. *Thoreau Abroad: Twelve Bibliographical Essays*. Hamden, CT: Archon Books, 1971.

Turner, Jack, ed. *A Political Companion to Henry David Thoreau*. Lexington, KY: University Press of Kentucky, 2009.

Walzer, Michael. *Exodus and Revolution*. NY: Basic Books, 1985.

Walker, Brian. "Thoreau's Alternative Economics: Work, Liberty, and Democratic Cultivation." *American Political Science Review* 92, no. 4 (December 1998): 845–856.

White, E. B. "Walden – 1954." *Yale Review* 44 (1954): 13–22.

Wolff, Robert Paul. *In Defense of Anarchism*. NY: Harper and Row, 1976.

Wood, Gordon. *Empire of Liberty*. NY: Oxford University Press, 2009.

# Index